COMPUTER NETWORKING
FOR
SYSTEMS PROGRAMMERS

WILEY SERIES IN
DATA COMMUNICATIONS AND NETWORKING
FOR COMPUTER PROGRAMMERS

SERIES EDITOR:
Gerald D. Cole, Independent Consultant

David Claiborne • Mathematical Preliminaries for Computer Networking
Gerald D. Cole • Computer Networking for Systems Programmers
David Claiborne • Personal Computer Networking
Gerald D. Cole • Open Systems Interconnection (OSI) for the Computer Professional

COMPUTER NETWORKING
FOR
SYSTEMS PROGRAMMERS

GERALD D. COLE

John Wiley & Sons, Inc.

NEW YORK / CHICHESTER / BRISBANE / TORONTO / SINGAPORE

Library of Congress Cataloging in Publication Data:

Cole, Gerald D.
    Computer networking for systems programmers / by Gerald D. Cole.
        p.   cm. – (Data communications and networking for computer
    programers)
        1. Computer networks. 2. Systems programming (Computer science)
    I. Title. II. Series.
    TK5105.5.C577 1990
    004.6 – dc20
    ISBN 0-471-51057-2

                                                    90-44238
                                                        CIP

Printed in the United States of America

10 9 8 7 6 5 4 3 2 1

For information about our audio products, write us at:
Newbridge Book Clubs, 3000 Cindel Drive, Delran, NJ 08370

CONTENTS

3

SYSTEMS DESIGN AND PROGRAMMING WITH OPEN SYSTEMS   24

4

DEVELOPMENT ISSUES FOR THE BOTTOM TWO LAYERS

5

DEVELOPMENT ISSUES AT THE NETWORK LAYER 76

6

THE TRANSPORT LAYER   107

7

HIGHER LAYER PROTOCOLS
IN END SYSTEMS   141

8

INTERCONNECTION, INTEROPERABILITY, AND MIGRATION STRATEGIES 179

9

DEVELOPING NETWORK SYSTEMS   187

10

NETWORK MANAGEMENT   206

11

TRENDS IN DATA COMMUNICATIONS AND NETWORKING   218

BIBLIOGRAPHY   228

INDEX   232

SERIES PREFACE

The Data Communications and Networking for Computer Programmers Series provides the information programmers and software engineers need to effectively deal with new data communications and networking technology. The series focuses on the educational needs of the computer systems analyst, systems programmer, and systems engineer, building on their existing computer knowledge base. The series, as a whole, provides an integrated view of such real-world topics as analyzing networks, implementing network protocols, developing local area and wide area networks, interconnecting networks, creating multivendor networks, and understanding network standards.

Because the breadth of the data communications field is beyond the scope of a single book, the information is presented in a series of books. Each book deals with a different aspect of the wide range of data communications topics. This division of information allows the different books to build on a level of knowledge defined by the other books in the series. When one book is used by a programmer, the other books in the series provide an established source for additional information. Overlap between the books is limited to essential information.

The authors of the series are working professionals in different networking and data communications areas. Each author writes using his or her experience in solving actual data communications problems in system development. The authors relate the data communications aspects to concepts already understood by experienced programmers, using similarities to extend the programmer's understanding from familiar computer programming concepts to different aspects of data communications networking. In many respects, data communications and networking can be viewed as a specialized form of I/O systems.

The complexity of data communications and networking, however, is not overly simplified. Unique data communications topics such as network error control and recovery, sequence and flow control management, distributed fault recovery mechanisms, and concurrent operation of atomic actions across the multiple resources of a network, are all addressed in detail. While the books emphasize similarities, aspects that differ are highlighted, still allowing the programmer to maximize the benefits from his existing knowledge.

Gerald D. Cole
Series editor

PREFACE

The objective of this book is to explain data communications and computer networking in terms of concepts that are already known to computer systems analysts, computer systems programmers, and computer systems engineers. The emphasis is on practical examples that are encountered in today's networks and on the evolution to Open Systems Interconnection (OSI). The book is not limited to OSI, but considers today's open environments of multiple protocol approaches. Other books in this series will discuss OSI in particular.

A main concern is the use of both industry and OSI standards. They are important because they provide the key to multivendor networking today and in the future, getting away from the awkward, limited forms of networking through device emulation; instead, true peer-to-peer intercommunication is possible.

This book is organized to convey information about computer networking in a way that is optimal for readers who have existing knowledge of computer systems, but little or no prior knowledge about computer networks. The intent is to avoid wasting the reader's time discussing bits, bytes, and buffering and instead to emphasize networking concerns such as flow control, reliable transmission, crash recovery, file transfer, remote log-in, and other networking matter.

The book is structured in a way that introduces concepts at relatively simple layers of the architecture of networks, and then builds upon these concepts to expand to the complex aspects of higher-layer protocols. The topics include interoperability, security, implementation issues, migration strategies, and future trends in networking. This approach has been successful in courses taught by the author at universities including UCLA Extension and the University of Southern California and more recently for Learning Tree International.

The author would like to acknowledge the cooperation of Learning Tree International for permission to utilize figures from their networking courses which have been developed by the author, and which have been utilized in this book.

Gerald D. Cole

1

INTRODUCTORY CONCEPTS

This book is concerned with data communications and networking as viewed from the perspective of one who is familiar with computer systems. This familiarity may be in the form of systems engineering concerns, systems analyst concerns, or systems programmer concerns. Any of these viewpoints provides a good starting point for understanding the extensions that come about when adding data communications and networking to these systems.

DATA COMMUNICATIONS AND NETWORKING

The exact dividing line between data communications and networking is not well defined. *Data communications* tends to be the preferred term to describe the lower level concerns of moving data directly from one computer to another over a point-to-point circuit. In contrast, *networking* is concerned with intermediate switching systems and the higher level matters of making systems interoperate.

One might say that data communications involves the movement of bits and bytes from one computing environment to another as an expedient alternative to moving floppy disks between machines. However, networking provides inter-connectivity and interoperability mechanisms to allow a variety of resources to be shared across the network. These resources include computing power, peripheral devices, programs, and data in the form of files and data bases. The ultimate objective of networking is to provide enterprise-wide interoperability and access to all resources for which there is a need to know.

The resources made available as a result of networking appear in many forms. Electronic messaging, in the form of electronic mail or bulletin boards, provides a free exchange of ideas and correspondence. Remote transactions provide instantaneous updates to data bases, preserving the integrity of distributed copies. Data collection systems provide a real-time assimilation of data into the overall understanding of what the corporation or agency is doing. Remote file access allows information to be retrieved and utilized regardless of its location on the network.

Many of the forms of networking involve an extension to the interprocess communication (IPC) capabilities to span networks. These IPC facilities are utilized to perform file transfers and remote log-ins, and to support electronic mail transfers. Others go a step further and implement the equivalent of remote procedure calls. These resemble local procedure calls in form and function, but with the added delay of network transmissions. Still others go beyond this to provide transparent access to resources; e.g., accessing files the same way whether local or remote. (The concept of *transparency* is that the existence of networking mechanisms need not be dealt with explicitly or seen by the user of the service.)

Underlying all of these data communications and networking applications is a set of hardware and software mechanisms. These are typically packaged into two forms:

1. Hardware/software devices, which are separate components on the network.
2. Software that runs on the mainframe or other end system. These end systems are often called *hosts*.

The separate hardware/software devices of the network include terminals, multiplexers, terminal access nodes, hosts, front-end processors, routers, bridges, and other such components. We focus initially on the class of devices called *terminals*.

Terminals can be either character or page mode. Character mode terminals send each character separately, although they may be grouped at the receiving computer into lines of text for processing. Other systems process each character on a character-by-character basis. At the other extreme in terminal handling is the page mode terminal. In this case, editing is done at the terminal, and data are only sent to the computer when the user indicates that it is to be sent by pressing a "transmit" key.

Several terminals may have their output combined for transmission by a multiplexer, thus sharing an expensive point-to-point communications channel. A similar device at the computer end sorts out the characters from each terminal and sends them to the proper input port on the computer. Output information is handled in the same manner.

Several terminals can share the network equivalent of a point-to-point channel by means of a *terminal concentrator*. This device is sometimes called a *Packet Assembler/Disassembler* or *PAD*, because it assembles a string of individual characters into a unit called a *packet* for transmission across the network, and it disassembles packets into a string of individual characters upon reception.

The packets that are formed by the PAD are sent to a server computer, typically called a host. A host may be any computer from a mainframe to a PC. The only distinguishing characteristic is that it is capable of providing services of one form or another to network users.

Some hosts, typically mainframes, may be interfaced to the network by means of a *front-end processor*. The front-end processor off-loads the data communications and networking processing from the host.

There are a variety of other interconnection devices, including routers to interconnect arbitrary networks, bridges to interconnect similar Local Area Networks (LANs), and repeaters to interconnect segments of a common LAN technology. All of these interconnection devices share two sets of concerns:

1. How to interconnect networks.
2. How to provide "fire walls" to isolate problems and to keep them from propagating to other portions of the interconnected system.

These devices will be discussed in detail in later chapters.

Considering the number of vendors involved in a typical network system, it is important to consider the effect of standards in providing interoperability. Standards are very important. Imagine the chaos one would face if there were no standards for light bulbs, camera film, or other day-to-day needs. Data communications and networking require, and are developing, standards to ease the interoperability problems, but we are far from the standards such as exist for light bulbs and film. However, progress has been made. Some important standards include the American Standard Code for Information Interchange (ASCII) character code, the High-level Data Link Control (HDLC) protocol, the network service and interface specifications of X.25, the intercomputer transport protocols, and the LAN protocols. Each of these will be discussed in detail in subsequent chapters. All fit into the concept of Open Systems Interconnection (OSI), which is the focus of attention of interoperability strategies of major computer vendors.

In addition to interoperability, there are other concerns in the implementation of data communications and networking. The cost of communications links provided by telephone companies has not dropped close to the extent that computing has. Therefore, many tradeoffs are decided in favor of more efficient use of communications at the expense of added computational power. The exception tends to be in LANs in which communications capability is very inexpensive and is often traded for simplicity of computing resources, particularly with PCs. The tradeoffs between communications and processing are analogous in many ways to the traditional tradeoffs that programmers have made between processing and memory utilization. We will see several examples of these tradeoffs, which are typical of the focus of this book, namely, to build upon an existing knowledge base in computers and computer programming in learning data communications and networking.

BASIC DATA COMMUNICATIONS AND NETWORKING DEVELOPMENT ISSUES

You may or may not have previously been involved in the development of computer systems with heavy real-time, input/output, and an embedded system emphasis, but if you have, you will find that data communications and networking have much similarity with things that you already know. We will try to build on that existing knowledge base, because this similarity provides a useful departure point from which one can rapidly learn about data communications and networking. Many of the common issues and methods include the following.

Interrupt handlers are an important part of data communications programming. The arrival of a data packet is typically signalled by an interrupt, which causes an interrupt service routine to set up a new buffer and to place the new arrival on a queue for processing as a schedulable task or process. At high data rates, there is not enough time to set up the next buffer in the interrupt routine, so the hardware must have at least a second buffer, and possibly several buffers, to be able to handle back-to-back packets that arrive tens of microseconds after the end of the previous packet.

Buffering is a second very similar aspect of data communications. As new information arrives, it is placed in buffer memory. The buffer approach may be either as a circular buffer or as a set of fixed-size blocks. If the latter is chosen, the block size is typically set as the maximum size packet. This avoids having to switch buffers during the input of a single packet.

Terminal handlers also involve buffering, but at much lesser data rates. Other terminal handling concerns include whether or not characters are echoed; i.e., sent back to the terminal. There are two modes:

1. *Local echo* or *half-duplex*, in which characters are printed on the screen as they are typed.

Or,

   2. *Remote echo*, in which characters are only printed on the screen after they
      have been sent to the computer and echoed (sent back) to the terminal.
      One purpose of remote echo is to provide the terminal user with assurance
      that the character was not corrupted during transmission.

Echoing is also utilized in some command and edit modes. Echoing is typically
disabled for password entry, so that it is not displayed on the screen.

   Another major area of terminal processing is the handling of control codes.
Because the terminal handler has two different contexts, processing user data
and processing user commands, some way of distinguishing the two is necessary.
Typically, an *escape character* is defined, which causes the next character(s) to
be interpreted as control. This escape character is usually a character that the
user would not typically type in his or her data, e.g., "^]".

   In addition to terminal-entered controls, there are also computer-generated
controls. These are often in the form of control blocks, i.e., buffers containing
control information instead of user data.

   Interprocess communication (IPC) across the network is an extension of that
provided by an operating system. The network IPC typically involves either connections (long-term associations) or remote procedure calls (one-time associations). In any case, interprocess communication is always by means of an
explicitly passed block of information, not by means of shared memory.

   Timers are an important element of data communications and networking.
There are several timers (e.g., for retransmissions of packets) and several different strategies on how they should be implemented. For example, there might be
a separate retransmission timer per packet, or one timer could be shared by all
packets from the same connection.

   Hardware support for data communications consists of both board-level and
chip-level products. The board-level products often will run one or more
protocol(s), and will deliver well-formed packets to the system. They will also
send packets, including retransmissions when they are included in the
protocol(s). The software interface is typically in the form of an I/O driver.

   Chip-level products are a part of a user-developed communications interface.
These chips range from rather basic data communications support to a full protocol. The chips often operate as a coprocessor with a microcomputer to perform
the data communications function.

   The above brief descriptions have been intended to make the learning of data
communications and networking an extension of things that you already know.
Next we will consider the basics of data communications and networking in the
more traditional manner of introducing the terminology and concepts.

2

BASIC DATA
COMMUNICATIONS AND
NETWORKING CONCEPTS

In this chapter, our intention is to introduce several important concepts of data communications and networking, and to use examples to illustrate how they relate to computer systems and systems programming. These analogies will be the basis for building on your existing knowledge base. You will find that data communications and networking processes are not very different from what you have been doing for some time. However, the multiple systems approach will cause some new aspects, and these are pointed out as exceptions to the analogies.

COMMUNICATIONS CHANNELS

One of the most important concepts in data communications and networking is the notion of a communications channel. You are undoubtedly familiar with the I/O channel(s) of a computer, and there are many similarities between computer channels and data communications channels. Both are often shared (multiplexed), both involve control information and data transfers, and both involve I/O handler software that builds on special hardware.

However, there are a number of major differences between computer channels and data communications channels. One of the most significant differences is the appearance of the channel concept at several different levels of abstraction. At the lowest levels, the channel may be a physical pair of wires or a portion of the data-carrying capacity of a coaxial cable. At a somewhat higher level of abstraction, the channel may be the software utilized in the direct interconnection of two computers. This software-implemented channel may have characteristics that the physical (hardware) channel would not have, such as an extremely low error rate.

Initialization of a channel often includes a *handshake* between the two ends of the channel. During this handshake exchange of messages, the two sides reach an agreement on the characteristics of the channel, such as the maximum packet size that will be sent across the channel. Many other configuration parameters also may be established at this time, which will be discussed in subsequent chapters.

VIRTUAL CIRCUIT AND DATAGRAM SERVICES ACROSS CHANNELS

We often use the word "virtual" in conjunction with the properties that a channel seems to have, even when the hardware support does not. Thus, a virtual circuit has desirable properties that the physical circuit does not have. This is analogous to the concept of virtual memory, in which the programmer can develop programs that utilize a very large address space, despite much smaller limitations of the actual memory hardware. Properties typically associated with a virtual circuit are reliability and the sequenced delivery of information (i.e., very few bad bits, nothing missing, and everything delivered in its proper sequence). Virtual circuits usually have additional properties, such as the ability for the receiving side to control the rate at which the sender actually transmits data. We have seen three basic mechanisms in our virtual circuits:

1. Error control.
2. Sequence control.
3. Flow control.

Each of these mechanisms will be discussed in detail at the several different levels of abstraction at which we find virtual circuits.

Virtual circuits require that a *connection* be established between two communicating parties. Associated with each connection are a set of optional services that can be negotiated when the connection is established. These negotiated services typically include non-default parameter settings, such as the maximum packet size that can be exchanged.

Virtual circuits, and connections in general, involve *state information*, such as knowledge of the next packet's expected sequence number. This state information is the fundamental characteristic of a connection-oriented communication channel that distinguishes it from its alternative, namely a connectionless communications channel.

The data units that are sent across a connectionless channel are often called *datagrams*. They provide a "best efforts delivery" service. Datagram service is called *connectionless* because it does not include the services (or the state information) of a connection, and there is no assurance of reliability or sequenced delivery. Instead, the connectionless datagrams are delivered to the extent that the provider of the service is able to do so, which will vary from network to network. Connectionless networks are preferred when the small amount of data to be transferred does not justify the overhead of a connection establishment, when the networks that are involved in the communications provide differing levels of service, and when network problems such as congestion are handled simply by discarding packets.

BIT SERIAL TRANSMISSION AND IN-BAND CONTROL

A difference between the I/O channel of a typical computer and the data communications channel is the nature of the data transfer. The I/O channel of a computer will often transfer one or more bytes in parallel and have separate lines for control information. This is called *out of band control*, because the control and data lines are separate. In some other computer I/O channels, control and data may share the same lines, with the receiving devices differentiating them based on their relative time of arrival in a control/data transfer sequence. This would be *in-band control*.

Telephone companies provide us with a good example of in-band control, which they have utilized for many years. When you dial a telephone number, you hear the clicks of an old-style pulse dial system or the tones of the current dial system. These are in-band control, because you can hear them in the voice channel. The in-band control is not limited to the telephone number, but also includes billing information, such as the free "800" numbers. This form of in-band control has caused telephone companies considerable grief over the years, because telephone hackers have produced these signals at the right times and tones to access any telephone in the world without charge. The future will show if data communications and networking in-band channels will suffer from such potentially serious side effects!

Another difference between I/O channels and data communications channels is that, unlike the parallel data transfer of the computer I/O channel, a data communications channel is almost always bit serial. Control and data share the same communications media. Thus, control is in-band. All of the bits look alike. The issue is how to differentiate control bits from data bits. The key to sorting them out is having a way to identify the start of a sequence of bits, and then having a known protocol for interpreting the format of the bit pattern. An example is shown in Figure 2-1, which indicates how a single character is sent in what is called *character asynchronous transmission*.

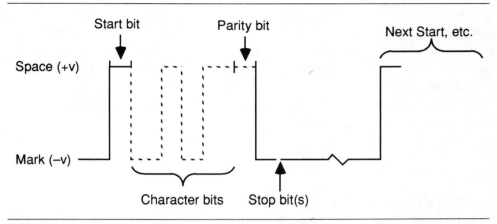

FIGURE 2-1 Character asynchronous communications are self synchronizing.

The arrival of the character is indicated by the transition from the steady-state *mark level* to the *space level* for one bit time. This is called the *start bit*. A transition that occurs for less than the full bit time would be rejected as a noise pulse. Following the start bit is a sequence of seven data bits, followed by one control bit. In this case, it is an error control bit called a *parity bit*. The parity bit is followed by at least one bit time at the mark level, called the *stop bit(s)*. The stop bit(s) might be considered to be control information also, but their only purpose is to put the line back to the mark level to allow recognition of another start bit transition. The time between characters is unknown. The next character could occur immediately after the stop bit(s) or at any arbitrary time thereafter. This is known as *asynchronous transmission*, but the asynchrony only applies to the characters. For example, the timing between the bits of a character is known because one bit follows immediately after another.

ASYNCHRONOUS AND SYNCHRONOUS TRANSMISSION

The word "asynchronous" is used in data communications in the same way as in real-time and other computer systems. Asynchronous events happen at unpredictable times. In data communications, the "event" is the arrival of a character in our current discussion, but it could be the arrival of some grouping of characters in another context. That grouping could be an individual packet of information or it could be the arrival and/or reading of an electronic mail message.

The alternative to asynchronous communication is synchronous communication. The typical use of the words *synchronous communication* is to refer to a grouping of characters into a packet, such that characters are transmitted one immediately after another. Thus, the timing between characters is known. The receiver knows when to expect each character because they arrive contiguously, just as the bits within a character did in our earlier example. As before, the word "synchronous" applies to the characters, but in this case it applies to the bits as well. You may find this form of communications referred to as either *character synchronous* or *bit synchronous*.

THE DIRECTION OF DATA FLOW

The flow of information across a computer I/O channel is typically in one direction at a time. Control (commands) may be sent to a disk controller, followed by a reversal of the direction of flow to have data returned. This is the equivalent of what is called *half-duplex* transmission in data communications. The alternative is to have simultaneous and possibly independent flows in the two directions. This is called *full-duplex*, or sometimes simply *duplex*. Of course it is possible to have one-way channels as well, which are called *simplex* channels. In effect, one might consider a full-duplex channel to be two simplex channels in opposite directions.

In addition to whether it is half- or full-duplex, another important characteristic of a channel is its data rate. In data communications, the data rate is measured in bits per second or bps. (Occasionally, the metric will be bytes per second or Bps.) The data rate of a channel is limited by the *bandwidth* of the physical circuit. The bandwidth of a channel is the range of frequencies that the circuit can pass. For example, the bandwidth of a typical telephone channel is shown in Figure 2-2.

The telephone channel passes frequencies (measured in hertz [Hz] or cycles per second) between 300 Hz and 3,300 Hz. The bandwidth is their difference, or 3,000 Hz. A useful rule of thumb is that one can obtain about one bit per second for each hertz of bandwidth. Therefore, we would expect to transmit data at about 3,000 bps over a telephone channel. Of course, there are examples of lesser and greater data rates, such as the common 1,200 bps transmission or the 9,600 bps rate. The differences are basically one of the technology utilized and the resulting costs of the device that adapts data transmissions to fit within the telephone bandwidth. This device is called a *modem* (modulator/demodulator). Modems and their programmable interfaces are discussed in Chapter 4.

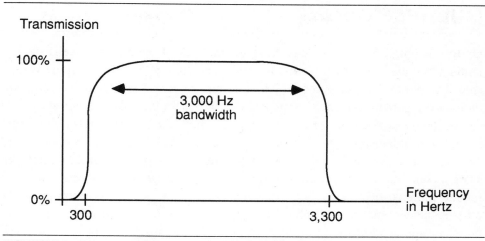

FIGURE 2-2   A telephone channel provides a 3,000 Hz bandwidth.

DATA RATE, BANDWIDTH, AND ERROR RATE

From the above example of the available data rates across a telephone channel, one can see that while there is a relationship between data rate and bandwidth, a wide range of data rates can be obtained for any given bandwidth. The maximum data rate that can be obtained on a channel with a given bandwidth is stated theoretically by Shannon's law,

Max data rate (bps) = BW log [1 + S/N]

where the logarithm is to the base 2, and S/N is the signal to noise ratio. For example, a S/N value of 15 means that the signal power is 15 times the noise power level. For this value of S/N, the equation states that the maximum theoretical data rate is four times the bandwidth. Higher signal to noise ratios would produce somewhat higher values of the data rate to bandwidth ratio.

The existence of noise causes occasional transmission errors in the form of bad bits, that is, bits that are changed from binary one to zero or vice versa. The error characteristics of a data communications channel are measured in terms of the *bit error rate (BER)*, which is the fraction of bits in error. For example, an average bit error rate for a telephone channel is one bad bit in every 100,000 bits that are transmitted, giving a BER of 10^{-5}. Other media, such as those utilized in LANs, often have extremely low BERs, such as 10^{-9} for coaxial cable and 10^{-10} for fiber-optic cable.

MULTIPLEXING

Up to this point, we have discussed characteristics of the channel itself, such as its data rate and error rate. Another set of concerns are how the channel is utilized. For example, a channel may be dedicated to one particular pair of communicating parties, but more commonly it shares a channel. In a computer I/O system, these are often called *multiplexer* (or multiplexor) channels. Multiplexing is the mechanism used to share a communications channel. It can take on any of several forms, but its fundamental purpose is always the same; namely, to share a common communications resource. In some cases, this sharing is done to reduce the cost of communications, such as remote access to a computer. In other instances, such as in LANs, sharing a common medium provides intercomputer communications. Regardless of the motivation, sharing a common communications channel is called multiplexing.

Two very common forms of multiplexing are Frequency Division Multiplexing (FDM) and Time Division Multiplexing (TDM). They differ in the way they divide the channel resources. FDM divides the frequency into individual sub-channels. Each sub-channel is assigned to one user, i.e., one pair of communicating entities. TDM takes the opposite approach, dividing access time but giving full-channel capacity to each user for a portion of the time. Both forms are shown in Figure 2-3.

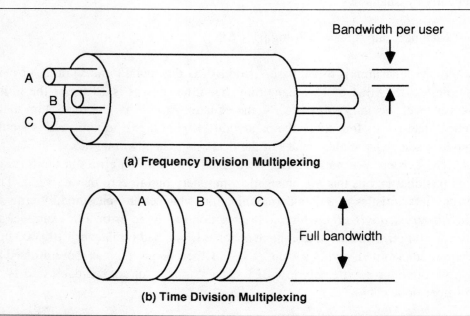

(a) Frequency Division Multiplexing

(b) Time Division Multiplexing

FIGURE 2-3   Frequency and Time Division Multiplexing provide two different ways to share a physical channel.

Frequency division multiplexing is uncommon in computing systems, but is very common in other parts of our lives. For example, the FDM sub-channels of Figure 2-3 might be the frequency bands assigned to television channels in either broadcast or cable TV fashion. In cable TV, the 300 to 400 Mhz (megahertz) bandwidth would be divided into a large number of 6-Mhz sub-channels assigned to TV channels 2, 3, 4, etc.

Time division multiplexing is common in computing systems, including the I/O channel multiplexing. First one user is given access to the full data carrying capacity of the channel, and then later, another is given such access.

Neither FDM nor TDM is inherently better than the other, but we tend to find more data communications examples of TDM than of FDM. This is primarily because of the use of digital channels. TDM is much more suitable for use with digital channels, while FDM is a good approach for analog channels. However, as we will see later, there are examples in which **both** FDM and TDM are utilized, for example, using FDM to divide the bandwidth of a coaxial cable network into sub-channels, and then using TDM over one or more of these sub-channels.

A rather common usage of multiplexing in data communications is in transmitting characters from terminals to a computer. As shown in Figure 2-4, terminals could be connected to a computer either directly, across individual telephone lines, or across a shared communications link. In the latter case, a multiplexer is used to share the common line.

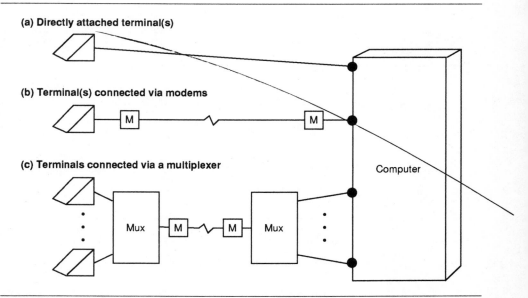

FIGURE 2-4   Terminals may be attached in several ways. All appear the same to the computer.

If a TDM multiplexer is utilized, it might divide time into *frames*, allowing each terminal to send one character per frame. If a terminal had nothing to send, a null character would be sent in the TDM slot assigned to that user. A frame structure of this sort would tend to be very inefficient, because there are many time intervals in which a given terminal is not sending (or receiving) data. This approach is shown in Figure 2-5 along with an alternative called *statistical time division multiplexing*. Such a multiplexing device is often called a *StatMux*, and it is the predominant form of multiplexer for terminal to host usage.

A typical StatMux configuration is shown in Figure 2-6. Note that the combined data rate of the attached devices is about four times the capacity of the channel. This is fairly typical for such uses. The major concern is not with users typing at terminals, but rather with output from the computer, which can result in large bursts of traffic. What happens if the aggregate amount of the computer-generated traffic exceeds the channel capacity? The first mechanism to come into operation is the buffering capability of the StatMux. Information will be stored for subsequent delivery. However, the amount of memory in the StatMux is finite, so another type of mechanism must be called upon if the buffers start to get full. Suppose that when buffers are 50% full, we want to tell the computer to stop sending temporarily. We would like to stop the flow on any heavy usage sub-channels but allow it to continue on low usage sub-channels. We rely on the XOFF/XON mechanism to provide flow control on the individual sub-channels. An XOFF ASCII character is sent to the major source of data. Others are

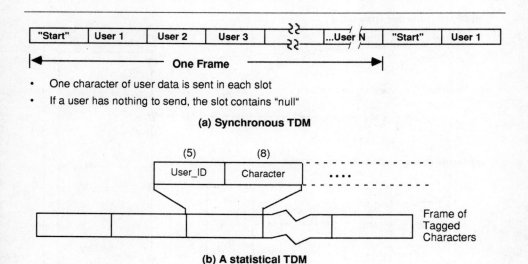

* One character of user data is sent in each slot
* If a user has nothing to send, the slot contains "null"

(a) Synchronous TDM

(b) A statistical TDM

Graphic courtesy of Learning Tree International.

FIGURE 2-5   Time Division Multiplexing (TDM).

allowed to continue to send. If another is also sending lots of data, it will receive an XOFF also. Eventually the StatMux will catch up, the buffer contents will reduce to an acceptable size, and we will send an XON ASCII character on the sub-channel(s) that had been stopped with XOFF(s).

The StatMux operates on the assumption that traffic is "bursty," i.e., that information flow occurs in spurts, with gaps of time in between. Therefore, additional users can be supported by allocating the idle resources to them. The price we pay for this statistical multiplexing is the need to send a *tag* with each character. In the example shown in Figure 2-6, five tag bits were sent with each eight-bit character. This allows up to 32 terminals and computer ports to be uniquely identified. In the approach using slots in a frame and a static allocation, the terminal and port were implicit in the location of a character in the frame.

In either the StatMux or the preassigned slot approach, the existence of the multiplexers is *transparent* to the host. The host hardware and software do not need to be changed to accept terminal input via the multiplexer, as opposed to having a separate line per terminal. The concept of transparency is very important in data communications and networking. Its exact meaning will depend on the context in which it is utilized, but it will always mean that some mechanism exists without the user of a service having to deal with it. In our multiplexer example, the host and terminals did not have to do anything differently when the multiplexers were placed between them.

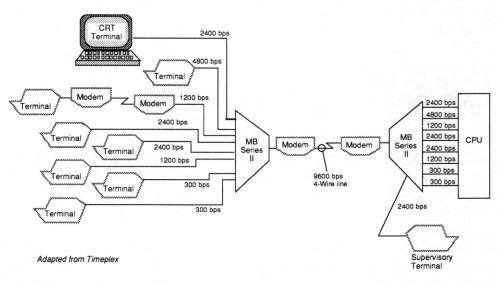

Adapted from Timeplex

Graphic courtesy of Learning Tree International.

FIGURE 2-6 A representative example of a StatMux.

PACKET SWITCHING

Statistical multiplexing at the level of individual characters added control information (the tag) to each data character. This concept can be broadened. Suppose we allow several characters to be sent with one tag. Then we need to include one more piece of control information; namely, the number of characters in this particular group. In a more general network environment, in which groups of characters might get out of order, we might also include a sequence number with each group of characters. The net effect is that our groups of characters become what we call *packets*. A packet might contain a few control bytes and a few hundred data bytes. This is essentially what packet-switching is—simply an extension of statistical multiplexing to a more general network environment.

While a StatMux typically operates with vendor-unique (and proprietary) protocols, packet-switching has been standardized, at least to the extent of the network interface. However, the internal packet-switch protocols continue to be vendor-unique and proprietary. The standardized network interface is X.25, which will be discussed in detail in Chapter 5.

The network protocols are concerned with delivery of packets of information across one or more networks. For example, a network user in the U.S. may be accessing a data base of information in Canada, and thus may be going across both Telenet (in the U.S.) and Datapac (in Canada). Both within and between networks, there is a common set of concerns. How large can the packets be? How do you tell the sender to stop sending for awhile? Who handles error recovery? How do we keep packets in the right sequence? These and other issues will also be discussed in detail in Chapter 5.

DATA COMMUNICATIONS AND NETWORK PERFORMANCE

The mechanics of how the network operates are defined in its protocols. How well it operates is determined by both its protocols and how they are implemented. Given that the protocol has some basic capabilities, such as the ability to send several packets before having to wait for acknowledgments, the implementation approach is the more important of the two. However, knowledge of both aspects is required for successful implementation and adaptation for a given environment. A poorly implemented protocol can make very inefficient use of the network and degrade the performance of the network. The most critical network performance metrics are:

1. Delay.
2. Throughput.
3. Availability.
4. Security.

They are discussed below.

The delay is the amount of time that is required to transmit a unit of information (e.g., a packet) across the network. For ease of measurement, this is normally measured as round-trip time, with the packet echoed back upon receipt. The reason for the round-trip measurement, instead of a one-way trip, is that you can avoid having to synchronize the clocks of the sending and receiving hosts, because the round-trip send and receive time stamps are at the same site. The echoing host can time stamp its received and sent times to be able to subtract the host delay from the overall delay. Because only the time difference is of concern, the two hosts' clocks do not need to be synchronized.

The delay is a function of the packet size, the path across the network, the data rate of the links along the path, and the competing traffic (i.e., queueing delay). Any specification of network delay should state the values of these parameters. The delay specification also should include whether it is to be the average delay, 95th percentile delay, or worst case delay.

The throughput is the sustained rate at which data can be transmitted across the network. In effect, it is the number of bits transmitted divided by the time for the transfer(s). However, this is an oversimplification, because there are issues in which bits actually count toward throughput, and in which factors are beyond the control of the network.

The issue of which bits count is one of protocol overhead. On the average, there may be as many protocol header bits as there are data bits. Does the throughput measurement include these protocol overhead bits? A vendor of an X.25 network service might argue convincingly that only the X.25 protocol overhead should be excluded from the throughput calculation; that the higher layer protocol bits were "data" as far as X.25 networks are concerned. The key point is that these issues should be resolved in the definition stage of development, not when the testing is being performed.

The throughput may also be limited by factors beyond the control of the network. Suppose that the two hosts are operating with a "stop and wait" protocol. The achieved throughput will be small when the network delay has the sender waiting for a relatively long time for acknowledgments (ACKs) to be returned. Only when the ACK is returned can the next packet be sent. (This is why it is called stop and wait.)

The availability of the network service is the fraction of time that the service is available for use by the subscribers. A 99% or 0.99 availability means that 99% of the time that network access is attempted, service is there. High availability is desirable but can be costly, because it is obtained by expensive system characteristics: high component reliability, rapid fault detection and repair, and redundancy of components.

Availability of a network is a complicated matter, because networks tend to fail a small piece at a time. One failure does not cause a loss of service to all users. Availability calculations must include such partial losses.

The security of a network is difficult to quantify and measure. Only attributes such as accidental misdelivery of packets can be assigned numeric values. Most of the security concerns are related to hostile threats. In this case, after a successful penetration attack has been devised, it breaks into the system in almost 100% of the attempts. Therefore, network security is typically specified in terms of the mechanisms to be provided, rather than numeric values of security protection.

SECURITY IN DATA COMMUNICATIONS AND NETWORKING

Security in data communications and networking is an extension of the security concerns of a single computer. All of the same basic concerns apply, but the components are geographically distributed. Unfortunately, these components are also often distributed administratively, which is more of a problem than being distributed geographically!

The reason why distributed administration can be a major problem can be shown using the basic "three-legged stool" model of security. There are three equally important supporting aspects that form the "legs" in our analogy. The first leg is the security policy: you need a common security policy across all of the interconnected components. This is difficult if they are administratively separate. The second leg is the security mechanisms to be applied. Here again, unless there are a number of common mechanisms across the network, security interoperation is unlikely. Separate administrations, with separate concerns, policies, and budgets, will undoubtedly have different security mechanisms. The third leg of the stool is assurances. How confident are you that the mechanisms are consistently applied, have the required integrity, and do indeed enforce the intended policy?

Like with any three-legged stool, all legs are equally important: all must be there and solid to support the user. In addition, there is no point in making one leg very strong if one of the others is weak.

The security policy must address many aspects of the network system. Which assets must be protected? What are the potential threat sources? Who are the authorized users, and what are they authorized to access? In that sense, what are the subjects and objects of the access control matrix? The security policy must address your definition of security. It almost always includes confidentiality of certain data, but often integrity also should be a concern. Who is authorized to modify and/or downgrade data? Security may also involve some level of assured service.

Security mechanisms comprise an equally important part of the second leg of the stool. These security mechanisms form a set of security services that enforce the policy. The services are typically considered to be those listed below. The first three directly reflect the major security policy concerns.

- **Confidentiality service:** Keeping information secret unless the recipient is authorized to receive it
- **Integrity service:** Being able to detect any unauthorized change to the information, including its labels or source indication
- **Service assurance:** Being able to detect an attempt at denial of service, to operate in a degraded mode, and eventually to recover to full service

The remaining security services support the above direct policy concerns.

- **Authentication service:** Proof that a person is who he/she claims to be, or that a message source is what it states
- **Access control service:** Ensuring that access to resources is only allowed when authorized, including permissions for read, write, and/or execute of a computer resource
- **Audit service:** The capability of collecting and analyzing data that indicates who accessed what and when
- **Non-repudiation service:** The ability to prove that an object was actually sent or that it was actually received. These correspond to notary and registered mail functions respectively

Security services and mechanisms are intended to restrict access, which may seem to be the extreme opposite of Open Systems Interconnection (OSI), in that it attempts to provide complete interoperability and access capabilities. The two sets of concerns are not contradictory, however. They simply state that the barriers which restrict access should be limited to those that are intentionally placed there for security purposes. Without these security barriers, the systems should be as open as possible. However, what if two vendors implement the same networking protocols that should be able to communicate, but each implements security differently, perhaps at different layers? The differences in security protocols present a barrier, but not the one desired. This barrier is complete rather than selective.

Standards for security services and mechanisms are still evolving. As a part of this evolution, guidance on which OSI layers should implement which security services also is being determined. The general approaches that are becoming accepted are described below.

- **Confidentiality service:** Provide between network switches at the Physical Layer (link encryption), and/or at the Network or Transport Layer. Some selective field encryption may also be at the Application Layer.
- **Integrity service:** Provide at the Network or Transport Layer by cryptographic error checking, which is sometimes called "crypto sealing" because it protects against unauthorized modification. It also may be provided at the Application Layer where there is more understanding of the relative importance of pieces of information.
- **Service assurance:** There is little industry-wide guidance on service assurance. Its solution tends to be application-specific.
- **Authentication service:** These services may be needed at a variety of protocol layers, whenever there is a need to be sure exactly who you are communicating with.
- **Access control service:** The access control service provides mandatory (label-based) and discretionary (need-to-know-based) controls over access to objects.
- **Audit service:** The audit service accumulates records about the attempted accesses of objects by subjects. These records include both authorized (allowed) and unauthorized (unallowed) access attempts.
- **Non-repudiation service:** The Application Layer is a commonly accepted location for the non-repudiation service.

There are a number of general principles that should govern the design and implementation of the security services and mechanisms. They are described in the following items.

- **Reference monitor:** A well-defined, isolated, small portion of the system should provide the basic access controls that control the access by programs to objects. The reference monitor should be developed with three properties: it must always be invoked (on every access attempt), it must be tamperproof (isolated in some way), and it must be small enough to be verifiable (to the degree required by the situation).

- **Least privilege:** No user, administrator, developer, or maintainer of the system should have privileged capabilities beyond his or her needs to perform a designated function.
- **Two-person control:** For particularly sensitive security situations that involve people, require that two independent persons be involved in the actions. No single individual is trusted to perform such functions.
- **Multiple "Fire Walls":** There should be two or more independent security mechanisms that must fail (or be broken) before unauthorized access occurs. This goes beyond two-person control to include multiple different security mechanisms.
- **Mutual suspicion:** All parts of the system should treat the other parts of the system as being potentially bogus until confirmed otherwise. This is especially true for sources of critical commands, such as a network control center or a network security center. However, in some systems this concern applies to **all** system components.

In this section, we have attempted to point out some of the highlights involved in producing a secure network. These aspects range from the often abstract concerns of a security policy to the nuts and bolts aspects of design, implementation, and operation of a secure system. All phases of the system life cycle must be included to end up with a secure system.

ADMINISTRATION OF DATA COMMUNICATIONS AND NETWORKING

Any system that provides a much needed resource, such as data communications and networking, must be administered. This is especially true when the scope of networking expands to include shared server computers and access to outside networks. The administration has many different areas of concern, as discussed in the following paragraphs.

Network administration involves network monitoring with questions such as: How well is the network operating? Where are the bottlenecks? How close is the traffic level to causing congestion? Which users are accessing which resources? All of these questions, and hundreds more, are answered through network monitoring, which involves the receipt, processing, and display of information that is collected from the individual network components. This information may include counts, such as total number of packets sent and number of retransmissions. The information also may include running totals, such as the sum of the byte counts of all packets sent or received.

Network administration also involves control. When the network monitoring indicates that there is a problem, network control comes into play to diagnose the problem and to isolate the malfunctioning component. Test methods include the sending of artificial traffic and looping traffic back at selected points until the problem is isolated.

There are a number of configuration related concerns of network administration. Devices must be attached to or removed from the network. Tables that indicate the current configuration must be built and maintained. Parameters have to be set and their values made available to the network administrator. A suggestion here is to automate every such configuration related mechanism. Do not try to manually maintain routing tables, timeout values, etc., except in the simplest, small-scale networks. You will see examples of this automation in various aspects of network administration and network management.

Network administrators will be concerned with some areas that are placed in separate chapters of this book. Examples include network security, which was discussed previously, and network testing, which is discussed in the following section.

DATA COMMUNICATIONS AND NETWORK TESTING

Data communications and network testing is important for four reasons. First, you need to know how well your network is operating. For example, is the network actually sending every packet twice because of inappropriately set timer values? If so, although traffic is delivered successfully, it consumes far more of the network resources than it should.

The second major reason for testing is for debugging network problems. In a typical multivendor network, it is the responsibility of network management to detect problems and isolate their cause to a replaceable unit or a vendor-provided service. Fault isolation often relies on forms of loop-back testing, to gradually include or exclude portions of the network from the test.

The third reason is that stress testing of a network maximizes the chances that the network will perform correctly in a crisis (e.g., peak load) period. This form of testing is often overlooked. Too often testing focuses on demonstrating that formal requirements have been met (i.e., does the network meet every one of the "shall statements" of the procurement document?). Such tests are necessary, but do not neglect tests that try to "beat the hell out of the network." It is better to find out if there are potential problems than to assume that ignorance is bliss.

Finally, there is a need to provide conformance testing, to evaluate protocol implementations against some accepted standard implementation, and test suite. Such conformance tests are becoming more common.

Various forms of data communications and network testing are distributed throughout the chapters that follow, but in each case, testing fills one or more of the abovementioned needs.

3

SYSTEMS DESIGN
AND PROGRAMMING
WITH OPEN SYSTEMS

This chapter introduces the concepts of open systems, which are the key to multivendor interoperability. Eventually we will have the internationally standardized *Open Systems Interconnection (OSI) protocols*, which all vendors are expected to support. These protocols have been developed as a part of a grand plan to develop networking from scratch without the hindrance of concerns such as backwards compatibility. It all started with the OSI *Reference Model (RM)*, which provided a framework for the development of agreed-to standards for computer networking. Many aspects of the OSI networking approach are still evolving, and some parts remain to be developed.

Meanwhile, we can expect to see continued usage of other open products, such as the *TCP/IP protocol suite* (Transmission Control Protocol/ Internet Protocol), which provides the basic needs of networking. Use of the official OSI protocols in data communications and networking will continue to gain popularity, and OSI will continue to be utilized both in the development of OSI protocols and as a gauge for comparison with other protocols.

BACKGROUND, OBJECTIVES, AND SUMMARY OF OPEN SYSTEMS

Open systems, in contrast to vendor-specific approaches to networking, have been used for more than a decade. As mentioned above, TCP/IP is a dominant set of protocols for communications with almost any vendor's hardware and software variations. Eventually, true international standards will be utilized universally, although this has not yet occurred. That is not the case today. However, we must be very concerned about this transition era, which may last for most of the decade. What should we utilize today, and how should we plan for the future transition? This is an important consideration to keep in mind as we discuss protocols in general.

The starting point for open systems was in the late 1960s with the development of networks such as the ARPAnet. A wide variety of different computer systems were to be interconnected, with computer-to-computer communications. Before that, most networking was simple terminal-to-host communications. The direct interconnection of hosts required that new host-to-host protocols be defined and implemented on this variety of machines. This effort lead to what was probably the first transport protocol, the Network Control Protocol (NCP). It was an open system protocol in that it was made widely available across many different machines.

About that same time, IBM was developing *System Network Architecture* (*SNA*) and DEC was developing *DECnet*. These were proprietary protocol suites in that they were under the control of IBM and DEC, respectively. However, they were not kept as trade secrets. Presumably, other companies could implement these protocols as well, and at least portions of them (particularly SNA) were implemented by other companies. Does this make these protocols open? One could argue that protocols can be proprietary, but still open. Indeed, one vendor makes this argument regarding their LAN server system. "Proprietary" means that it is under their control; "open" means that others can utilize it. This works fine until the vendor who controls the networking protocols changes them, for example, by adding a new enhancement. The other companies that have implemented the protocols now have to catch up and are at a disadvantage.

Whatever the arguments about proprietary versus open might lead to, we will limit our usage of the word "open" to those protocols that are not under the control of a single commercial enterprise. Unfortunately, that typically means they are controlled by a committee, but that is the price for openness in this case. The early NCP protocol was designed by a committee consisting of representatives from the ARPAnet host sites. Its successor, TCP, was initially designed by Vint Cerf and Robert Kahn but was soon put under a committee mode of refinement. The OSI protocols have followed this same approach of starting with a reasonably well-planned protocol (usually from the European Computer Manufacturing Association), and refining it in a committee.

The original OSI committee was quite small, at one time consisting of three persons. This effort during 1977 to 1979 produced the OSI Reference Model (RM), based on existing computer network architectures such as SNA, DECnet, and TCP/IP, as well as reflecting the wisdom and foresight of its developers. Although this model is more than a decade old, it has become a living set of documents, as various addenda have attempted to keep pace with other emerging aspects of networking technology. Depending on who you talk to, the expanding set of RM developers may or may not have actually kept up with recent advances in technology. In any case, the RM still serves several valuable purposes.

The OSI RM was developed to serve only one basic purpose: to provide a framework for the development of computer networking standards. As such, it was important to strictly follow the specific services and mechanisms defined in the RM. (The latter were called "functions" in the RM.) However, the RM also has provided a very convenient structure for describing more general forms of networking approaches. Therefore, existing protocol suites such as SNA, DECnet, and TCP/IP have traditionally been compared, on a layer by layer basis, with OSI.

Our use of the model in this book is as a structure or framework for discussion. This should not imply that only OSI-specific issues will be discussed. Instead, the framework is used more generally, including some issues that are necessary to know but do not fit in a strict OSI interpretation. The motivation is one of presenting information in an-easy-to-understand manner without strictly following the RM itself. This does not always set well with an avid OSI advocate, and you are advised to emulate this more broad-based interpretation at your own risk. It may lead to a visit by the OSI "protocol police"—that is, those self-appointed zealots who attempt to protect the purity of OSI concepts.

The RM provides a layered set of network services. In many ways it is analogous to the layers of an operating system. In both cases, the top layer provides services that directly concern the applications programmer. Similarly, the lowest layers provide detailed control of the hardware devices, such as disk controllers for the operating system or LAN interface boards for the network. In both cases, the intermediate layers provide increasing levels of service, one layer building on and adding to the services of the layer below it.

The OSI RM requires strict adherence to passing through all the layers. It is considered a violation of OSI principles to skip over one or more layers, or for an application to operate directly on some lower layer. If you try it in an OSI environment, you may get another visit from the "protocol police." However, building on any appropriate lower layer service is common in some of the protocols, such as TCP/IP.

For the purposes of this book, we do not limit ourselves to only the specific definitions of the OSI services and mechanisms of each layer. These are addressed in another volume in this series. The concern here is more general, utilizing the RM only as a basis for discussion.

The RM is shown in Figure 3-1 in the form of a sample file transfer to be made. This example is discussed in a top-down manner, describing which services are provided at which layers. In subsequent layer-by-layer sections, however, follow the layers in a bottom-up manner, which is the traditional way to present layered services.

The bottom-up presentation is preferred for various reasons. First, it allows one to follow the value-added aspect of each layer. What services did the lower

7	Application	Provides appropriate service for application
6	Presentation	Provides data formatting (syntax)
5	Session	Provides service facilities to the application
4	Transport	Provides for end-to-end data transmission integrity
3	Network	Switches and routes information units
2	Link	Provides transfer functions for units of information to other end of physical link
1	Physical	Transmits bit stream on physical medium

Graphic courtesy of Learning Tree International.

FIGURE 3-1   The OSI RM provides a seven-layered set of services.

layer provide, and what new services did the layer of concern add? Second, it allows you to learn concepts, such as flow control, error control, timers, and parameter initialization, starting with very simple (lower layer) approaches, and moving to complex (higher layer) implementations of the same basic issues.

You might wonder about having the same issues at several different layers. Why not provide each service once, and then simply utilize it at higher layers? The reason is often one of granularity. For example, lower layer flow control may stop the data flow from an entire computer, while higher layer flow control would stop or reduce the flow from a single application. This will be explained later.

The example application was to perform a file transfer. An Application Program Interface, or API, in the form of a service call, maps the user request into the required commands at the FTAM (File Transfer, Access, and Management) protocol. In this example, only the file transfer capabilities are being utilized. For example, going to "get" the file (i.e., read it to have a local copy). Alternatively, an access could be made to a single record or the file could be managed; for example, its name could be changed. In the given example, the goal is transferring the entire file.

FTAM "knows" about operations related to files, but it does not know about the specific implementation of files at the other host. However, FTAM provides the appearance of a *virtual file*, and all operations are performed based on this virtual representation of the actual file. It is the responsibility of FTAM at the other host to map the virtual file related requests into a form that is suitable for the file being accessed. In other words, the user is unaware of the background processes handled by FTAM.

FTAM relies on the services of the Presentation Layer to convey the information from the remote computer to the local computer in a way that preserves the *semantics* (meaning) of the information, but maps, as required, the *syntax* (form and format) from one machine environment to another. These required services are negotiated at the time the logical connection between the two end systems is established.

The Session Layer provides its service next, which in this example is twofold. First, the two computers have negotiated (i.e., agreed) that the flow of information will be half-duplex (two-way alternate). The Session Layer allows this service to be negotiated and subsequently enforces the flow by means of a *token* which only one computer has at any given time. The second service provided by the Session Layer in this example is the provision of *check points* for crash recovery. If either computer crashes during the transfer, the most recent *synchronization point* can be used for restart.

The Session Layer builds upon the Transport Layer services, which include data integrity. Data will be transferred in Transport Layer packets, called *Protocol Data Units* in OSI. Data integrity means there are no defective packets (i.e., no missing or bad bits), no packets are missing, none are out of order, and none are duplicated. Only one correct copy of each packet is delivered to the recipient.

The Network Layer provides a service to the Transport Layer such that the Transport Layer does not have to know about the nature and interconnectivity of the network(s) over which the data is transferred. It does not have to know about maximum packet size limitations or how to find a path across the network(s). These services are provided by the Network Layer.

Data Link Layer protocols provide a data delivery service along several cascaded point-to-point links. These include links within the network, between the host and the network, and/or between hosts. The delivery service is in terms of blocks of data, i.e., some number of contiguous characters. These blocks have often been called "frames," although they could equally well be called packets or Protocol Data Units. The service may be that of a connection (virtual circuit) or it may be connectionless (datagram based). Examples of each are discussed later in this chapter.

At the very bottom the Physical Layer provides a mechanism for delivering bits. Its job is to adapt the bits into a form that is suitable for transmission over the media, which may be a telephone circuit, a satellite link, a LAN, or any of a number of different media. Some of these forms are analog; others are digital. The media choices and tradeoffs are generally not considered to be an OSI concern. However, they are discussed here in the context of the Physical Layer because of the strategic importance of selecting the proper media in a network. This is an example of going beyond the normal boundaries of the RM, when appropriate, to introduce additional needed material.

Subsequent chapters begin more detailed discussions of the protocol and implementation issues of the layers by starting at the bottom and working up. The bottom-up approach allows you to understand the basic concepts before the complexities of higher layer mechanisms are encountered. The increasing sophistication and complexity of the networking mechanisms become apparent as you move from the Physical Layer up through the Transport Layer. Above the Transport Layer, you will find a new, rather different set of concerns. In the meantime, you will continue to investigate the RM itself and attempt to benefit from its well-defined set of terminology and concepts, which should continue to serve beyond the next decade. For the first time, the RM's terms and concepts will have a single interpretation, without using the vague terms of messages, packets, frames, blocks, and units. These terms may not have meant the same thing, but a Protocol Data Unit (the OSI term) has only one meaning.

OSI TERMINOLOGY, CONCEPTS, AND CONSTRAINTS

The OSI RM not only provides a framework for the definition of computer networking protocols, it also implicitly provides a new and common set of terminology and concepts. As mentioned previously, these can be very useful from a technical communication point of view, but these terms and concepts also can take on a more definitive role in contractual matters related to networking.

OSI Terminology

OSI terminology initially seems rather verbose. OSI says Protocol Data Unit or PDU instead of packet or its other variations such as frame. Why use three words when one word will do the job? The answer is clearly, "When you want to be precise about what you are saying."

OSI appends a letter to PDU to relate it to a specific layer. Therefore, TPDU means Transport PDU, while NPDU means Network PDU. This further specifies the data unit of concern in a given discussion. In general, the PDU is the unit of information that is passed between peer protocol entities.

There is also a Service Data Unit or SDU. The SDU is the unit of information that passes across a layer boundary. By definition, the data unit that passes from layer N to layer N–1 at the sending end (computer) will be the exact same SDU that is passed from layer N–1 to layer N at the receiving end.

Application data finds its way down through the protocol layers on one end system, and back up through the layers of the receiving end system by following a sequence of Service Access Points or SAPs. A SAP may be either an internal software address or an external hardware address. It is a generalization of other ad hoc mechanisms that have been found in previous non-OSI protocols, which have gone by names such as a "type field," "next protocol," "port number," and "socket number." Again, there is a common, well-defined meaning associated with the terms.

The characteristics of a SAP can be seen from an analogy. Consider the case of an airline's reservation telephone number—it is a SAP. Several users may be simultaneously accessing this SAP, with each user distinguished by a unique number, called a Reference Point Identifier in OSI. In the analogy, this uniqueness is characterized by the name of the operator with whom you are talking. This concept of a SAP is shown in Figure 3-2, in which the ellipse is the SAP and the dots are the Reference Point Identifiers. In Figure 3-2, the different SAPs at a layer will represent different types of service. One may be a secure service, while another may be a high throughput service, for example.

This section's discussions are representative of OSI terminology that are believed to be the principal terms of concern in most network systems.

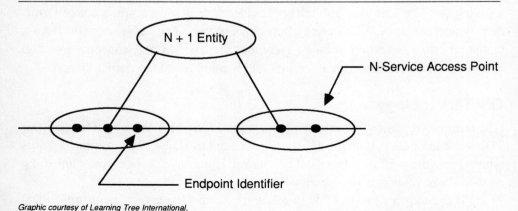

Graphic courtesy of Learning Tree International.

FIGURE 3-2   A Service Access Point (SAP) provides a known location for a given type of service.

OSI Concepts

Just as new terminology was introduced with OSI, some additional concepts also were introduced. The main contribution here, however, was to codify previous concepts that had existed in various forms and under various names. OSI introduced the concept of very strict layering: Every layer should be involved in every application usage of the OSI protocol suite. In many previous protocol suites, concern was limited to retaining a hierarchical structure, but allowing applications to build upon whatever layer, or subset of layers, that was considered to be appropriate.

OSI also introduced the concept of *sublayers*—a layer within a layer. For example, the internet protocol is a sublayer within the Network Layer. Similarly, the electronic mail delivery protocol is a sublayer of the Application Layer.

Each layer (or sublayer) is described in terms of two documents: a service definition and a protocol specification. The service definition defines the services that are provided by this layer (or sublayer) to the next higher layer. The protocol specification defines the set of conventions for communications between the peer level entities in the two systems that are communicating.

The initial OSI services and protocols are all connection-oriented. Some connectionless versions exist today, but more will be developed over time. Currently, however, most OSI protocols operate on the basis of establishing a connection and negotiating the properties of the connection at that time. Data units are transferred, and eventually the connection is released.

The connection establishment is typically based on a full OSI handshake, which consists of an originator *request*, which is delivered to the other system as an *indication*. This is followed by a *response*, which is delivered across the network and arrives as a *confirmation* at the originating end system. During this exchange, there is an agreement regarding if a connection will occur, and if so, what its parameters (such as maximum packet size) will be. This is called *negotiation*.

Connections are established between end systems. Other systems also may be involved between these two end systems, which are called *intermediate systems*. They are relay systems because they simply send the protocol data units toward the destination end system. These relay systems may be simple repeaters (at the Physical Layer), bridges between local area networks, or routers (gateways) between any kinds of networks. These are discussed in detail in Chapter 5.

Connections may include the capability to send *expedited data*. Expedited data transfer involves the ability to establish a second data channel over which special "urgent" data can be sent without being subject to flow control over the principal channel. The idea is not to have a completely separate control channel, but to have a minimal capability to express the special concern for a packet that is being sent.

Connections at a given protocol layer usually provide a well-defined service. This is especially true at the Network and Transport Layers, which are often considered together. If the Network Layer provides a service, it can be propagated directly upwards as a Transport Layer service. Reliable and sequenced delivery are two such examples. If the Network Layer provides a service, the Transport Layer can simply pass it along. These are sometimes called "pass through services." Therefore, we find different classes of Transport protocols that provide the same service in different mixes of Transport versus Network provided services.

Unlike the Transport/Network Layers, the higher layers do not provide a common (single) service level. Instead they provide a variety of Functional Units that can be negotiated at connection establishment. Each functional unit provides a different service. One functional unit may control which end system can communicate in a half-duplex manner; another may be related to crash recovery in a file transfer. Not all applications need all functional units, thus they are negotiable. However, there is a "kernel" component that is considered to be required in all implementations, and it is not negotiable.

The discussions above are representative of the concepts introduced and/ or codified by OSI. The next major section discusses some of the implementation considerations related to the fact that OSI protocols do not spring to life overnight. Each protocol is subjected to a lengthy process, and the implementer must be careful not to initiate implementation too soon or too late. The section "Implementation Issues in Open Systems" describes this development process and the succeeding section makes recommendations as to when it is safe to implement the evolving protocols.

OSI Constraints

OSI layering rules impose rather severe constraints on the allowed use of lower layer services. Each layer must be invoked as one passes through the layers. These constraints, however, can be counterproductive in some protocols. This was a major concern in the Manufacturing Automation Protocol (MAP) community, and a subsequent Mini-MAP recommendation did away with this layering constraint, eliminating many of the middle OSI layers.

Other protocols, such as the TCP/IP protocol suite, have found strict layering is a hindrance in obtaining the needed interrelationship between the layers of a protocol suite. For example, the TCP/IP protocols tend to share information between layers much beyond what would be expected of the OSI layering.

For example, error reports at the Internet Protocol are typically passed on to the Transport Layer for action, but this does not strictly follow OSI layering constraints.

IMPLEMENTATION ISSUES IN OPEN SYSTEMS

You might expect that a system running a closed, vendor-specific, network implementation could easily interoperate with another copy of that same implementation. After all, the two end systems would be running the same program. Life is not that simple for vendors with proprietary networking software, but it certainly is simpler than the open systems environment in which many different implementers are involved.

The service definitions and the protocol specifications at each layer are not sufficient in and of themselves for a multi-implementer environment. Implementation agreements are also required. Many of these implementation agreements are with regard to if and how options should be implemented. Many protocols have numerous options, and an implementer need not necessarily include all of them. But if one implementer does include an option and another does not, will they be interoperable? Deciding which options to include and which to exclude is one aspect of the implementer agreements, and will affect interoperability.

The most active implementer groups are those of the Manufacturing Automation Protocol and its related Technical and Office Protocol (TOP). This work has been performed in conjunction with the National Institute for Standards and Technology, formerly the National Bureau of Standards.

In addition to the formal implementer agreements, there are also a set of implementation guidelines, or rules of thumb, that have evolved over the years as protocols have been implemented by multiple organizations. One of the most useful of these guidelines was developed and published in the early TCP specifications. It is called the "robustness principle," and it is still valid in today's implementations. The robustness principle states that implementers should be very cautious and conservative about how they interpret a specification, but those same implementers should assume that others will bend all the rules.

Another guideline for implementers is to minimize the need for human involvement in the day-to-day operations of the network. Systems should be self-configuring when booted or restarted. Systems should, for example, automatically learn about other network neighbors, the characteristics of the network(s) over which data passes, and the timeouts that are appropriate for each path. Expecting a human being to manually enter such information across the network results in expensive, labor-intensive operations that are error prone.

IMPLEMENTATION CONCERNS RELATIVE TO THE STANDARDIZATION PROCESS

Many data communication and networking implementers face a common problem. When should they expend the effort to implement a new and evolving protocol? If they start too soon, they will have to rework their implementation, perhaps to the extent of starting all over. If they wait too long to get started, their company or organization will be behind and may have lost a possible major competitive advantage in the marketplace. When is it **safe** to begin the implementation?

To answer this question, you need to understand the protocol standardization process. First of all, there are many "players." For example, in Local Area Networks, the IEEE (Institute of Electrical and Electronic Engineers) is a major participant. But the 100 Mbps version of LANs is coming from the ANSI (American National Standards Institute) committee, working with the IEEE. These efforts are also being tracked by the International Standardization Organization (ISO) committees, with similar ISO standards being developed. On the other hand, the higher level protocols typically have come from ECMA (the European Computer Manufacturers Association, which includes several U.S. companies). The IEEE and ECMA efforts have fed into the international standardization bodies, namely ISO and CCITT (Consultative Committee for International Telephone and Telegraph). With all of these groups involved, when is a standard really a standard, and when should you implement it with some assurance that you will not have to discard your implementation and start over at some later time?

There are several key indicators as to when a protocol has become reliable and can be implemented with minimal risk. These indicators include inclusion of the protocol in major vendor products, such as the use of token ring LANs in IBM products or the use of Ethernet/IEEE LANs in DEC products. Another indicator is the adoption of protocols in major user-oriented protocol stacks, such as MAP/TOP (Manufacturing Automation Protocol/Technical Office Protocol). A related indicator is when protocols are widely utilized in the implementer groups as discussed above. Another indicator is the status of the protocol in the international standardization committees. The most easily recognized status is in ISO, in which there is a well-defined sequence of protocol formalization steps.

In ISO, as shown in Figure 3-3, a concept starts out as a Working Paper and moves to a Draft Proposal (DP). Many changes are apt to occur during these deliberations. Advanced development groups tend to implement the DP. It may eventually reach the stage of Draft International Standard (DIS). At this point it is normally stable, with only editorial and minor technical changes expected. Although commercial companies may have been involved from the early stages, this is when the commercial implementations often are begun in terms of products. If all goes well, the final International Standard (IS) differs in a very small way, and OSI products can be released quickly into the marketplace.

As can be expected from the above brief discussion of the standardization process, the evolution of a standard may include the introduction of several compromise positions. You will see examples of "warts" or other strange aspects of

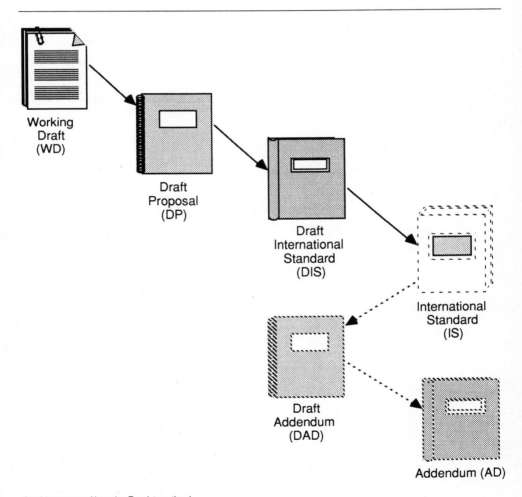

Working
Draft
(WD)

Draft
Proposal
(DP)

Draft
International
Standard
(DIS)

International
Standard
(IS)

Draft
Addendum
(DAD)

Addendum (AD)

Graphic courtesy of Learning Tree International.

FIGURE 3-3   The ISO development process proceeds along a well-defined sequence of steps.

the standardized protocols in later discussions. You should not expect to have the most elegant protocols coming out of standardization committees. An agreed-to standard has been characterized as a compromise that each participant feels is equally poor. The important aspects are that standards actually do come out of the committees and that the national or other implementer groups define meaningful subsets of the protocols for subsequent implementations. At least some of the warts can be eliminated in this way. And, in the end, would you rather have your networking protocols with a few warts or have them dictated by a single, dominant vendor?

4

DEVELOPMENT ISSUES FOR
THE BOTTOM TWO LAYERS

The Physical and Data Link Layers were well in place when the OSI RM was developed and still are basically intact. The major changes have occurred in LANs, which have profoundly added to the lower layer concepts. These two layers are the subject of this chapter.

THE PHYSICAL LAYER

The purpose of the Physical Layer is to get bits delivered from one computer to another directly connected computer. These computers may be the end systems (e.g., hosts), or they may be switching computers (e.g., packet switches). The Physical Layer functions by adapting the representation of bits into an appropriate form for the communications.

Representing Data and Control Characters

The concept of representing bits is broadened to include representing characters to introduce some concepts and capabilities that need to be built upon, namely those of a character set such as ASCII. The ASCII (American Standard Code for Information Interchange) code set is shown in Figure 4-1.

The ASCII code set includes 128 symbols, representing the seven-bit coded values. Many of these symbols are the familiar letters and numbers of normal user-to-user data. Also included are punctuation symbols, which humans could consider as "control characters." When does a sentence stop? When is there a pause between connected ideas? Symbols such as "." and "," provide this control. Another portion of the ASCII character set can control terminals. These include carriage return, line feed, form feed, and bell.

In addition to terminal control characters, there are Data Link Layer control characters, such as Start of TeXt (STX) and End of TeXt (ETX), which start and end a block of contiguous characters that represent the information being sent.

b7 →					0	0	+6 0	0	1	1	1	1
b6 →					0	0	1	1	0	0	1	1
b5 →					0	1	0	1	0	1	0	1
Bits	b4	b3	b2	b1	col row	0	1	2	3	4	5	6	7
	0	0	0	0	**0**	NUL	DLE	SP	0	@	P	`	p
	0	0	0	1	**1**	SOH	DC1	!	1	A	Q	a	q
	0	0	1	0	**2**	STX	DC2	"	2	B	R	b	r
	0	0	1	1	**3**	ETX	DC3	#	3	C	S	c	s
	0	1	0	0	**4**	EOT	DC4	$	4	D	T	d	t
	0	1	0	1	**5**	ENQ	NAK	%	5	E	U	e	u
	0	1	1	0	**6**	ACK	SYN	&	6	F	V	f	v
	0	1	1	1	**7**	BEL	ETB	'	7	G	W	g	w
	1	0	0	0	**8**	BS	CAN	(	8	H	X	h	x
	1	0	0	1	**9**	HT	EM	)	9	I	Y	i	y
	1	0	1	0	**10**	LF	SUB	*	:	J	Z	j	z
	1	0	1	1	**11**	VT	ESC	+	;	K	[	k	{
	1	1	0	0	**12**	FF	FS	,	<	L	\	l		
	1	1	0	1	**13**	CR	GS	−	=	M	]	m	}
	1	1	1	0	**14**	SO	RS	.	>	N	^	n	-
	1	1	1	1	**15**	SI	US	/	?	O	_	o	DEL

Graphic courtesy of Learning Tree International.

FIGURE 4-1   The American Standard Code for Information Interchange (ASCII) provides data and control representations.

At the Physical Layer, this block of characters is viewed as a sequence of bits that must be represented in a way that can be recognized by the receiver.

Encoding Bits for Transmission

The transmitting device puts the physical representation of the bits on the transmission line bit by bit. This representation might be a positive five volts to represent a binary one and a negative five volts to represent binary zero. This would be very simple for the transmitter, but it would make life very difficult for the receiver, which would have to be able to determine if a long string of binary ones was, say, 22 bits in length versus 21 or 23 bits in length. The receiver needs an occasional reference point to accurately read in the bits. These reference points are typically transitions in the data representation. A transition allows the receiver to accurately determine the boundary between two bits and to resynchronize its receive clock with that of the transmitter.

In the above representation, a long string of binary 1s or 0s would not have any transitions, and clock recovery might be inadequate, resulting in loss of actual bits or the insertion of extraneous bits. Therefore, the bits are encoded to ensure that there are a sufficient number of transitions in the signal for accurate clock recovery. Two such methods, shown in Figure 4-2, are called *Manchester encoding* and *NRZI* (*Non-Return to Zero Inverted*) encoding.

Manchester encoding provides a signal transition for every bit, all that anyone could ever want. The problem, however, is that Manchester encoding provides more transitions than are needed, and the excess transitions consume bandwidth. There is a tradeoff between ease of clock recovery and the efficient use of bandwidth. Manchester encoding is utilized in systems that have more than enough bandwidth and want simple, low-cost clock recovery. Baseband LANs provide examples of such systems with excess bandwidth.

An encoding scheme that requires less bandwidth is NRZI, which in this example has a transition on every binary 0 but does not have a transition on a binary 1. Would that present a problem for a long string of binary 1s? Yes, but a way around that problem is found in the Data Link Layer, where some extra zeros are inserted in the transmitted data stream and then discarded at the receiver. This answers a particular concern of the Data Link Layer; namely, to ensure that a specific bit pattern does not appear in the data stream. It also has a positive side effect of ensuring that the NRZI-encoded Physical Layer gets its transitions sufficiently often (by ensuring that a zero, and therefore a transition, occurs frequently).

A variation of this encoding scheme is utilized in the 4B/5B encoding as used in the 100 Mbps FDDI (Fiber Distributed Data Interface) LAN. FDDI converts every four bits that are to be sent into a five-bit pattern for actual

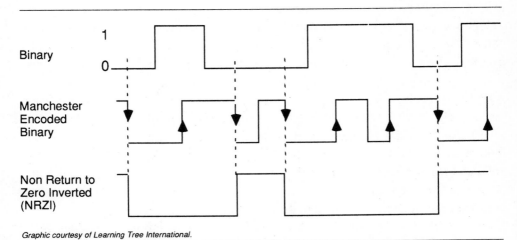

Binary

Manchester
Encoded
Binary

Non Return to
Zero Inverted
(NRZI)

Graphic courtesy of Learning Tree International.

FIGURE 4-2 Binary data may be encoded for better clock recovery.

transmission. The coded five-bit patterns are selected to ensure that zeros will occur at least once per every four bits sent. Then, NRZI encoding is utilized in addition to the 4B/5B encoding. This allows inexpensive fiber-optic transmitters to be used for the LAN, which would not have been the case if Manchester encoding were utilized.

After encoding the binary signal, it can be placed directly on a baseband (i.e., direct digital) system such as a LAN. However, for an analog system such as a telephone channel, the signal must be further adapted for other bandwidth reasons. This necessitates limiting the required bandwidth as well as ensuring that the entire transmitted signal fits within the particular bandwidth of the telephone channel.

The process of converting a digital signal into an analog signal for communications is called *modulation*, and the corresponding return from analog into digital form is called *demodulation*. These two words give the contraction *modem*, or modulator/demodulator. Modems are discussed later in this chapter.

Media Alternatives and Implications

Although OSI considers itself to be independent of media concerns, system/ software designers must include these media-related details in their "tool kits" regarding the implementation of actual networks. Therefore, the media alternatives and their various tradeoffs should be discussed.

There are many different communications media alternatives. The most common segregation of these alternatives is telephone company-provided capabilities and locally installed media capabilities.

Use of Telephone Company Channels

Telephone company channels may be either of two types, direct dial or dedicated. The latter may also be known as leased circuits. Direct dial circuits are established on an as-needed basis. Dialing may be manual, but it is most commonly done using a computerized provision of the appropriate tone pairs to represent the various digits of the telephone number being called. The computer also should abide by the call progress signals, for example, waiting for a dial tone before sending the number. In contrast, leased telephone channels do not require a dial tone and phone number exchange. The connection is always available, and ready for use, and paid for—whether used or not. The breakeven point on usage is at about three or four hours per day but can vary considerably based on fixed costs at each end, line length, and tariffs.

However, there is more to consider than cost. Leased circuits are better quality because they do not have to go through switching apparatus and can be tuned to provide more effective usage of the bandwidth than with direct dial circuits.

As a result, more bits per second are obtainable on leased circuits than on direct dial circuits.

Use of Locally Installed Media

Instead of utilizing telephone company channels, the network implementer can build upon one or more of a variety of media. To avoid having too wide a range of media and the accompanying required wiring technician skills, most wiring approaches are limited to no more than three different media approaches. The following are the most common media choices.

1. Telephone company **unshielded twisted pair wiring** is utilized widely, because it is often already in place and available for use. There are often extra pairs in the 25-pair cables that the telephone company has installed. With deregulation, you can probably use some of this wiring for your LAN. Mixing data and telephone cables in the same bundle sometimes causes cross talk, however, particularly with the relatively high voltages of the ringing signal coupling into the data circuits.

    Even if existing telephone twisted pair wires are not currently available or not considered suitable for usage, unshielded twisted pairs can be installed simply and inexpensively. The media itself is very inexpensive, and skilled technicians are readily available.

2. The other form of twisted pair wiring is **shielded data grade wiring**. In addition to the shielding, the wire has less resistance, as reflected by its wire gauge number. Normal telephone twisted pair wiring is AWG 24 (American Wire Gauge size 24); data grade wiring is AWG 22. The smaller the AWG number, the lower the resistance. Electrical properties of cables are discussed again in the section "Baseband Operation."

3. Unlike the similar appearance of the two wires of a twisted pair cable, a **coaxial cable** has distinctly different configurations for its two conductors. One is typically an internal (solid) copper wire, and the second is a braided and/or foil shield around the insulated central conductor. This form of cable is commonly used with television receivers, particularly with cable television.

Fiber Optics

One of the most promising data communications media is *fiber optics*. It has been used by telephone companies for several years and is beginning to make major inroads into the data communications and networking world. It has become a major emerging technology in LANs as well. You should not overlook the possibilities provided by utilizing fiber optics. However, you will find that some new technology and terminology must be learned. Some of the key issues are discussed below.

Optical fibers are very small, hairlike strands of pure glass or a similar material. The strands are covered by a thin, protective plastic-like material, and transmit light from one end to the other. Light is inserted at the transmitting end by coupling the light from an LED (light emitting diode) or a laser into the small core of the fiber strand. At the receiving end, the light is converted back to electrical signals. Envision that an illuminated receiver pulse indicates a binary 1 and a dark signal represents a binary 0. However, the encoding schemes tend to be more complicated than this simple example. One such example is in the previous brief mention of the FDDI network.

The diameter of fiber optic cables is measured in microns, or millionths of a meter. Two diameters are involved: the inner core diameter and the outer cladding diameter which is separable from the plastic coating. Both the core and the cladding are glass, but they have different optical properties that keep the light inside the central core. Common core diameters are 50, 62.5, and 85 microns. All of these share a common 125-micron cladding diameter for the convenience of utilizing a common set of connectors. These cables are designated using these two numbers, such as 62.5/125 micron, which is the AT&T de facto standard. IBM uses a different size fiber, namely 100/140 micron. The characteristics of these different fiber sizes are compared in Figure 4-3, which shows the sizes, loss per Km, and bandwidth-distance product.

The loss per Km is given in decibels (dB). The dB is a ratio, with 10 dB being a factor of ten. Therefore, a 10-dB loss of light power is reduction in signal strength of a factor of ten; a 20-dB loss would be a reduction of signal power of a factor of 100, or 10^2. The signal must be regenerated before it has attenuated beyond recovery. In the following examples, a factor of ten in signal strength reduction is used as the point at which a signal regenerator must be inserted.

Figure 4-3 shows that the loss per Km is about 3 dB for 50-micron fiber and about twice that for 100-micron fiber. Therefore, if a repeater is placed every 10 dB of loss, one would have to be placed at about 3-Km intervals for the 50-micron fiber, and twice as frequently for 100-micron fiber. The MHz × Km product column also shows that the data rate can be greater for the 50-micron fiber compared to the larger core diameters. This makes 50-micron fiber better on both counts. The other consideration is the angle of light that can be coupled into the core, which would mean 100-micron fiber (the larger core size) is superior. A compromise between the two concerns is the 62.5-micron fiber, which has gained wide acceptance. It is also part of AT&T's approach to utilizing fiber optics.

Figure 4-3 also shows the effects of using a longer wavelength of light. The dB/Km and MHz × Km parameters are both improved considerably by using

A Comparison of Fiber-Optic Cables				
Core size (μm)	Cladding size (μm)	Numerical Aperture	Attenuation dB/km	Bandwidth MHz • km
50	125	0.20	3	600
62.5	125	0.275	4	160
85	125	0.26	5	200
100	140	0.29	6	100

All data at 850 nm, graded index cable

- For 62.5 micron fiber,

	850 nm	1300 nm
dB/km	4	2
MHz • km	160	500

Improved performance →

Graphic courtesy of Learning Tree International.

FIGURE 4-3 A comparison of common fiber-optic media.

1,300-nm (nanometer) light instead of 850 nm. A better alternative is 1,500 nm, but 850 nm is mature technology and relatively inexpensive. Use of 1,300 nm can be found in current state-of-the-art products but is considerably more expensive. Use of 1,500 nm is still being developed.

One of the difficulties with fiber optics is the number of choices necessary. In addition to the core/cladding diameter, you must select between different light source wavelengths, multi- versus single-mode transmission, and connector styles.

As described above, the light wavelength choices are for 850, 1,300, or 1,500 nm. This is just outside of the human visual spectrum of about 350 to 800 nm, residing in infrared light. You should utilize the least expensive technology that meets your requirements. A current leading edge fiber optic network standard is the FDDI (Fiber Distributed Data Interface), which utilizes 1,300 nm.

Another required choice in fiber optic networks regards multimode or single-mode cable. *Multimode* means that two or more colors of light are used to convey the signal, while *single mode* means that one coherent color is utilized. (Of course, the light is beyond the spectrum of visible light, and therefore does not have a color noticeable to the human eye.) The concern with multimode is that different colors have different propagation delay times, thus the signal representation tends to spread, limiting the data rate and the distance between repeaters. Most LANs use multimode fiber; many high-speed, long-distance, point-to-point telephone circuits utilize single-mode fiber. LANs often utilize a special form of multimode called *graded index*, which compensates for the differing propagation times of different wavelengths. Expect to see a mixture of multimode, graded index, and single-mode fiber-optic systems in future data networks.

The connector choices present another set of complex options. There are at least a half-dozen major fiber-optic connector types. They vary in ease of installation, lifetime of connect/disconnect cycles, insertion loss, variability of insertion loss, and a number of other factors. Some of the major fiber-optic connector styles are the SMA, ST, and biconic connectors.

Other Media

There are a number of other data communications media of lesser and/or more specialized usage than already described. These include radio broadcast links, satellite links, use of power lines, and infrared transmission.

Radio broadcast links often are in the form of private microwave links. These point-to-point circuits can be useful but also have a few negative aspects. First, they require a license to operate. The license may be difficult to obtain, because there are often more requests than there is available bandwidth. The most readily available bandwidth is within the 20 Ghz frequency range, which can be degraded by rain or fog.

Satellite links are a form of radio broadcast and share the advantages and disadvantages described above. However, satellites have two significant additional characteristics. On the positive side, satellites can have a very large "footprint"; that is, the geographical range of transmission and/or reception can encompass an entire country. On the negative side, there is a long propagation delay for signals, which must go up to the satellite and back down again. For satellites that appear to be stationary with respect to the earth, the up and back delay is about a quarter of a second.

Another miscellaneous communications media is the use of power lines for data communications. The technology is an extension of systems that turn lights on and off by sending signals over the power lines themselves. These systems are convenient to install but have very limited data rates, such as 10,000 bps.

The final example is infrared transmission. This form of communication is an extension of that used in cordless television remote controls. Signals are sent utilizing infrared light, which works well as long as there is one transmitter and one receiver. The availability of extensions to multiple transmitters and selected receivers is significant but limited, although some products are available today. These are primarily in the form of LANs within one floor of a building.

The range of available media choices is quite large, and the optimal choices are very dependent on site-specific considerations. The choice, therefore, is not to be taken lightly.

Baseband Operation

In digital circuits, baseband means that the digital signal is placed directly on the channel without any modulation. This is not possible with normal telephone channels, because their bandwidth is inadequate for the digital signal, which contains frequency components both above and below the frequency cutoff of the telephone channel. However, it is possible over the twisted pair (or other) wiring that may be in place.

Given that a digital signal can be placed directly on a cable, what determines the limits of this transmission? How high can the data rate go? How long can the cable be? What other factors are involved? These are important questions that must be dealt with.

There are several factors that create limits on the baseband data channel. Two of the most prominent are the *cable resistance* and *capacitance*. Cable resistance is measured in ohms/foot, while capacitance is measured in picofarads/foot. Both resistance and capacitance are bad in that they limit utilization of the cable. Ideally, both should be as small as possible.

The negative effects of resistance and capacitance are that when combined they make it difficult to cause a signal to rapidly change from a binary 1 to a binary 0 representation, and vice versa. Rapid changes are necessary to convey high data rates. If you have an electrical engineering background, you will probably want to skip over the next paragraph, which describes this phenomenon in terms of a water pipe analogy. Otherwise, you may want to read the analogy and skip the subsequent description in electrical engineering terms.

The water pipe analogy for baseband operation is based on the simple example of filling a tub with water using a garden hose. How long will it take to fill the tub? This depends on the resistance, with a small diameter hose having more resistance than a large-diameter hose. Similarly, the time depends on the capacitance of the tub. What really matters is the product of the resistance and the capacitance. If we want to raise and lower the water level in the tub, we will need a low-resistance (large-diameter) hose and/or a small-capacitance tub.

For an engineering example, consider the specific example of a 100-foot length of #24 gauge wire, a common telephone company cable. It will have a resistance (R) (for the 100-foot length) of about 26 ohms and have a capacitance (C) of about 25 picofarads per foot for a capacitance of 2.5 microfarads.

The critical parameter is the product of the resistance and capacitance, which is the time constant for the RC electrical circuit of this cable. The effect of the time constant is shown in Figure 4-4, in which a 50-Kbps binary baseband signal is applied to the cable.

The effect of the time constant is to delay the signal's rise and fall. Electrical engineering theory tells us that the signal is up to its full value in about three time constants, which in this example is just in time to go back down again. If the pulses were significantly shorter (i.e., with a higher data rate), the pulse might not rise high enough to be detected as a 1. An error might be introduced. At lower data rates, the same rise and fall times are not a concern. The net effect is that repeaters must be placed in the circuit periodically and often enough to restore the signal levels before they are lost.

Therefore, the achievable data rate and distance between repeaters can relate to the quality of the cable in terms of its resistance and capacitance. Data grade cable is usually #22 rather than #24 gauge. The #22 gauge wire would have a resistance of 1.6 ohms per 100 feet instead of the 2.6 ohms per 100 feet seen with the #24 gauge. In general, the resistance changes by a factor of two for every three wire gauges. For example:

Wire Gauge #	Resistance per 100 feet
17	0.5 ohms
20	1.0
23	2.0
26	4.0

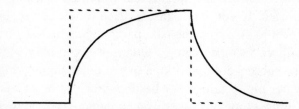

(a) Rise and fall time degradation due to an RC time constant

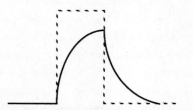

(b) The same RC time constant on a narrow pulse

FIGURE 4-4   Resistance and capacitance degrade a digital signal.

Other considerations include the susceptibility of the cable to outside sources of electrical noise and its production of such interfering signals. For example, the Federal Communications Commission (FCC) is very concerned when a cable radiates signals at or above 30 MHz.

Modulation and Modems

The term "modulation" means to vary some property of a signal, such as its amplitude or frequency, to convey information. An everyday example of such modulation is AM (Amplitude Modulation) and FM (Frequency Modulation) radio receivers. With radios, the information is typically voice or music. With data communications, the information is in the form of a bit-serial digital data stream.

Modulation is used to adapt a digital signal so it can be sent across an analog channel, such as a voice grade telephone channel. In some LAN examples, one or more adjacent television channels may be used to convey very high data rate digital signals.

There is a direct relationship between the data rate and the analog bandwidth to convey it. As a rule of thumb, you can obtain about one bit per second of data rate for each hertz of bandwidth. Therefore, you could expect to get about 3,000 bps over a 3,000 Hz bandwidth telephone channel. Sometimes the yield is better and sometimes it is considerably less. The differences are caused by the compromise made between the evolving technology (to obtain higher data rates) and the desire for very low-cost modulation (operate at lower bps rates).

When a modulated signal is received, it must be demodulated, which returns the signal to its original digital form. The device that performs modulation (on sending) and demodulation (on reception) is called a modem, which was described earlier as being a contraction of the words modulation and demodulation.

The following section describes one of the low-end modems, the Bell 103. It provides a simple, but representative introduction to how modems work. Discussion then builds on this example and covers more complex modem technology and devices.

A Simple Modem Example

The Bell 103 modem has been used for at least two decades, primarily to connect low-speed terminals to computers. The most likely encounter that you may have today with a 103 modem is as a fallback mode of operation in your PC modem. Most usage today is with more advanced technology. However, the 103 is the easiest modem to understand and serves as a good point of departure into the more complex issues of state-of-the-art modems.

Like many other modems, the 103 starts by dividing the 3,000 Hz bandwidth of telephone channels into two smaller bandwidth channels. One is used for transmission and the other for reception. The decision of which modem sends on which channel is based on which modem initiated the call for direct dial, or is administratively determined by switch settings for a leased circuit. Each sub-channel is then utilized to convey binary 1s and 0s by switching the tone (i.e., frequency) of a signal to represent binary 1s and 0s. This is shown in Figure 4-5. Because the frequency is shifted to represent the signal, this approach is called *Frequency Shift Keying* or *FSK*.

When one modem calls another, an initial tone is sent. The receiving modem returns another tone, and the conversation is initialized. This is called a hand-shake. You will see many more examples of the handshake concept, which is important in data communications and networking.

The Bell 103 does not do very well in terms of the rule of thumb of 1 bps per hertz of bandwidth. Why do you only get 300 bps out of a 3,000-Hz bandwidth? First of all, the 3,000 hertz is cut into two pieces, to send and receive in a full-duplex manner. Some of the bandwidth is lost to serve as a guard band between the two portions of bandwidth. But this still seems to have pretty poor perform-ance, maybe 0.3 bps per hertz. The missing factors are:

1. The technology available at the time the 103 modem was defined.
2. The desire for low cost.

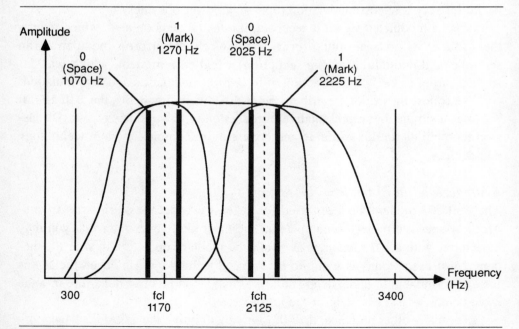

FIGURE 4-5   Bell 103A modem frequency assignments.

3. The desire for low error rates over relatively poor quality (noisy) telephone lines.

The next section builds upon this simple starting point, and describes more state-of-the-art modems.

Operation of Modern Modems

Modern modems share a common concern with the Bell 103; namely, fitting the data representation into the telephone channel bandwidth. However, they differ considerably in how this is done, the level of technology involved, and in the achievable data rate.

One of the ways to achieve higher data rates is to utilize the entire voice grade bandwidth in one direction, which can more than double the data rate. Two channels are utilized, one in each direction. This is sometimes called a "four-wire circuit," with two wires in each direction. However, there is confusion regarding two-wire and four-wire circuits, because any circuit that is long enough to require repeaters (amplifiers) is a four-wire circuit. This results because amplifiers only work in one direction. This is shown in Figure 4-6, which shows a two-wire, end-to-end circuit, with an intermediate section having a four-wire circuit. The "hybrids" at each end of the four-wire circuit potentially can provide unintended feedback, causing echo. You probably have heard this echo when using the telephone for voice communications. Because echo bothers humans, the telephone company puts echo suppressors on such circuits. If there is a signal in one direction, the other direction is clamped off to eliminate the echo from returning. For full-duplex operation, the Bell 103 modem transmits a tone to disable the echo suppressors and achieve the full-duplex transmission that is required. Any resulting echo will be ignored by the 103 modem, because the echo will be returned to a transmitter, not a receiver.

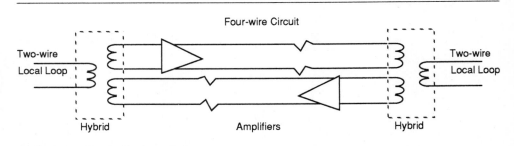

Graphic courtesy of Learning Tree International.

FIGURE 4-6   Two-wire and four-wire circuits are often combined, requiring the network implementer to know about both.

Many modern modems utilize four-wire circuits. Use of full four-wire circuits from end to end can provide the full bandwidth in each direction, significantly improving the data rate.

Another principal improvement over the 300 bps data rate of the 103 modem is the use of better modulation techniques. Modern modems utilize *Phase Shift Keying (PSK)* instead of FSK. The phase of a signal is a more complex concept than either amplitude or frequency. A phase shift between two signals is shown in Figure 4-7. In effect, the two sine waves appear to be identical except for being shifted along the horizontal axis. One full cycle of the sine wave is considered to be 360 degrees, thus the scale is in degrees of phase shift. Unlike the FSK example, it is possible to have more than a single bit represented in each signalling change. For example, if we have four different phases, we can represent two bits in each signalling interval. This doubles the bps for a given *baud* rate. The baud rate is the rate at which the signal changes its rate, i.e., its phase in this case. (Baud rate is often used synonymously with bps, and although this is incorrect, it is so common that its misuse is accepted.)

More advanced modems go beyond PSK to include combinations of PSK and amplitude modulation. This further increases the number of distinguishable states that the signal can have in any one signalling interval. The patterns of possible amplitude/phase combinations are called "constellations" because they resemble a regular pattern of stars in the night sky. An example constellation pattern is shown in Figure 4-8.

Modern high performance modems often utilize additional techniques to further increase the data rate that can be achieved. So-called Quadrature Amplitude Modulation (QAM) modems have two carrier signals that are identical except for a 90-degree phase shift. This 90-degree separation is called quadrature because the two signals are at right angles to each other. (This is the same reason we call a pad of paper a "quad pad" when it has lines in both horizontal and vertical directions, with a 90-degree separation of the lines.)

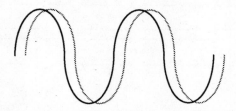

FIGURE 4-7   Two sine waves may be identical except for their phase. Phase information conveys digital data.

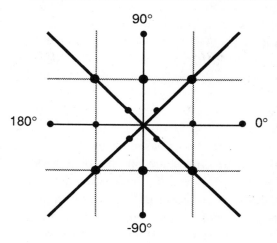

Graphic courtesy of Learning Tree International.

FIGURE 4-8 A constellation pattern combining phase and amplitude modulation.

The desire to get more bits per baud eventually leads to a problem with noise-induced variations in a signal's amplitude and/or phase. To address this problem, many modern modems have introduced a form of forward error correction. Most errors are detected and automatically corrected by adding redundant bits in the transmitted patterns. The most common form is Trellis Code Modulation (TCM), in which each four-bit pattern to be sent has a fifth bit appended based on an algorithm that operates over the sequence of many such four-bit nibbles. It gets its name from the sequence of bit positions over time in the constellation pattern. They tend to resemble the twisting of a rose bush climbing up a trellis.

Despite all of the best modulation methods, forward error correction, and other design features, sometimes a telephone channel simply will not support the desired high data rate. In this case, many modems have the capability to fallback to a lesser rate. Our familiar 2,400 bps PC modems will fall back to 1,200 bps if they cannot operate at 2,400 bps. A further fallback is to 300 bps, utilizing the Bell 103 methods.

To obtain high data rates, some modems require that the telephone channel be a leased or dedicated circuit instead of a direct dial circuit. The better line quality of the leased circuit occurs because it does not have to go through the switching equipment, and it can be tuned for optimal performance. This tuning is called *equalization*. It improves the effective bandwidth of the channel, making higher data rates possible. The current data rate limits of most commercial products are 19.2 Kbps for leased lines and 9.6 Kbps for direct dial circuits. Other data rates are also common, such as 12 Kbps and 14.4 Kbps. These rather strange numeric values are all multiples of 2.4 K, which is the most common baud rate for such modems. The higher values represent 2, 3, 4, or more bits per baud. Higher data rates are achievable by means of either data compression algorithms or even higher forms of signal processing technology.

Modem Standards

Our discussion of the Bell 103 was based on the Bell System de facto standard. In addition to Bell standards, there are international standards for modems. For some years, the Bell standards and the international standards were similar but incompatible. One of the more recent Bell standards is the Bell 212A, which operates at 1,200 bps and is compatible with the international standard V.22 modem at that data rate. More recent modems are either the international standards or are vendor proprietary approaches, such as the Trailblazer modem.

Extensions to modem capabilities are tagged with "bis" to indicate a second version or "ter" to indicate a third version. For example, V.22bis operates at 2,400 bps, but can fall back to the 1,200 bps operation of the V.22 modem.

A summary of current modems is shown in Figure 4-9. The CCITT and Bell System (where available) designations are listed, along with an indication of the degree of compatibility and the operating characteristics.

Modem Interfaces

The interface between a modem and a piece of data processing equipment has historically been an important demarcation point. In earlier days, this was the dividing line between what you leased from the telephone company and what you bought (or leased) from a computer company. Today, this dividing line has blurred considerably, but it is still an important interface, because it provides a convenient troubleshooting breakout point, and it is the key to the direct interconnection of many pieces of data processing equipment.

In the modem world, data processing equipment is known by the CCITT designation of Data Terminal Equipment or DTE. Modems are known as Data Circuit termination Equipment or DCE. It is probably easier to remember it as Data Communications Equipment, but that is not its official name. The present name dates back to when that was indeed the termination point of the telephone company's circuit, because they always provided the modem as well. It was an expensive but certainly simpler world. Your communications came from AT&T, and your computer came from IBM or perhaps one of the "seven dwarfs." Now you may get your communications from IBM and your computers from AT&T, or more likely from any of several other combinations of vendors.

Summary of CCITT and Bell Modems							
CCITT Rec'DTN	Data Rate (bps)		Circuit		Modulation		Bell Version
	Normal	Fallback	2-Wire	4-Wire	Method	Sync/Async	
V.21	300	–	Duplex	–	FSK	Async	~ 103
–	300	–	Duplex	–	FSK	Async	~ 212A
V.22	1200	–	Duplex	–	DPSK	Sync or Async	= 212A
V.22$_{bis}$	2400	1200	Duplex	–	QAM	Sync or Async	None
V.23	1200	600	Half	Duplex	FSK	Async	* 202
V.26	2400	–	–	Duplex	DPSK	Sync	= 201
V.26$_{bis}$	2400	–	Half	Duplex	DPSK	Sync	
V.26$_{ter}$	2400	1200	Duplex	–	DPSK	Sync	
V.27	4800	–	Manual equal. (leased)		DPSK	Sync	~ 208
V.27$_{bis}$	4800	2400	Auto equal. (leased)		DPSK	Sync	
V.27$_{ter}$	4800	2400	Switched line		DPSK	Sync	
V.29	9600	7200/4800	–	Duplex	QAM	Sync	~ 209
V.32	9600	4800/2400	Duplex	–	QAM/TCM	Sync	None
V.33	14400	–		Duplex	QAM/TCM	Sync	None

"~" means similar, but not compatible
"=" means equivalent
"*" *means compatible in some uses*

Graphic courtesy of Learning Tree International.

FIGURE 4-9 A summary of current modems.

Regardless of the source of equipment and services, the DTE-to-DCE interface is still a standard. Unfortunately, it is not a well-standardized standard. For example, it has both 25-pin and 9-pin implementations. This semi-standard interface is known as RS-232. The RS means Recommended Standard, and the 232 is the assigned number. Sometimes it is called RS-232C, which is the C version of the standard. The "bis" and "ter" notations of CCITT are not used. Who said that standardization groups must do things in a standard way? More recently, RS-232C has been updated to RS-232D, which is now often called EIA-232D, which will be discussed in more detail later in this section.

RS-232 is limited in two basic areas. First, the maximum cable length between the DTE and DCE is usually stated as 50 feet (15 meters). Better quality cables can at least double this length, but it still is a limiting factor. The second upper limit for RS-232C is a data rate of 19.2 Kbps. Above that data rate, the V.35 interface typically is utilized in today's implementations.

To go beyond the 50 feet and 19.2 Kbps limits, the Electronics Industries Association (EIA) developed new modem interface standards. They divided RS-232 into two parts, the signal semantics and their electrical characteristics. This lead to the EIA standards RS-449 and RS-422/423, respectively. RS-449 defined some new test signals, such as loopback tests. RS-422 defined new balanced electrical signals that allowed longer cable lengths and much higher data rates. RS-423 provided interoperability with, and hence an upgrade path to, RS-232. The electrical interfaces were meant to be switchable between RS-422 and 423, providing either higher performance, or for the sake of transition, interoperability with RS-232. All of this seemed like a superb engineering approach to expanding beyond the RS-232 limits. However, it met with limited acceptance; thus we still have RS-232 and very limited usage of RS-449.

Some recent alternatives have been introduced, including RS-530, which is a variation of the 25-pin connector of RS-232. The idea is to revise the utilization of some of the less frequently used signals/pins to provide a second wire for balanced signals. This may add to the current confusion about the intended function of the connector on the back of your workstation or PC. Is it an RS-232 port, a parallel printer port, or perhaps an RS-530 port?

The interface signals of the RS-232 interface can be divided into a few general categories. First, there are the basic signals required for any operation, including the most simple asynchronous communications. These include:

Transmitted Data (pin 2)
Received Data (pin 3)
Common Ground (pin 7)
Request To Send (pin 4)
Clear To Send (pin 5)
Data Terminal Ready (pin 20)
Data Set (Modem) Ready (pin 6)
Carrier Detect (pin 8)
Ring Indicator (pin 22)

For most applications, that is all you need to know about RS-232 data and control lines. With the exception of the ring indicator, these are the signals you will need to understand to build a *null-modem* to interconnect two DTEs by means of RS-232, but without any modems. This is done frequently when devices are physically close and need to be connected. A typical null-modem is shown in Figure 4-10.

RS-232C lines, in addition to those discussed above, relate to synchronous operation and secondary channel usage, as discussed in the following paragraphs.

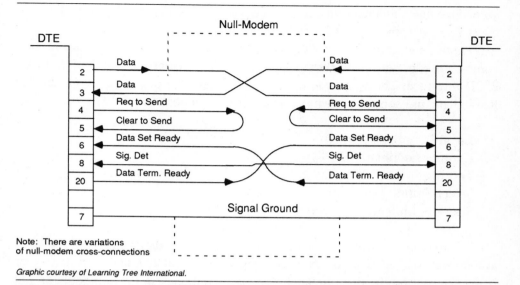

FIGURE 4-10   A basic null-modem involves these signals. One possible wiring configuration is shown.

The additional control lines that are required for synchronous operation provide clocking. These were not required in asynchronous operation, because the sending and receiving ends provided their own clocks with sufficient accuracy to read in a single character. The clocking for each character is resynchronized at the start bit of each character. This simple approach is not possible in synchronous transmission in which characters are packed one right after the other for long strings of characters. Clocking must be controlled more tightly. There are two options for the source of transmit clock in synchronous transmission—the modem (on pin 15) or the DTE (on pin 24). If the modem provides the clock, it is called Transmission Signal Element Timing (DCE source), or sometimes "internal clock." If the DTE provides the clock, it is called Transmission Signal Element Timing (DTE source), or sometimes "external clock." Note that the terms internal and external are often confused, because they depend on the perspective. Their use always should be clarified. In contrast, there is only one possibility for the receive clock. In synchronous operation, receive clock is always provided by the modem (on pin 17). This clock is recovered from transitions in the received data.

Another set of control lines are required when a secondary channel is utilized. The secondary channel is in the reverse direction and capable of handling a limited amount of data, typically 75 bps. It can operate as a signalling channel for half-duplex line turnaround or for modem monitoring and maintenance. The secondary lines include Transmitted Data (pin 14), Received Data (pin 16), Request To Send (pin 19), and Clear To Send (pin 13).

Three new control lines were added in RS-449 and are expected to gain common use, because they are available in CCITT modems and in the RS (EIA)-232D interface. These include the following list. The pin assignments are for RS-449 and use some pins designated for other functions in RS-232.

Local Loopback (pin 10)
Remote Loopback (pin 14)
Test Mode (pin 18)
Select Standby (pin 32)
Standby Indicator (pin 36)

Local loopback refers to a form of testing in which the signal is looped back at the local modem. That is, the digital signal is modulated, and then instead of being sent out on the line, the analog signal is fed back to the demodulator and returned to the DTE. This is sometimes called "analog loopback." It provides a test of the local modem, independent of the line or the remote modem. The loopback condition can be initiated by either activating the RS-449 control pin or by manual action at the modem control panel. Artificial traffic would then be sent and compared with the returned data.

Remote loopback is a similar test in which the signal is sent to the local modem where it is modulated, then sent to the remote modem, and then demodulated as usual. But instead of delivering the signal to the remote DTE, the digital signal is then looped back, remodulated, and returned to the source DTE. This is sometimes called "digital loopback." It too can be caused by either activating the RS-449 control pin or by manual operation at the panel. In some modems, this operation can be performed on the remote modem by a panel operation at the local modem, allowing both tests to be run from one location.

Modem-Related Programming

The RS-232 or RS-449 control signals can be manipulated under program control. Typical examples are the Request To Send/Clear To Send handshake, responding to the Ring Indicator, and activating the loopback control signals. Certain other controls can be performed on "smart modems" by sending commands across the transmit data line. The most common such set of commands is the AT command set, which was pioneered by Hayes Corporation. Modems that perform this set of commands are called "Hayes compatible."

The AT command set gets its name from the AT prefix on the commands. This presumably stands for Attention, because its purpose is to get the modem's attention and treat the following information as mode control. The modem is either in data mode or command mode. One enters command mode by a combination of timing and character transmissions. Then commands can be entered as indicated below.

The command format is **AT** followed by a letter representing the command, which is followed by a parameter (when needed). As an example,

```
ATDT 1-(800)-123-4567
```

is the AT command for **Dial (D)** using **Tone (T)** dialing and calling the number **1-(800)-123-4567**, where the dashes and parentheses are ignored by the modem. A result code will be returned to the computer supplied the command. In our example, this result code might be **6** or **BUSY**, or it might be **1** or **CONNECT**. The number or word response is selected by a configuration setting.

Other AT commands are available for controlling character echo, terminating a call, controlling the use of the built-in speaker, and to run diagnostic tests, to mention a few.

Some other modem internals need to be understood, because they can have direct programming implications. In these cases, a reliable transmission protocol is built into the modem. Therefore, the system designer or programmer can take advantage of this reliable communication and not duplicate it in software. A common example is the V.42 modem standard from CCITT. It includes both the MNP (Microcom Network Protocol) and the LAPD (Link Access Protocol, D channel). Both are included because the standardization group was divided between the two approaches and could not select one. If a vendor provides either MNP or LAPD, that vendor can advertise that the modem is V.42-compatible. Only if a vendor implements both can it claim to be V.42-compliant. Therefore, two V.42-compatible modems may be unable to communicate, because one may implement MNP while the other may implement LAPD. Data communications can get tricky! There must have been some marketers on the committee.

ISDN

The *Integrated Services Digital Network (ISDN)* integrates voice, data, and other forms of communications into a common circuit switched network environment. All such communications are digital, even when the signals themselves are inherently analog. Such is the case for voice, which is sampled 8,000 times per second, and the samples are then digitized into either seven-bit or eight-bit values. The combination of the 8,000 samples per second and the seven or eight bits per sample gives rise to the familiar 56 Kbps or 64 Kbps digital data rates provided by telephone companies. In North America, 56 Kbps has been more common; in Europe, 64 Kbps is utilized.

Adaptation of an analog voice signal to make it fit on a digital carrier sounds like just the opposite of what was done before to adapt a digital signal to fit onto an analog channel. In that previous example, the operation was called modulation/demodulation and the device that performed the operation a modem. In this opposite situation, the analog signal is coded and subsequently decoded, and the device that does this is called a *codec*.

A Basic Rate ISDN channel includes two of these 64 Kbps channels, one for voice and one for data. It also includes a 16-Kbps channel that can be multiplexed to provide a variety of services, but one of its main functions is to send signalling information, like the telephone number you may be dialing. The 64-Kbps channels are referred to as B channels. Two are provided in an ISDN basic rate channel, one for digitized voice and one for data. They share a common D channel for signalling and other uses. The overall Basic Rate channel is therefore often called **2B + D**.

ISDN also provides a higher data rate Primary Rate channel. It consists of either 23 B channels and one D channel (**23 B + D**), or 30 B channels and one D channel (**30 B + D**). The D channels in these cases operate at 64 Kbps rather than 16 Kbps. In North America, the primary rate is the **23 B + D**, which corresponds to a T1 channel at 1.544 Mbps. In Europe, the primary rate is the **30 B + D**, which corresponds to 2.048 Mbps circuits. (One slot in the **30 B + D** channel is utilized for synchronization, leading to a 32-slot frame. In North America, a single bit is utilized in each frame for signalling.)

A key aspect of the integration of ISDN into our voice and data systems is the PABX (Private Automatic Branch Exchange). Modern PABXs always perform voice or data switching in a digital form. When an analog voice signal reaches the PABX, it is immediately digitized. Any subsequent switching is by means of digital, time division multiplexing. Therefore, the PABX is already like ISDN in many ways.

Many people have argued that by the time ISDN is readily available, it will be obsolete. A 64-Kbps data channel is no longer adequate for many needs, such as high performance workstations. However, ISDN is not limited to 64 Kbps. A higher data rate primary rate channel could be utilized, and higher data rate channels are available. We are seeing the beginnings of very high data rate ISDN in what ISDN developers call "broadband" ISDN channels. (These should not be confused with broadband LANs.) In ISDN jargon, broadband means very high data rate. The ISDN concern for high data rates has reached the point of beginning to introduce fiber optics into the local loop communications to one's house. Uses may include very high definition television, video telephones, or yet to be determined applications.

VLSI Support at the Physical Layer

Many VLSI (Very Large Scale Integration) chips are available to ease the development of low level data communications functions. One such chip is the USART (Universal Synchronous, Asynchronous, Receiver, Transmitter). As the name Universal indicates, this type of chip covers a wide range of applications. However, it is limited to the bit timing, synchronization, sending, and receiving kinds of functions. The more complex issues such as error recovery and flow control are left to support software.

We will see more substantial portions of the communications being cast into silicon at the Data Link Layer.

Security at the Physical Layer

Security services and mechanisms may be placed at the Physical Layer when protection of the raw bit stream is required. This protection may be by means of electromechanical safeguards, such as running the cables through an alarmed conduit, or in any other tightly controlled circuit. When it is not possible to provide such protection for the cable, encryption is utilized typically to make the exposed data appear as completely random bits. This form of encryption is often called link encryption, but it is not actually done at the Data Link Layer. Instead, it is performed at the Physical Layer, modifying the signal for transmission in a manner analogous to modulation and demodulation.

Encryption on the line may be full-period, i.e., encrypted "fill" characters are sent between packets thus hiding the existence of actual traffic. This provides protection against traffic flow analysis in which an adversary infers something about our status, readiness condition, etc., by monitoring the occurrence, length, and other properties of point-to-point traffic.

Test Tools at the Physical Layer

There are a variety of test tools that one can purchase or develop to gain insight into implementation at the Physical Layer. These tools typically allow the developer to see the signal status (e.g., with LED [Light Emiting Diode] readouts), to patch the signals (e.g., with jumper wires), and to simulate signals (e.g., test generators).

One familiar tool is the *breakout box* which fits between a modem and a terminal or computer. The breakout box provides both the monitor LEDs and a patch panel capability at the RS-232 interface. It can be utilized to force control signals to a defined state for debugging purposes, and allows critical signals to be monitored continuously. A more significant patch panel capability may also be provided to patch into a different line or different modem for troubleshooting.

If one questions the quality of a communications line, a *Bit Error Rate Test* (*BERT*) can be run. This can be a simple program that you write to send data out, have it echoed back, and compare what was sent with what was returned. Alternatively, many pieces of test equipment have a built-in BERT test with test generators and test analysis capabilities. Not only can the average bit error rate be determined, but other parameters such as the number of "error-free seconds" can be collected.

In some cases, a more important measure than BER is the *Block Error Rate* (*BLER*) and its corresponding *Block Error Rate Test* (*BLERT*). Blocks might be groupings of 1,000 bits that are sent as one unit. In data communications and networking, these are usually called packets. If our error recovery strategy is to retransmit a block if it has at least one erroneous bit, then we do not really care if there are one or more bits in the block. The BLER will not differ depending on the number of bad bits in the block, but the BER will vary. Both tests are available. You use the one that best meets your needs.

THE DATA LINK LAYER

The Data Link Layer of the OSI RM is concerned with point-to-point communications between any two directly connected computers. These point-to-point computers may consist of two hosts with a communications circuit between them, two adjacent packet-switches, two hosts on a LAN, or a host-to-packet switch communication. All of these are candidate situations for a data link protocol.

Connection and Connectionless Operation

Most data link protocols are connection-oriented and thus provide reliable, sequenced delivery. However, some data link protocols within packet-switched networks have been designed as connectionless, and more recently, LANs have been developed with connectionless data link protocols. The packet-switch data link protocols include those of ARPAnet, which provided reliability but not sequence control. The LAN examples are characterized by the IEEE standard 802.2 type 1, which provides neither reliability nor sequenced delivery. The strong error checking of the LAN ensures that bad data are almost never delivered, but there is no error recovery when bad packets are detected. The IEEE 802.2 also provides a type 2, optional, connection-oriented data link protocol. Every IEEE 802.2 implementation must include support for connectionless data link control, and may or may not also provide the support for connection-oriented controls. Most implementations, except the IBM token ring LAN, utilize only the connectionless capability. IBM has historically wanted link level error controls and so includes it in token ring LANs.

Advocates of connectionless LAN data link controls argue that errors are infrequent in the LAN environment, and recovery can be provided easily at the Transport Layer (i.e., there is no reason to duplicate this capability at the Data Link Layer). IBM token ring advocates would argue that errors should be detected and corrected as quickly as possible (i.e., there is no reason to propagate bad data across an internet only to have it discarded). They would argue further that error detection and correction on the spot provides insight into where the errors are being introduced. Well, the jury is still out, and in the meantime, we have both.

Polling and Peer-to-Peer Data Link Protocols

In the LAN versions of data link protocols, all nodes on the network are considered to be peers; that is, to be equals in terms of the protocols they implement. No party is considered to be a slave to another, nor is there any terminal-to-host concept of communications. Being a peer does not mean that one necessarily has the same computing horsepower as other nodes; it simply means that each peer is running the same protocols and has no specific master/slave control over the communications.

In contrast, there are polling networks. One node is designated as the master (or primary) while the other nodes are considered to be slaves or secondaries. This configuration has been around for decades and will continue as long as it serves a purpose in existing systems, extends those systems, or replicates such systems. However, the master/slave configuration is not believed to be of sufficient long-term concern to developers of networks and network software to include more than this brief comment. If you want to clone a copy of these "dinosaur" networks, make a direct copy. Particularly, do not reinvent!

This does not mean that you will never again encounter master/slave relations in networks, but that they are old technology at the Data Link Layer. You will continue to find master/slave relationships at the Application Layer, such as in concurrency control and updating replicated, distributed data bases. There is more on this in Chapter 7.

Framing in the Data Link Protocol

The data link protocol is unique in its special problem of having to find the beginning and end of packets. At other protocol layers, there is nothing before the beginning byte of the packet to obscure the matter, and the length is often passed with the packet. Why does the data link protocol have this special problem?

The answer involves several aspects of the data link layer. First, typically it is a bit serial protocol, which means that data, control, and receive clock must all be recovered from the bit stream. This causes some loss at the beginning of the packet. Some bits are lost recovering receive clock synchronization. Then, there is typically a search for some special pattern to provide byte synchronization, and finally frame (packet) synchronization. The front-end portion of the packet can be considered to be a preamble, which is long enough to allow all of the above described synchronization. Every other protocol will have its packets neatly delivered with clearly defined boundaries without this searching.

For the same reasons that you had to search for the beginning of a packet, you must now search for its end. You do not know how long the packet is in advance. The trick is how to indicate the end of a packet when you must be able to transmit any possible pattern of 1s and 0s in the data portion of the packet. The four common approaches are described below.

The first approach is the Binary Synchronous (Bisync) protocol which dates back to the 1960s. When the Bisync protocol needed to transmit arbitrary data patterns, called binary data or transparent data, it utilized a special control character called DLE (Data Link Escape). Occurrence of a DLE pattern in the packet signalled the receiver to interpret the next character in a special way. The next character would be either a control character or the same DLE bit pattern in the data. If the transmitter wanted to indicate the beginning of a packet, it would do so with a Start of Text (STX) character preceded by DLE. At the end of the packet, the transmitter would send End of Text (ETX) preceded by DLE. When the transmitter wanted to send the equivalent bit pattern of DLR4E in the text, it would send DLE, DLE. Upon reception, one of these DLE patterns would be discarded. This approach is shown in Figure 4-11. You may have found it to be similar in concept to the literal print statement in a programming language in which quotes are used to delimit the print string as well as be part of the print string. The solution is to double the quotes within the print string. Only single quotes actually delimit the string. These DLEs are utilized in exactly the same way.

The second approach to finding the end of a bit serial packet is to convey its length in the control portion of the packet. DECnet utilized this approach in its data link protocol, DDCMP (Digital Data Control Message protocol). It contains a count field in its header. As a precaution, the header is error checked before utilizing this count value.

The third approach to handling arbitrary bit patterns in the data stream is to modify the bit pattern to breakup any accidental occurrences of a special flag pattern that will terminate the stream. In the HDLC (High-level Data Link Control) protocol, the flag pattern is 01111110. If this pattern appears in the packet itself, it is broken up by the following algorithm. Upon transmission, the sender looks for strings of binary 1s in the packet. If it finds five 1s in a row, it inserts a 0. The receiver does the inverse: it looks for five 1s in a row and discards a 0 if found. Only the real flag pattern will not have a 0 after five 1s.

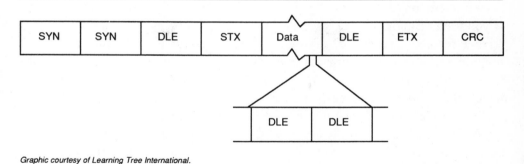

Graphic courtesy of Learning Tree International.

FIGURE 4-11   The Data Link Escape (DLE) character is important in providing transparent operation.

LANs have yet another solution to this problem. The designers of LANs have utilized encoding schemes for binary 1s and 0s that also include other non-data symbols. These non-data symbols, called "encode violations," can indicate special cases, such as the end of a packet. These violations, however, will not cause a visit from the "protocol police." They are looking for other things, as will be discussed elsewhere.

Connection-Related Mechanisms in the Data Link Protocol

As indicated above, many data link protocols provide connection-oriented services. These protocols provide reliable, sequenced delivery with flow control. These services and the mechanisms that provide them are discussed below.

Error control mechanisms provide reliable delivery service. The techniques for providing reliable delivery may be either retransmission or forward error correction. We apply these same mechanisms in a person-to-person telephone conversation. If something is not understood, you indicate that it should be repeated. We tend to acknowledge the successful reception of conversations with periodic remarks such as "yes" or "OK." We also can prompt a retransmission by asking for the statement to be repeated. The analogy breaks down a bit at this point.

The other form of error control is forward error correction. In this case, there is enough redundancy in the transmitted data to allow it to be corrected without requiring a retransmission. This is common in languages such as English. In spite of some noise on the line, we can often understand what was said.

The data link protocol typically deals with errors by means of a Positive Acknowledgment, Retransmission protocol. When a packet is received, its error check field is confirmed as being correct. If not, the packet is discarded. If it is received correctly, it is acknowledged (ACKed). If no ACK is received within a timeout period, the sender of the packet will retransmit it. This does not fit the person-to-person telephone analogy, but it is how most data link protocols work. If you tried this approach in the personal use of a telephone, you might get some strange results. If instead of saying "yes" or "what was that?" you simply said nothing and waited for a timeout, the other party would probably be quite confused as to what was going on. Computers never learned how people talk on telephones, so this does not affect them.

The sender will retransmit a packet if an ACK is not received within a timeout period. But what if the ACK gets lost, not the original packet? In this circumstance, you would deliver two copies of the same packet. Suppose that each such packet is a debit to someone's bank account. Does this seriously confuse the bank records? Clearly, some way to detect duplicate packets is needed; so, control numbers are added with each packet. This is packet number one, the next is packet number two, etc., uniquely numbering the packets. Unique numbers, however, imply a very large field. All that is really required is the ability to detect a duplicate within the expected time, during which it might be retransmitted.

To manage the lifetime of sequence numbers, a "window" mechanism is used. At any given time, only a subset of the possible sequence numbers is allowed to be sent. This should eliminate confusion, even if sequence numbers are later reused. This is analogous to the odometer in a not-so-new car rolling over after 100,000 miles. No one would believe it is suddenly a new car!

There is a need to associate ACKs with the specific packets that are being acknowledged. Therefore, a sequence number is included with ACKs as well as with data packets. The logical choice might seem to be to say that ACK number 5 acknowledges packet number 5. This is done sometimes, but more often than not, the ACK number is the next expected packet sequence number. This allows an ACK number to be returned, even when no packets have been received. This capability is needed when ACKs are piggybacked on normal traffic. You will see various examples of this piggybacking.

Associated with the sequence control mechanisms are the flow control mechanisms. While they build on a common framework, the intent of flow control is to make sure that the sender does not transmit more rapidly than the receiver can accept the packets. This typically relates to buffering at the receiving end. Occasionally, the receiver must indicate that it can no longer accept more packets. Do not send anything more until it tells you that it can accept it. Flow control is in other aspects of daily life. You may be on an airplane waiting to take off but unable to depart from the gate. This may be because the runway queues are full, thus flow control has been invoked. On the other hand, you may be able to see that this is not the case. Perhaps the reason that you cannot depart is because of congestion at your destination airport. Unless you have a landing slot at the destination airport, it is futile to take off. These are examples of the pervasive nature of flow control.

Basic HDLC Operation

The HDLC protocol began as a modern replacement for older data link protocols such as Bisync. However, HDLC has evolved into a family of data link protocols, covering everything from polled terminals to LANs and PCs to mainframes via modems.

There are three basic forms of HDLC that correspond to the meaningful combinations of polled versus non-polled and master/slave versus peer-to-peer. These three combinations and their official HDLC names are:

1. **Polled, Master/Slave** = Normal response mode.
2. **Non-Polled, Master/Slave** = Asynchronous response mode.
3. **Non-Polled, Peer-to-Peer** = Asynchronous balanced mode.

The **polled, master/slave** mode is called normal response mode because this polling was the normal way of doing business in the mid-1970s when this protocol was standardized.

The **non-polled, master/slave** mode was called asynchronous response mode because the slave could transmit without waiting for a poll. The transmission of a packet from slave to master is asynchronous, because there is no predetermined time when it will be sent. This is the same sense as utilized in talking about asynchronous characters.

The **non-polled, peer-to-peer** mode is called asynchronous balanced mode. It has the asynchronous characteristics with respect to sending packets and has balanced control. That is, neither end is the master nor is it the slave; both share these roles.

The remainder of this discussion will focus on the asynchronous balanced mode, which has become a dominant Data Link Layer protocol. However, much of this information also applies to the other modes.

An HDLC packet is framed with multiple occurrences of a special bit pattern called the flag, which is 01111110. When one wants to send an HDLC packet, it is preceded by a few flags. The first flag is usually not recognized because the receiver takes a few bit times to recognize that something new is coming in and then to recover clock synchronization. After incoming bits are reliably detected, the receiver starts to search for the flag pattern. The second flag may then be detected. To verify that this was not just a random occurrence of this bit pattern, the receiver also checks the next eight bits. It continues to check eight bits at a time until it finds a non-flag pattern. This is assumed to be the start of the packet. The next flag pattern detected by the receiver will indicate that the end of the packet has been received, including its CRC (Cyclic Redundancy Check) error check. Any accidental occurrence of the flag pattern in the packet itself is broken up by the transmitting hardware by inserting a 0 after any string of five 1s. These inserted 0s are removed at the receiving end. Only the real end symbol actually arrives at the receiver as 01111110. This framing of an HDLC packet is shown in Figure 4-12.

This figure also indicates that once you know the start and end points of an HDLC packet, you can find the relevant address, control, and error check portions. Of particular concern here is the control field, which is shown in greater detail in Figure 4-13.

Three types of packets (or frames as they are often called in HDLC) are shown in the figure. They are described in the following paragraphs.

Information frames convey user data. Each frame has a sequence number to ensure that all data are received, in order, and with no duplicates. The sequence number space also provides a vehicle for the ACKs, which represent the next expected sequence number. In an information frame, the sequence number and ACK number relate to different directions of data flow. The sequence number is the number that we are assigning to this packet. In contrast, the ACK number is the next sequence number we expect the other side to utilize.

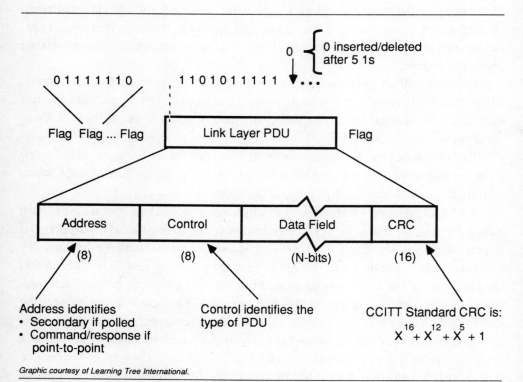

Graphic courtesy of Learning Tree International.

FIGURE 4-12   HDLC has flag-based framing.

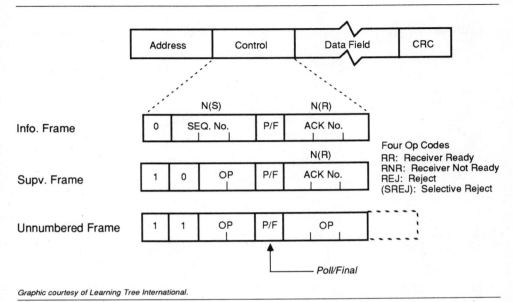

Graphic courtesy of Learning Tree International.

FIGURE 4-13 HDLC control is in three forms.

Supervisory frames are used to convey ACKs when there is no data to send and to convey flow control signals. Flow control signals are:

1. **Receiver Ready (RR)**—you may send more packets.
2. **Receiver Not Ready (RNR)**—you may not send any more packets until we indicate (with an RR) that it's alright to do so.
3. **Reject (Rej)**—you did not send the next expected packet number. Go back and send this one and all that followed it. (Reject is not always available.)
4. **Selective Reject (SRej)**—go back and send just this one packet. (Selective reject is not always available.)

Unnumbered frames are utilized to control the initialization, fault recovery, and termination of the packet exchange. Recovery here refers to major problems such as erroneous commands. Normal bit errors are recovered by retransmissions. An example exchange of an unnumbered command and its corresponding unnumbered ACK is shown in Figure 4-14.

The unnumbered command SABM, or Set Asynchronous Balanced Mode, causes both ends of the link to become initialized and set to operate with this mode. The initialization consists of setting the sequence and next ACK numbers to zero.

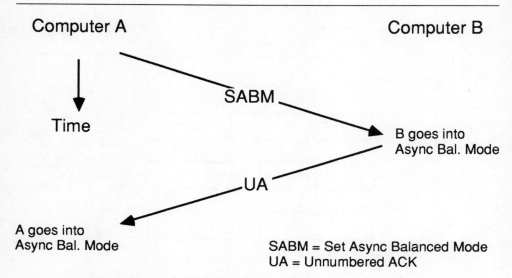

Graphic courtesy of Learning Tree International.

FIGURE 4-14   An HDLC link is initialized by a handshake exchange.

Note that the unnumbered commands and ACKs do not have sequence numbers. This, of course, is why they are called unnumbered. But how can they operate properly without the safety net of sequence numbers to detect missing, duplicated, or out of order packets? What happens if the SABM command is a duplicate and the command gets repeated? Then we end up in Asynchronous Balanced Mode, which is exactly what would happen if you only got one such command. Your only concern is that the command was executed **at least** once. The more difficult concern of **exactly** once is not required based on the protocol design.

Information frames are not so forgiving. They are to be delivered **exactly** once with only one copy of each packet being accepted at the receiver. Sequence numbers are provided in the information frames for this purpose. They are the only Data Link Layer packets that contain sequence numbers and consequently this exactly once property. Note that supervisory packets, like unnumbered packets, do not cause problems if they are duplicated. Telling the sender to stop sending twice is no problem. However, supervisory packets, unlike information or unnumbered packets, do not have timeouts and retransmissions. They can be lost. If an RNR is lost, the other side tries to send later, and the RNR is sent back. The packet can be discarded, because it will be retransmitted (but not until the RR is sent back). This does not work so neatly if an RR gets lost. Suppose that this RR is the one that will allow the other side to start sending after our last RNR. If the RR is lost, how will the other side get the message that it is OK to send? Why would you expect to have to retransmit it? Implementations must account for such what-if conditions.

When you do receive an RR, there is a fixed upper bound on how many packets you can send before you have to wait for an ACK. This upper bound is called a window. The window size value typically is set at two, meaning that you can send two packets and then wait for an ACK to come back. The ACK provides a new, updated left edge for the window, but the window size remains fixed at two, which is its default value. It is a sysgen parameter, and if you want to change it, you must recompile and link the software with that new parameter value.

Other sysgen parameters include the timer values and the maximum packet size. Higher layer protocols, which have similar features, have much more flexibility in the ability to adapt, i.e., change them. That is because the higher layers must deal with a wider range of user needs and network environments. Meanwhile, at the Data Link Layer, these are rather static values.

One remaining feature of our basic HDLC is the P/F (Poll/Final) flag. This control flag has a variety of meanings, depending on the mode of operation and the specific context within that mode. The one interpretation discussed here is selected as a departure point for later discussions of similar concepts; namely, an end-of-record delimiter. A multi-packet poll message, or a multi-packet response could be delimited by setting this flag on the last packet of such a sequence. The discussion will pick up on that idea with the X.25 "more" flag and the transport protocol "end" flag.

What has been described is the basic form of HDLC. Many extensions are possible, as discussed in the following section, "Expanded HDLC Features."

Expanded HDLC Features

HDLC has been expanded to include a number of optional functions. These extensions include the following.

1. **Exchange Identification (XID)**—The two nodes can provide each other with information about them and their ability to operate in certain modes.
2. **Reject (Rej)**—As discussed earlier, reject may be available optionally to speed up retransmission of packets.

3. **Selective Reject (SRej)**—As discussed earlier, this capability allows you to ask for a particular packet to be retransmitted. It is particularly useful in applications with large window sizes in which the retransmission of all subsequent packets is not efficient or required.

4. **Unnumbered Information**—The ability to send user data in unnumbered packets. This is especially useful in connectionless Data Link Layer variations, like those often utilized in LANs.

5. **Initialization**—Sets link control functions to an initial value.

6. **Unnumbered Polling**—Used to request that control information be returned.

7. **Extended Addressing**—Multi-byte address fields, using a "more" bit in each extended byte except the last.

8. **Extended Sequence Numbers**—Use of seven-bit sequence and ACK numbers.

9. **Mode Reset**—Resets sequence and ACK numbers.

10. **Test**—An echo function to test that you can communicate with another link entity.

11. **Request Disconnect**—Request for a disconnect command.

12. **Longer** (32-bit) **CRC Error Check**—Use of a 32-bit frame check sequence (CRC).

Various groupings of these optional extensions to HDLC have been named and are widely utilized in selected areas. Examples include LAPB (Link Access Procedure Balanced), which is utilized in X.25; LAPD (for D channel), which is utilized in ISDN; LAPM (for modem or micro-to-mainframe); and the IEEE 802.2 Logical Link Control.

Related V.42 Matters

A set of protocols that are related to the Data Link Layer are those considered as CCITT's V.42 and V.42bis. V.42 was intended to be a standard protocol for the reliable transfer of data between mainframes and microcomputers, with implementations typically included in the modems that are involved in the transfers. The CCITT committee was unable to select a single solution and ended up with two. Some parties wanted the LAPD protocol to be the basis for this protocol as well; others believed that the large installed base of the Microcom Network Protocol (MNP) dictated that it should become the standard. Both became part of the standard. A V.42-**compliant** modem must implement both; a V.42-**compatible** modem can implement either one but need not implement both. Therefore, a V.42-compliant modem can talk to any other V.42-compliant or compatible modem, but two V.42-compatible modems cannot necessarily communicate. One may implement only MNP while the other implements only LAPD. They are certainly not compatible with each other, but that's not what the fine print requires. Let the buyer beware.

The next release of V.42 is V.42bis which includes data compression. A 2-to-1 compression is generally considered to be possible.

Special Issues of Local Area Networks

LANs have special Data Link Layer needs, the most unusual being the need to have either connectionless or connection-oriented data link services. Actually, all of the IEEE 802 LANs must be able to operate with a connectionless Data Link Layer protocol. This is called the Type 1 protocol. Others may optionally operate with a connection-oriented Type 2 protocol as well. In those cases, the data flow may be any mixture of connection and connectionless packets. As shown in Figure 4-15, the implementation of only Type 1 is called Class 1, while the implementation of both is called Class 2.

The reason for having the two classes of LAN data link protocols is based on very different views of what should be going on at the Data Link Layer of a LAN. Some groups, such as the Ethernet™ community, argued strongly that the Data Link Layer service should be a best effort, connectionless service with the ultimate reliable sequenced delivery being provided by a higher layer. Others, IBM in particular, argued that reliable, sequenced delivery was the responsibility of the Data Link Layer, and that one should not have to rely on a higher level protocol for such recovery. There are technical and existing product motivations

	Type	Commands		Responses		Format
Class 1	Type 1	UI	(unnumbered information)	–		U
		XID	(exchange identification)	XID		
		TEST		TEST		
Class 2	Type 2	I	(information)	I		I
		RR	(receiver ready)	EE		S
		RNR	(receiver not ready)	RNR		
		REJ	(reject)	REJ		
		SABME	(see below)	UA	(unnumbered ACK)	U
		DISC	(disconnect)	DM	(disconnected mode)	
				FRMR	(frame reject)	

Graphic courtesy of Learning Tree International.

FIGURE 4-15   Local Area Networks utilize two variatiosn of HDLC, Class 1 and Class 2.

for both sides of the argument. The net result was that the IEEE committee decided that both should be allowed, but that only the connectionless approach was required. The IEEE 802.2 data link protocol builds heavily on HDLC and includes all three frame formats, as shown in Figure 4-16.

The Type 1 (connectionless) protocol involves only the unnumbered frame format, allowing user data to be sent via this mechanism. The Type 2 (connection-oriented) protocol utilizes the information frame and the supervisory frame formats as well.

VLSI Support at the Data Link Layer

There are a number of vendors that provide VLSI semiconductor chips to support common data link protocols, which have a potential for high-volume usage.

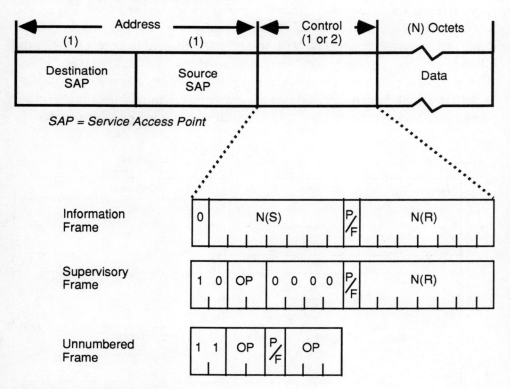

HDLC has been the basis for IEEE 802 standardization at the data link layer (i.e., logical link control)

Graphic courtesy of Learning Tree International.

FIGURE 4-16   IEEE LANs utilize a variation of the HDLC frame format.

One example is LAPB. The first company to provide such chips was Western Digital, followed by Motorola. This is a complex protocol, and the VLSI implementation historically has not been a simple "plug and play" way to avoid any need to know what is going on at the Data Link Layer. Instead, it has been an alternative and often convenient way to avoid writing the program to implement this protocol.

Test Tools for the Developer

The hardware/software developer of the Data Link Layer is well supplied with test tools. One of the most powerful is the data link protocol analyzer, which can emulate one end of the point-to-point protocol. As such, the tester can simulate a data source, it can loopback data, or it can simply monitor and display the data it receives.

An example of a low-cost data link protocol analyzer is illustrated in Figure 4-17, in which the analyzer acts as one end of the data link. A sample of the protocol analyzer is shown in Figure 4-18. In this example, the protocol analyzer is set up to run a BERT.

One of the tests that can be run is a loopback of the data that are sent from the other end of the link. This is similar to the concept of a modem loopback, but here the loopback also includes the end system. Such a test could be used in conjunction with modem level loopback testing to isolate problems.

The data link tester also provides a test pattern generator, such as a repeated ASCII text sequence or a "fox pattern," which may be the familiar "quick brown fox" message or any variation that represents a test pattern of concern.

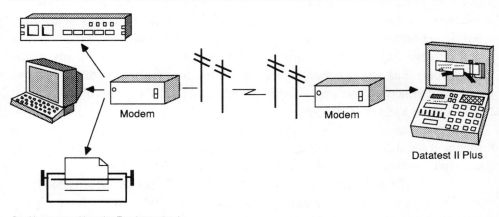

Datatest II Plus

Graphic courtesy of Learning Tree International.

FIGURE 4-17   An example of a data link tester.

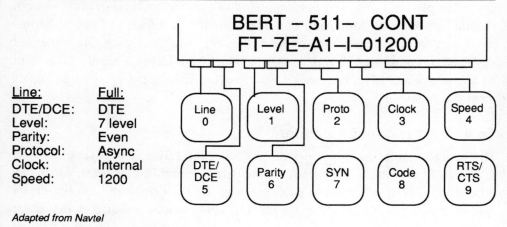

Line: Full:
DTE/DCE: DTE
Level: 7 level
Parity: Even
Protocol: Async
Clock: Internal
Speed: 1200

Adapted from Navtel

Graphic courtesy of Learning Tree International.

FIGURE 4-18   A specific example test for bit error rate.

Often times, the data link tester is used for a BERT. This test measures the average number of bad bits in a transmission. It also may collect other useful statistics, such as the number of error-free seconds during transmission.

A variation of the BERT is a Block Error Rate Test (BLERT). This test measures the average number of bad blocks in a transmission. The BERT and BLERT test results are related, because clearly there would be no bad blocks if there were no bad bits. However, the two measures differ considerably depending on the nature of the bad bit statistics.

If the bad bits are typical of that found in terrestrial circuits, the lines are either very good or very bad. The average may be a very infrequent occurrence. Most errors in these cases are burst errors, with a number of bad bits being clustered. Burst errors often are caused by atmospheric interference, cross talk, or "screwdrivers" being in the wrong place. An error burst, caused by any of the above events, has a length that is measured from the first bad bit to the last bad bit in a sequence of bad and good bits, during which the probability of a bit being good or bad is about 50-50.

However, an alternative error scenario occurs when bad bits are scattered throughout the data, with a fixed probability of any bit being good or bad. This is more typical of satellite circuits, with Gaussian noise characteristics.

The BLERT can be related to the BERT when the errors are equally likely on every bit; i.e., when the probability of a bad bit is equally likely for each bit. Although this does not account for burst errors, it does give us a first approximation to relate the two error statistics. In this case, the BLER is related to the BER by the following relationship.

Under these circumstances, the BLER is approximately the product of the BER and the packet length. This is the result of the following mathematical approximation. If the probability of a bad bit is p, then the probability of a good bit must be $(1 - p)$. The probability of N good bits in a row is $(1 - p)^N$, which can be approximated by the binomial theorem.

$$(1 - p)^N = 1 - N \times p + \cdots \text{(small terms)}$$

Therefore, the probability of a bad block is one minus this value, or

$$\text{Prob (bad block)} = N \times p$$

This approximation states that the probability of a bad block is the probability of a bad bit times the block length in bits. This clearly relates the probability of a bad block to its length. The longer the block, the more likely that it will have an error. This is intuitive but can be quantified for this special case of equally likely bad bits.

SUMMARY

The bottom two layers of the OSI RM provide a data delivery service between two directly connected devices. This delivery service includes the adaptation of the electrical signals to operate over the given type of channel and its associated bandwidth constraints. The Data Link Layer builds upon the Physical Layer services and provides either connection or connectionless delivery services to the Network Layer. What the Network Layer does with these services, and what other services add to them, is the subject of the next chapter.

5

DEVELOPMENT ISSUES
AT THE NETWORK LAYER

The Network Layer of the OSI RM is modelled after the concepts and functions of packet-switched, wide area network technology. Therefore, it fits well with networks such as Tymnet, Telenet, and Datapac, which are large-scale national and/or international networks. In contrast, more recently developed technology, such as LANs, may or may not have a network layer. When they do, it is typically the Internet sublayer within the Network Layer. We will discuss both of these variations of the Network Layer in this chapter.

The OSI Network Layer provides a connection-oriented service with its usual reliable, sequenced delivery characteristics. This contrasts with the connectionless best effort delivery service that we will see at the Internet sublayer and in many LANs.

The intent of providing a reliable, sequenced delivery service at the Network Layer is to off-load these communications concerns from the hosts. For many applications, this network-provided service is adequate. For other applications, in which there is a requirement for higher levels of data transfer integrity, the Transport Layer protocol must provide all the reliability and sequence mechanisms, making those of the network somewhat redundant. In these cases, the best effort delivery of a connectionless service is adequate, and it also provides benefits in terms of alternate routing (in which packets may get out of order) and congestion control (because packets may be discarded). Each of these topics will be discussed in detail later in this chapter.

INSIDE THE NETWORK LAYER

The network layer has three principal functions:

1. Finding a path across the one or more networks that connect the two end systems (hosts).

2. Segmenting data units into a size that can be handled by any of these networks along the path, but can still be reassembled upon reception.

3. Managing the transmission rate such that none of the nodes along the path becomes congested.

Routing In Networks

One of the principal functions of the Network Layer is *routing*, which means finding the proper path from host A to host Z, where "proper" includes the existence of a path, called "reachability," as well as the concept of a "best" path. Best may refer to a least delay path or one that meets any other predefined quality of service. Finding such a path across the network is the job of the network routing algorithm, in conjunction with a routing data base. The data base should contain both connectivity and cost data, where "cost" refers to any appropriate metric. As mentioned above, delay is the most common cost metric.

Most networks will have a topology that includes many potential paths from any host to any other host. This multiple connectivity is a form of redundancy, leading to a highly available network service in spite of packet-switch or link outages. A simple example is shown in Figure 5-1, which indicates that an outage along the preferred path has caused the packets to be routed along an

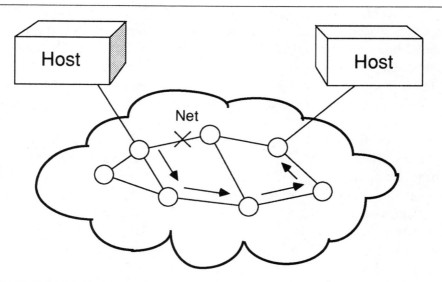

Graphic courtesy of Learning Tree International.

FIGURE 5-1   Dynamic alternate routing automatically finds a new path when an outage occurs.

alternate path. As before, finding the best currently available path is the routing problem.

The solution to the routing problem may be either static (manually set) or dynamic. When rapid recovery is a concern, dynamic alternate routing is required and is the only subsequent concern in this discussion. Routing also may be influenced by the mechanism that is utilized to provide a global picture of the network health and well-being. Almost all routing algorithms require some concept of this overall network status, but they differ in how they obtain the global information.

One approach to providing a global perspective is to have a routing server. It obtains status information from all packet-switches periodically, computes the best routes, and feeds this information back to the packet-switches. This approach has two major problems. First, it is vulnerable to a single point of failure (i.e., the routing control server). This problem can be addressed by a "hot standby." A potentially more serious problem with this approach is that the resulting routing information may be inaccurate by the time it is received and used by the packet-switches. Although the routing server approach has been applied in terminal-to-host-oriented networks, it is not a commonly utilized method.

An early approach to providing a global picture of the network was for each packet-switch to periodically inform each of its directly connected neighbors what it sees as the connectivity of the network. This is the simple hop-based approach to routing, where a hop is one store-and-forward relaying of a packet. The first ARPAnet routing algorithm had this form. It offered a simple, dynamic approach to detecting problems and routing around them. For example, consider the small four-node network of Figure 5-2. This was the original ARPAnet test configuration.

The hop-based scheme not only allows routing changes to be propagated; it also allows a new node to self-configure its routing tables. For example, assume that packet-switch node A has just been booted. After some other self-configuration, including determining that it has two communications lines, node A sends out a "Hello" packet. Nodes B and C now know that A is booted, and on the next routing update each sends a copy of its routing table to A. Node A then computes its routing table as shown in Figure 5-2. Node A finds the minimum hop count for each destination (other than itself) and adds one, because node A is one hop away from either node B or C. Node A also keeps a record of where this minimum was found, and this will be used to determine which path to take.

Suppose that later, node A fails to get information from node C, as shown in Figure 5-3. Node A does not know if the line to C is down or if node C itself is down, but the routing algorithm automatically switches to sending packets through node B, which is exactly what it should do.

• Node A updates its Hop Table

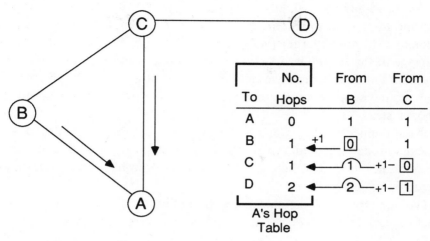

Hop algorithm:
    Find minimum from neighbors
    Add 1 and utilize as new hop count

• Node A subsequently sends to Node D via Node C

Graphic courtesy of Learning Tree International.

FIGURE 5-2   A simple hop-based routing scheme allows a node to self-configure.

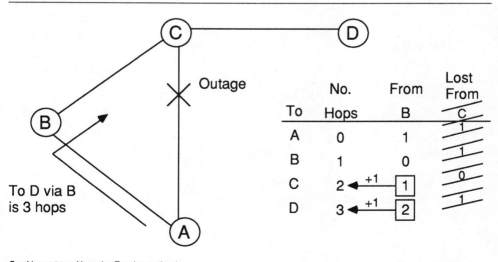

Graphic courtesy of Learning Tree International.

FIGURE 5-3   The loss of one neighbor causes a node to reroute packets.

Figure 5-4 takes this scenario a step further. Node B also has lost contact with node C. Now, nodes A and B exchange hop tables, each finding minimal values, adding one, sending them back where one is added again, etc. Eventually the hop count to reach either node C or D becomes very large, and in particular it becomes larger than the number of nodes in the network. When this happens, the hop count is trying to tell nodes A and B "You can't get there from here!" In other words, the other nodes are unreachable. It tells the packet-switch, do not continue to try; send a "destination unreachable" message back to the host instead.

If the connection from either A to C or B to C is reestablished, routing proceeds through the available paths. This seems to work well, and it may for very small networks, but there are definitely some problems with this simplistic approach.

The first problem is that the approach does not "scale" well. Bad news about outages spreads too slowly because it takes several routing update cycles to get

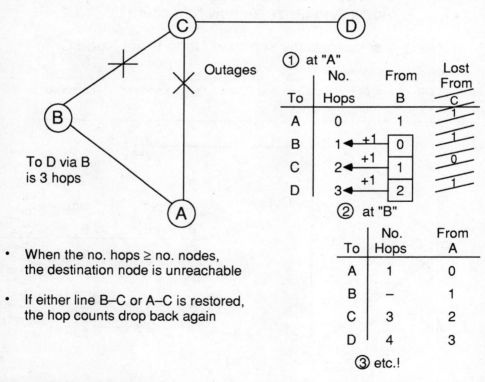

Graphic courtesy of Learning Tree International.

FIGURE 5-4   If the network becomes divided into two pieces, the hop count heads
for infinity.

the news to remote (many hops removed) nodes. In contrast, it responds to good news too quickly. When a line or node comes back up, it often is a bit unstable. After it is announced, it remains in the routing tables for a full update cycle, even if it has problems. A "hold down" timer has often been used to delay the introduction of reinstated nodes, which tends to solve this problem.

The approach also is prone to having routing loops, because until the new up/down status of a node or link is propagated to all nodes, there are inconsistencies in what amounts to a distributed routing data base. These routing loops clear up automatically as the information is finally propagated, and all nodes eventually have the same routing data base.

Probably the most significant problem with the simple hop-based routing scheme is that it is vulnerable to a problem called the "black hole." This problem occurs when one node tells all of its neighbors that it is directly connected to all hosts; that is, it is zero hops away from everybody! It may do this for any number of hardware/software failure conditions. The effect is disastrous. All neighbors send all traffic into this black hole, from which it can never recover. This has happened on many occasions during application of this simple routing algorithm. And this is not ancient history, because this algorithm is still widely used.

A variation of the hop-based scheme has been adopted by DEC in its DECnet protocol. DECnet uses the hop count only to determine reachability; the actual path is based on a separate table of link costs. Whenever a DECnet node discovers a routing change, it is immediately sent to each of its directly connected neighbors. Each of them updates their routing tables, and if the change exceeds a predefined threshold, each of them notifies their neighbors. Significant changes are therefore propagated very rapidly, while minor changes do not cause global routing updates and the associated processing.

Several years ago, ARPAnet adopted an alternative approach for routing updates. When a node discovers a problem, it sends this information to all other nodes by using a flooding scheme. Thus routing updates are sent to all neighbors, which then give the processing and transmission of these updates very high priority. The new information is spread very rapidly, avoiding the inconsistencies of the slower hop-based approach.

Giving routing updates such high priority caused a massive failure of the ARPAnet, however. This failure occurred when a defective packet-switch sent three erroneous routing updates to a neighbor packet-switch. Each of the three routing updates had a sequence number that made it look like a more recent update than the previous one. Because sequence numbers are expected to wrap-around, the three update packets formed an endless chain of apparent routing updates. When all of the packet-switches in the network gave these packets the highest priority for processing and communications, all other traffic nearly stopped.

The network control center determined the problem, after its monitoring detected the problem, along with numerous telephone complaints to assist in its detection. But even after the problem had been diagnosed, it took several hours to get the program patch distributed to all packet-switches, because they continued to process almost nothing but the erroneous routing updates until they finally received the correction.

Routing has been the Achilles heel of wide area networking for some time. Even when better algorithms have been developed, as in the ARPAnet, new failure modes have been discovered through the unexpected acts of nature.

The most recent developments in routing technology is known as the Open-Shortest-Path-First Routing Protocol. It has been developed by the Internet engineering working group and put into the public domain. It is expected to be resistant to routing loops and many other network routing problems. The basic idea is that every node in the net will receive information about the state of every link in the network, and from this they will compute the optimal routes. Because every node will have the same link state data base, all routing should be consistent.

We have seen a continuing improvement in routing algorithms as was required to handle problems of scale and proper reaction to errors and accidents. We also have noted that routing problems can have major consequences in figuratively bringing a network to its knees. Network designers and implementers should consider routing to be an area of major concern in their networks.

Segmentation and Reassembly

Segmentation (or *fragmentation*) consists of cutting a packet into pieces to have it transmitted across the network. This segmentation can occur at any network along the path, making it of particular concern in internetwork paths in which the exact path to be taken is never completely known in advance. Several variations of segmentation are shown in Figure 5-5.

The top example in Figure 5-5 uses a simple "more" flag. All segments except the last indicate that more pieces are coming. A variation of this approach has two flags, "first" and "last." If a single packet contains the entire unit of information, both flags are set. Otherwise, one packet indicates that it is the beginning of a sequence, all intermediate packets indicate that they are neither the first nor the last, and the packet with the last flag set terminates the sequence. The first flag is redundant, because the packet that follows a last packet is implicitly the first packet of a new sequence. Therefore, the top example does not include the first flag.

The second example in Figure 5-5 adds sequence numbers to the packets, because in this example they may get out of order. The third example in this figure not only handles the problem of out of order packets, it also permits the

- More flag with sequenced data

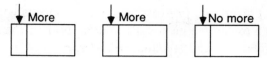

- Packet No. and "last packet" flag
  - When packets can get out of sequence

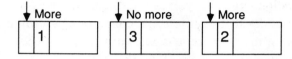

- Segment offset and "last segment" flag

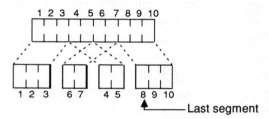

Graphic courtesy of Learning Tree International.

FIGURE 5-5 Various schemes are available for segmentation and reassembly.

segments to be further segmented at any point along the end-to-end path. Every byte has an associated sequence number. Only the sequence number of the first byte is actually conveyed with the packet, but that value, along with the length in terms of bytes, allows subsequent segmentation.

Regardless of how individual packets are segmented, the receiver must put all the pieces back together. This is called *reassembly*. Reassembly is the opposite of segmentation but is more complicated. Segmentation is analogous to taking a picture and cutting it into a jigsaw puzzle, whereas reassembly is analogous to receiving several such jigsaw puzzle pieces and trying to reassemble the multiple puzzles. The first concern is determining which piece belongs to which puzzle. This can be determined by a *datagram number* associated with each piece.

A more complicated concern is where the piece belongs in the overall datagram. A given piece may contain some new information and also may overlap some previous information that had been received already. We will return to reassembly when we discuss the specifics of the Internet Protocol, IP, which has this problem.

Congestion Control and Deadlock Prevention

In this section, we introduce two new concepts: *congestion control* and *deadlocks* and their prevention. Congestion is what happens when some intermediate device, such as a router, begins to take in more packets than it can send to others. This has been referred to as "all store and no forward."

Congestion control resembles flow control in many ways, and sometimes the same mechanisms can be utilized for both purposes. The two concepts differ in that flow control is between two nodes that are communicating with each other, while congestion control involves intermediate nodes that may be transparent. Examples of nodes that require some congestion control mechanism are packet-switches within the network and gateways (routers) between networks. Neither is seen by the end-to-end users of the network service.

One method of providing congestion control builds directly on flow control approaches. Suppose a packet-switch within the network becomes congested because it has received a large number of packets from one neighbor. It tells that neighbor that it must stop sending. The neighbor in turn tells its neighbor, which has been forwarding the packets, to stop sending. This "back pressure" builds up back to the source host, which is told by its packet-switch to stop sending. The simplicity of this approach is that no new mechanisms are needed. Congestion control uses this flow control mechanism. It may be slow to act, however, and it is not selective enough. Entire flows are stopped between nodes when only the offending host's traffic should be affected, which still would not be selective enough. Why stop the data flow of all users at a given host when only one such user is causing the problem?

A better congestion control scheme would be for the congested node to send a control packet directly to the offending host, advising it to stop sending on a particular end-to-end connection. It would be even better if the congested node could also discard the packet(s) that caused the congestion. You will see specific examples of these mechanisms in the IP protocol discussion.

A form of congestion that has catastrophic consequences, deadlock, occurs when one or more nodes in the network become so badly congested that they cannot continue to operate. A classic example of a network deadlock is the reassembly deadlock of the early ARPAnet days. In that network, messages up to 8,000 bits in length were sent from a host to a packet-switch. The packet-switch would take the first 1,000 bits and send them, while the next part of the message was still coming in. Eventually, all of the packets would end up at the destination packet-switch, which would reassemble them for delivery to the destination host. Only when a message was completely reassembled would it be sent to the host.

The ARPAnet deadlock example is shown in Figures 5-6 and 5-7. Figure 5-6 shows that packets are flowing from a host on the left to a host on the right

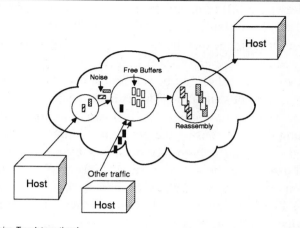

Graphic courtesy of Learning Tree International.

FIGURE 5-6   A reassembly deadlock condition starts.

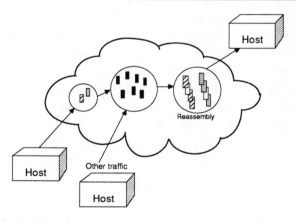

Graphic courtesy of Learning Tree International.

FIGURE 5-7   The reassembly deadlock has happened.

through an intermediate packet-switch. One packet from each of two messages has not yet been delivered. They were delayed because of line errors and are waiting for a retransmission timeout to expire. Normally, they would be received successfully upon retransmission, then forwarded to the destination packet-switch where the reassembly would be complete, and the messages would be sent to the host.

But in this scenario, while these packets are waiting for the timeout to re-transmit, packets from another source start to enter the network, and they are headed for the same destination packet-switch, which no longer has available reassembly buffer space. All of its buffers are tied up waiting for the partial reassemblies to be completed, but the two missing packets required for reassembly are unable to get through because the newest packets have congested the intermediate packet-switch's store-and-forward buffer space. The newest packets will be unable to move on until they can be sent to the destination packet-switch, but it cannot accept them in this situation. This is a deadlock.

The initial approach to avoiding deadlock was to curtail the high data rate (saturation) testing that was causing the problem, and then devise and implement a fix. The fix was to avoid reassembly deadlock by ensuring that, before the packets were allowed into the network, reassembly buffers would be available at the destination packet-switch. When the first packet of a multi-packet message was received by the sending packet-switch, it was sent off as a reassembly request. If adequate buffering was available, the other packets were allowed to enter the network. Otherwise, the request packet was sent back, telling the others to stay out of the network. This approach is analogous to having a hotel reservation before heading off to a big city for a convention.

The approach worked for awhile, then reassembly lockup occurred again. This time the culprit was not the lack of reassembly buffers but the lack of another required resource; namely, a reassembly control block. Each reassembly effort required one control block. When a reservation request came across the network, a full complement of reassembly buffers was set aside, but a reassembly control block was not allocated. This was the implementation error.

The new form of deadlock occurred when short, but multi-packet, messages were sent. As soon as the last packet was received, any buffers beyond that number could be returned to the free pool. This meant that an incoming request packet could be answered with "Yes, come ahead," even if no reassembly control block was available. Buffers were available, but not all other required resources were. As with the previous analogy, a hotel reservation does not ensure that transportation, food, and other needs are available.

After the problem was discovered, it was easy to fix—simply set aside a reassembly control block as well as the reassembly buffers. But how do you know if you have implemented everything necessary to avoid a future deadlock?

Perhaps the answer is not to be required to provide 100% assurance that you can avoid deadlocks, but rather to provide a recovery mechanism when deadlocks occur. The packets in the previous example that were trapped in the intermediate packet-switch could be discarded after a specified number of failed attempts to transmit. Or, the reassembly operations that were not completed within a predefined time limit could be discarded. These two approaches are analogous to having a maximum retry count in writing to a magnetic media or performing a "garbage collection" on resources that are otherwise unavailable.

X.25 NETWORKS

X.25 was intended as a host-to-network interface protocol when it was first written for inclusion in the 1976 CCITT recommendations. It was imperative that some such standard be introduced at that time, since the next opportunity in the CCITT publication process would be in 1980. During that four year interval, many public packet-switching networks would be coming on-line. Unless a standard was defined, every network would develop their own proprietary interface, and the chance for standardization might be lost for the foreseeable future. As a consequence, the 1976 X.25 recommendation was developed in a spirit of "If that's a feature you want, you've got it as long as you will vote Yes." The result was a flawed protocol that had arcane features that took many years to discard. Many of these features would never be removed and set a precedent for other "strange" features to be added.

Because of the nature of the X.25 development process and its development a few years before the OSI RM, it is not surprising that X.25 does not fit well within the OSI RM. This is shown in Figure 5-8, which indicates an overlap between the network and transport layers. This overlap is to account for end-to-end functions, such as delivery confirmation, which is clearly not an interface matter between the host and a network. Other end-to-end functions are discussed later in this section.

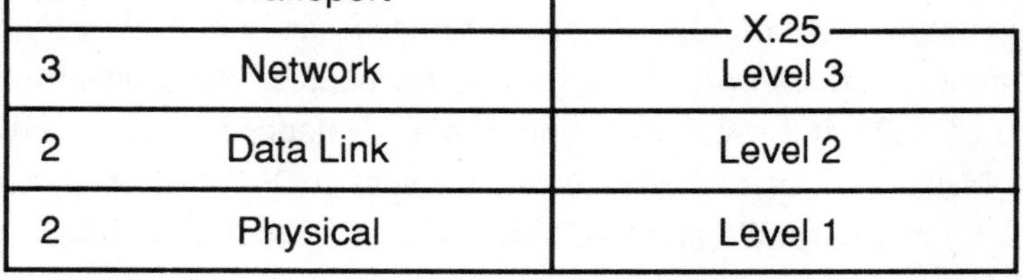

7	Application		
6	Presentation		
5	Session		
4	Transport		
3	Network	X.25 Level 3	
2	Data Link	Level 2	
2	Physical	Level 1	

The X.25 standard does not map well onto the OSI reference model. It emerged before the model was recommended and has been modified since then.

Graphic courtesy of Learning Tree International.

FIGURE 5-8 X.25 and OSI layering do not match at layers 3 and 4.

The X.25 recommended interface is described as being between a DTE (Data Terminal Equipment) and a DCE (Data Communications-terminating Equipment). Technically, CCITT also got this wrong, because by their own terminology, the packet-switch is DSE (Data Switching Equipment). The DCE is typically the modem at either end, i.e., at both the DTE and the DSE.

The Three Layers of X.25

The X.25 interface is a Network Layer protocol but includes protocols at the Data Link and Physical Layers as well. Therefore, X.25 consists of three different protocol layers, with a choice of two variations at each of the two lower layers. At layer three there are many variations, which have been built into the protocol as facilities that can be negotiated at the establishment of an X.25 connection. There are even variations in the way the negotiations are carried out.

As is probably clear by now, the X.25 protocol is considerably more complex than one might have expected a simple host-to-network interface to be. This author believes it is much more complex than it ever should have been. Although the industry is probably stuck with it for many years, there may be an opportunity to correct it when a new interface is defined for the very high data rate networks of the future.

In the meantime, you will find many X.25 networks with interfaces to hosts as shown in Figure 5-9, which indicates the three protocol layers of the interface. The Physical Layer consists of X.21, a digital, direct dial, synchronous communications capability; or X.21bis, which attempts to provide approximately the same capability over leased line RS-232 circuits. X.21bis is considered to be an interim solution until full X.21 circuits are available.

The Data Link Layer can be either a LAP (Link Access Procedure) or a LAPB (Link Access Procedure Balanced). LAP was a mistake and should not be utilized in any new design. It is carried along to grandfather clause earlier implementations. LAP was based on the Asynchronous Response Mode of HDLC, which had operational problems including an unnecessarily complex initialization and a potential deadlock condition. LAPB has been utilized on all modern implementations of X.25 and uses the Asynchronous Balanced Mode of HDLC.

Even at the Network Layer, there are two choices in X.25—Permanent Virtual Circuits (PVC) and Virtual Calls (VC). Permanent Virtual Circuits are analogous to leased telephone lines and Virtual Calls are analogous to direct-dial circuits. Like the analogs in the telephone world, PVC and VC capabilities are arranged for administratively and then requested as needed.

Notice that several PVCs and/or VCs can be multiplexed across the LAPB link layer connection. The level three PVCs and VCs utilize the error detection and recovery capabilities of the level two LAPB, but they do not rely strictly on

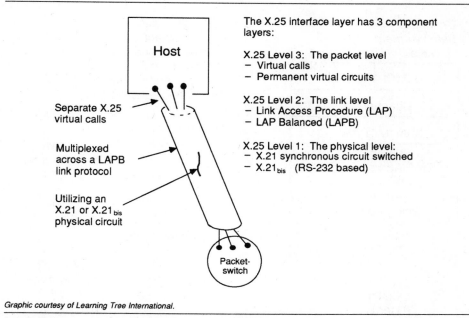

The X.25 interface layer has 3 component layers:

X.25 Level 3: The packet level
– Virtual calls
– Permanent virtual circuits

X.25 Level 2: The link level
– Link Access Procedure (LAP)
– LAP Balanced (LAPB)

X.25 Level 1: The physical level:
– X.21 synchronous circuit switched
– X.21$_{bis}$ (RS-232 based)

Host

Separate X.25
virtual calls

Multiplexed
across a LAPB
link protocol

Utilizing an
X.21 or X.21$_{bis}$
physical circuit

Packet-
switch

Graphic courtesy of Learning Tree International.

FIGURE 5-9   X.25 involves three protocol layers.

its other properties such as flow control. Each X.25 connection has its own flow control mechanisms, such that no single (high-usage) connection will lock out all of the other connections.

Establishing an X.25 Connection

When a PVC is utilized, all of the characteristics of the channel are administratively determined and do not need to be initialized when a connection is first used. However, VCs (like their dial-up analog) must be initialized on each start up. This requires control packets to establish the call and to negotiate the specific characteristics of each call. These characteristics include the size of the sequence numbers, the maximum packet sizes to be transferred, and which end will pay for the call. These negotiated capabilities are called *facilities*. If a parameter is not negotiated, it will default to a predefined value. The default sequence number size is three bits, and the default maximum packet size is 128 bytes. You can imagine what the default is in terms of who will pay for the call! The negotiation is always in the spirit of being able to request a wide variety of values while being willing to negotiate toward the default values, which everyone must be willing to accept. A connection request packet is shown in Figure 5-10, which indicates some example facilities to be negotiated. The call establishment handshake is shown in Figure 5-11.

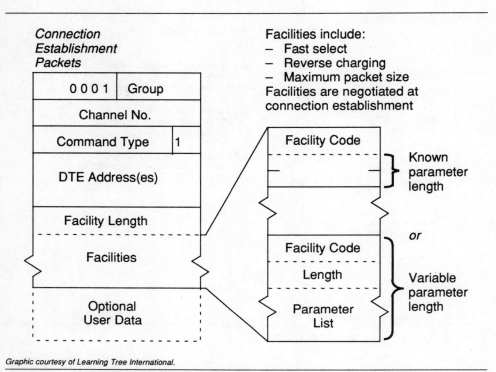

Graphic courtesy of Learning Tree International.

FIGURE 5-10   An X.25 connection request packet contains facilities to be negotiated.

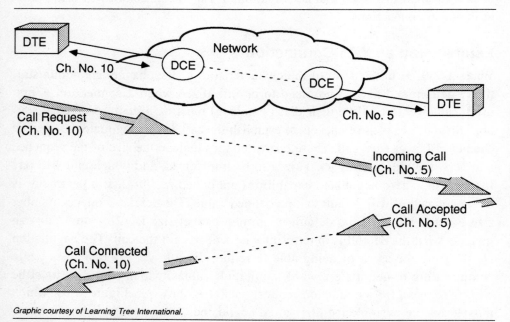

Graphic courtesy of Learning Tree International.

FIGURE 5-11   An X.25 connection open involves a full handshake.

The connection request/response exchange provides a convenient mechanism to negotiate certain parameters that will be held constant for the life of the connection. These include the maximum packet size to be exchanged, the window size, and the sequence number size (three or seven bits). All of these values have a default that will be used unless the negotiation causes them to change. The ground rules for negotiation are that the connection request can include requested non-default values and that the response can either accept these requested values or negotiate them toward the default values. For example, the default value of the window size is two, and the default maximum packet size is 128 bytes. If a connection request asked for a window size of six, and a maximum packet size of 32 bytes, the response might be to reduce the window size to three and to increase the packet size to 64 bytes. These values then would be applied for the duration of the connection, but any other connections may have different parameter values.

Note that the channel numbers also are selected during the handshake, but not by negotiation. Each end of the connection can select its own number to utilize. Clearly, this channel number does not have end-to-end significance. The initiating DTE selects the channel between it and the packet-switch, and the packet-switch at the other end selects the channel number between it and the other DTE. This selection process is managed as shown in Figure 5-12 to avoid (or minimize) the chance of a call collision, in which both a DTE and a packet-switch select the same number at the same end.

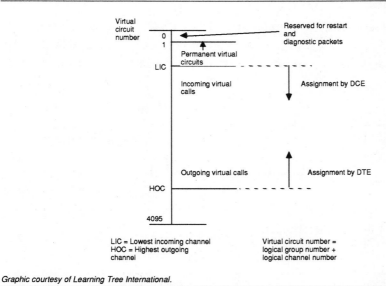

Graphic courtesy of Learning Tree International.

FIGURE 5-12   X.25 channel numbers are assigned by the DTE or DCE.

The channel number provides a shorthand way of referencing the connection, which is defined in the connection open request by the full addresse(s) of the destination host, and optionally of the source host. Presumably, the packet-switch might know the address of the host on the other end of a leased line, therefore this value need not be sent on each connection request packet.

Both addresses can be variable in length; like the telephone numbers, one only needs to send area code extensions when going outside of one's area. The address format is defined as CCITT recommendation X.121, which is summarized in Figure 5-13.

Note that the X.121 numbering system has three basic parts:

1. A country code.
2. A network number within that country.
3. An assigned number within that network.

The country and network codes are assigned internationally. The numbers within a network can be assigned in any way that the network decides. For example, the first digit may have some network-specific interpretation, such as whether the address is to be utilized directly or is to be mapped by the network into a physical address. Similarly, the network may decide to use only a portion of the address space, reserving the remainder for future enhancements. Any of these options are available to the network administration.

Utilizing an X.25 Connection

After a VC is established (or immediately for a PVC), data can be sent over the connection. Actually, a restricted amount of data can be sent with the connection request as well. But, immediate transmission in a VC is as unusual as

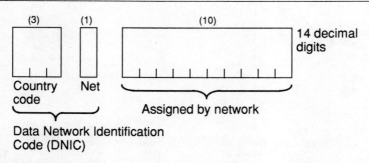

Graphic courtesy of Learning Tree International.

FIGURE 5-13   X.25 utilizes addresses with an X.121 format.

starting a telephone conversation before you had been acknowledged somehow. You will see an important exception to this later, in terms of "fast select" communications.

The data packet is shown in Figure 5-14. It contains only three bytes of control information in this form. (An extended six-byte version can be negotiated.) Note the similarity to HDLC in terms of the sequence number and ACK number fields. The M (more) flag replaces the poll/final flag of HDLC but has a similar meaning in marking the end of a group of packets. The D (delivery confirmation) flag and the Q (data qualifier) flag have been added.

The data to be sent over the connection may need to be segmented into packet sized data units to be transmitted. However, there is still a need to associate the data units as portions of a larger whole that the host wants to send. This is reflected in X.25 in its more flag, which indicates that more data units are coming, until the last packet (which indicates "no more").

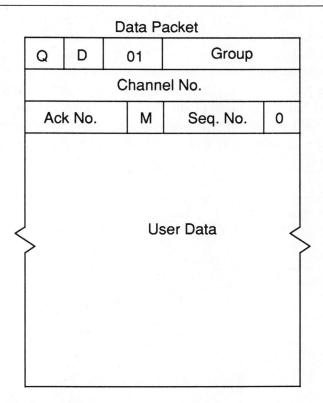

Graphic courtesy of Learning Tree International.

FIGURE 5-14   An X.25 data packet has a three-byte header.

The host is not the only entity that can manipulate the X.25 more flag, however. The network (packet-switches) also can apply this capability to either segment packets or to combine host-segmented packets. Suppose, as shown in Figure 5-15, that the sending host segments the transmission of a short file into two packets, each of which is further segmented into two smaller packets before delivery to the destination host. This would not seem to be necessary in X.25, because a mutually agreed-to maximum packet size is negotiated in the facilities negotiation when the connection was established—but such further segmentation is allowed in X.25. Alternatively, the network could have combined the two original packets that the host sent and delivered one complete packet to the destination host. The net effect in all of these cases is the same; namely, that the destination host receives a sequence of one or more packets that can be associated as one logical unit (i.e., the file that was sent).

The reason for the above level of concern about segmentation and where it can be performed is the result of the interaction of the more flag and another X.25 mechanism called *delivery confirmation*. The delivery confirmation mechanism provides a transmitting host with the option of asking that the returned ACK have end-to-end significance, thus indicating that the packet was delivered to the destination host. Otherwise, the ACK comes from the local packet-switch and indicates that the packet was successfully received by the network. The latter is an interface protocol message, while the delivery confirmation overlaps the usual Transport Layer functions. Figure 5-16 shows a typical single packet message example of delivery confirmation and also shows the dilemma when one tries to send packets utilizing **both** the more and the delivery confirmation mechanisms.

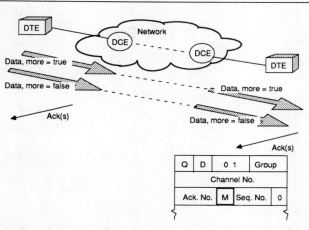

Graphic courtesy of Learning Tree International.

FIGURE 5-15   The X.25 more flag can be utilized to segment packets.

There are a special set of circumstances under which both the more and delivery confirmation mechanisms can be utilized, as exemplified in Figure 5-17. A group of packets can form a complete packet sequence, the end of which is clearly identified. However, there can be intermediate groupings of packets, with the delivery confirmation flag set at the end of each of these smaller groupings.

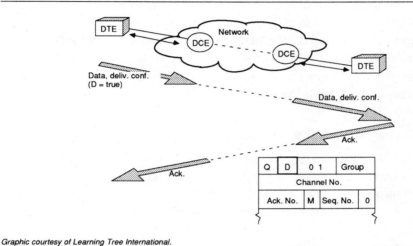

Graphic courtesy of Learning Tree International.

FIGURE 5-16   The X.25 delivery confirmation flag indicates that ACKs have end-to-end significance.

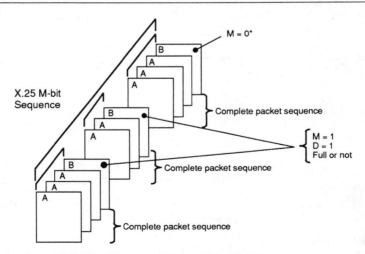

*Note: D = 0, M = 1 and < Full will also terminate the sequence, but will result in a reset of the logical channel

Graphic courtesy of Learning Tree International.

FIGURE 5-17   The more and delivery confirmation flags may be utilized together only under specific circumstances.

This allows assurance at these intermediate points that the data are being delivered to the destination host while still allowing the unambiguous indication of the end of the complete data unit (e.g., a file).

A third mechanism of X.25 is the *data qualifier* flag. As Figure 5-18 shows, this simple flag is merely "along for the ride" as far as X.25 is concerned. If the transmitting host sets the flag, it is delivered to the destination as being set, and vice versa. X.25 provides no definition of the flag setting, and there are no error-prone interactions between this flag and any other. If a packet is segmented, all of the new smaller packets have the data qualifier either set or not set to match that of the original packet. Similarly, packets of a more sequence could be combined. All packets of a segmented sequence must have the same data qualifier setting, or an error will be indicated.

Other X.25 Control Packet Mechanisms

At this point, the supply of flag bit mechanisms in the X.25 packet header is exhausted. However, there is still much to learn about X.25 mechanisms, because other control packets can affect X.25 operations, including expedited data, fast select, reset, and restart. These mechanisms are described in the following paragraphs.

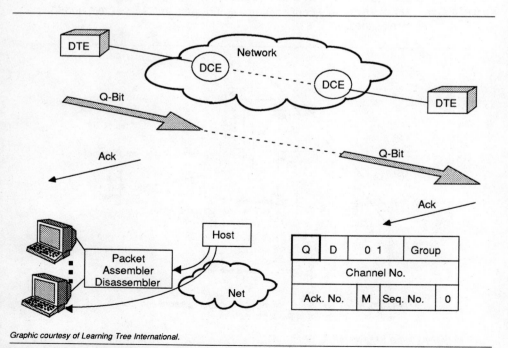

Graphic courtesy of Learning Tree International.

FIGURE 5-18   The data qualifier flag is carried by, but not interpreted by, the X.25 net.

Expedited data means what its name implies. This data is to be delivered as quickly as possible to the destination, perhaps overtaking ordinary data that has already been sent. However, because X.25 networks do not necessarily have internal priority mechanisms, all that can be guaranteed is that no subsequent normal data will overtake expedited data. This is ensured by simply not sending any more normal data until the expedited data has been ACKed (on an end-to-end basis). Similarly, no subsequent expedited data packet can be sent on this connection until the ACK is received. An exchange between expedited data and ACK are shown in Figure 5-19.

A limited amount of data can be sent in an expedited data packet. This value was originally set at one byte but was later extended to 32 bytes to match the similar needs of the transport protocol.

The *fast select* variation of X.25 was developed to support quicker transaction exchanges over X.25. If you performed the usual call establishment and clearing packet exchanges of X.25 for each simple transaction exchange, the overhead would be very large. There would be a full exchange to establish the call, followed by the one packet request/one packet response of the transaction, and then another full exchange to clear the call. Instead, fast select can be negotiated and operates as shown in Figure 5-20.

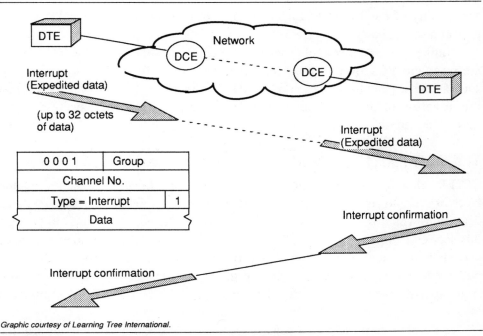

Graphic courtesy of Learning Tree International.

FIGURE 5-19   Expedited data has end-to-end significance in X.25.

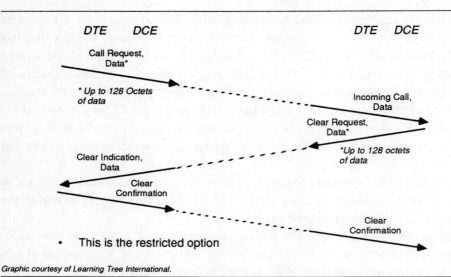

Graphic courtesy of Learning Tree International.

FIGURE 5-20   Fast select provides a transaction-like support by X.25.

An X.25 characteristic, if not a feature, is its ability to advise you of potentially lost packets. This mechanism is called *reset*. The effect of reset is limited to a single connection, but its sequence and ACK numbers are reset to zero. Interrupt (expedited data) and/or normal data packet(s) may be lost. It is the responsibility of the Transport Layer protocol to recover from this packet loss. A typical reset is shown in Figure 5-21.

Unlike reset, *restart* applies to all connections, both PVCs and VCs. PVCs are reset and VCs are cleared. A restart is performed for major fault recovery, such as the loss and re-creation of a LAPB connection, but also for the normal initialization of the X.25 (level three) connections when first bringing up a LAPB connection.

The CCITT X.213 Network Service Definition for X.25

CCITT defines a service definition and a protocol specification at each layer; the Network Layer is one major exception. It has a Network Layer service definition, which is X.213, but the protocol within the network that is to provide this service is not standardized. Tymnet does it one way, Telenet does it another way, and Datapac does it yet another way. The same would be true for the other public packet-switched networks around the world. How can they get by without standardizing the internal protocol to provide X.25 service? Why is only the interface specification (i.e., X.25 itself) required to be standard?

There are two principal reasons. First, it is not necessary if they all provide the same X.213 service. Second, they are the ones who make the rules, so when

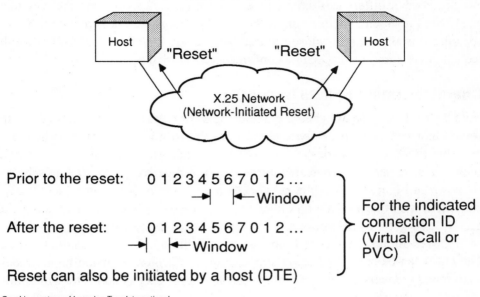

Prior to the reset: 0 1 2 3 4 5 6 7 0 1 2 ...
                              ⟶| |⟵ Window

After the reset: 0 1 2 3 4 5 6 7 0 1 2 ...
                        ⟶| |⟵ Window

Reset can also be initiated by a host (DTE)

For the indicated
connection ID
(Virtual Call or
PVC)

Graphic courtesy of Learning Tree International.

FIGURE 5-21   The X.25 reset indicates that packets may have been lost.

they decide that they do not want to do something, that is the way it is going to be. The PTT (Post Telegraph and Telephone) monopoly of each country is its voting member to CCITT. In the U.S. and Canada, there is no PTT. We are represented by the U.S. Department of State and Telecom Canada, respectively. We tend to be the exception rather than the rule in this regard.

In any case, it was important that all of the public packet-switched networks provided a comparable service such that they could be interconnected as required to provide international end-to-end service, necessitating the X.213 service definition, which came several years after X.25. This lead to a number of compromises. Some of the quirks of X.25 had to be changed; in other cases, some of the elegance of X.213 had to be sacrificed to adapt to X.25 mechanisms, which otherwise did not fit the model.

An example in which X.25 had to change is in its handling of expedited data, which X.25 calls "interrupt." Originally, X.25 limited interrupt packets to a single byte in the data field. This was increased to 32 bytes to be consistent with the desired size in X.213. After all, X.213 had to be consistent with what the transport protocol planned to send, which was 16 bytes of application data, plus the transport protocol overhead.

An example in which X.213 had to change was regarding the delivery confirmation of X.25. This was added as an option in X.213, but only because it already existed in some X.25 networks. Again, the PTTs make the rules.

Some other differences exist between the way X.25 works and the way that X.213 says it should. An example is the way that a connection is released. X.213 specifies this as a simple "close request" and "close indication"; X.25 has a full request, indication, response, and confirmation handshake.

Characterization of X.25 Networks

X.25 networks can be assigned a grade of A, B, or C, just like a school grade. In some other instances, it can be seen more as "pass/fail." Of concern is how acceptable the X.25 network is in terms of two characteristics: signalled errors, such as resets; and the undetected introduction of bit errors. The grading scheme is shown in Figure 5-22. If the network is acceptable in both categories, it gets an A. If it is not acceptable on either count, but gets most of the data across, it gets a C. To get a B, the network must have an acceptable number of undetected errors, even though it does not have an acceptable number of signalled errors. The latter can be recovered using simple transport protocols, while bit error detection and recovery involve more complicated error checks and retransmissions

---

Network Service Level

• Networks can be rated by their service level:

Network Type	Acceptable Signalled Errors (1)	Acceptable Residual Errors (2)	Summary Statement
A	Yes	Yes	Acceptable (low) number of errors
B	No	Yes	Errors occur, but the host is notified
C	No	No	Errors occur without notification

(1)   Signalled errors include resets (lost or duplicated packets)

(2)   Residual errors include erroneous bits, lost packets, etc., without any network indication

• The network service level will affect our choice of transport layer protocol

Graphic courtesy of Learning Tree International.

FIGURE 5-22   X.25 network services can be graded, affecting the choice of the transport protocol functions.

based on timers. The pass/fail approach is based on the network being either completely acceptable or requiring a recovery mechanism from either type of error. We will discuss the transport protocol selection more in Chapter 6.

INTERNETWORKS

Internet Protocols

Internet protocols connect networks to other networks. They come in two forms, connection and connectionless. Public networks, such as those of Tymnet, Telenet, and Datapac, are connection-oriented and utilize an extension of X.25 called X.75. In contrast, private networks use connectionless internet approaches called an Internet Protocol (IP) of any one of several variations. The most common is the IP associated with Transmission Control Protocol (TCP). This IP is typical of the others and will be the principal example here. The other protocols can be readily described as variations, subsets, or supersets of IP.

The X.75 Approach to Interconnecting Networks

Public packet-switched networks are expected to conform to the CCITT X.25 recommendation. Therefore they should all provide a common level of service; namely, that of CCITT X.213. It is therefore very simple, at least conceptually, to interconnect such networks. All that is required is a VC (a connection) between two networks, where this VC provides the same characteristics as X.25. This interconnection is CCITT X.75. It provides a packet structure similar to that of X.25, the principal difference being the addition of another variable length field in control packets. This additional control information is called *utilities*. It resembles the facilities field of X.25 but conveys additional information, such as the set of interconnection devices along the path.

The IP Approach to Interconnecting Networks

The IP is connectionless and consists of independent transmissions of datagrams. Each datagram must contain all of the control information that is needed for its delivery to the destination host. This information includes the internet address of both the source and the destination. These addresses are in the form "network address, host address," much like telephone numbers consist of area code and local phone number. The required information for delivery also includes the "type of service," which is analogous to air mail or special delivery in the mail system. These functions are included in each IP packet header as shown in Figure 5-23. The other fields in the header will be described later.

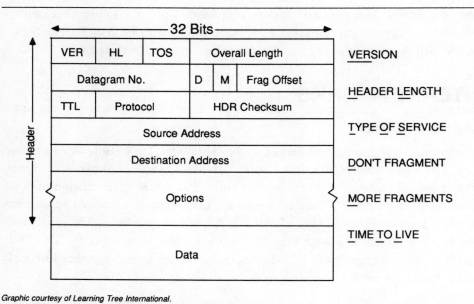

Graphic courtesy of Learning Tree International.

FIGURE 5-23   The internet protocol datagram.

The principal design goals of the IP were to support a wide variety of network services (not just X.25), and to provide host independent routing and segmentation across the interconnected networks. It also was intended to support a wide variety of higher level needs that have evolved to be both connection and connectionless transport protocols. These are TCP (Transmission Control Protocol) and UDP (User Datagram Protocol), respectively.

The principal reasons for the use of connectionless internet protocol were:

1. To allow dynamic alternate routing to rapidly find a new path when the current one is lost.
2. To provide a convenient method of congestion control by simply discarding packets under such conditions.

IP Options

Datagrams may convey options that can contain a variety of information related to the packets, including the route to take (called a "source route" and provided by the originator), the capture of the addresses of the intermediate systems that handle the packet (just the opposite of source route), time stamps at the intermediate systems, or a security label, to name a few. The IP options and their placement in the IP header are shown in Figure 5-23. It is not possible for all options to be conveyed in any one packet, because in IP these options cannot exceed 20 bytes in length (the entire header is limited to 40 bytes in length, and includes a mandatory 20 bytes). Although the data portion may vary in length, all IP implementations must be capable of handling a 576-byte datagram.

Segmentation (Fragmentation) of IP Datagrams

One of the principal design goals of IP was to provide host independence from matters such as the maximum packet size of the networks over which its packets are flowing. Because of dynamic alternate routing, the host does not know which networks are involved, so this independence is particularly important. Thus, IP packets can be segmented at any point along the path. The IP protocol description uses the term fragmentation, but it is same concept as segmentation. Segmentation can be performed by the originating host or at any router along the path.

One aspect of the IP datagram handling of segmentation seems similar to the X.25 more flag, but IP packets do not necessarily stay in order the way X.25 packets do. Therefore, it is necessary to add information to allow arbitrarily segmented packets to be combined even after getting out of sequence and/or being duplicated. The solution for IP is to allow any IP packet to be segmented (fragmented in IP terminology) along any eight-byte boundary, and still be reassembled. Because packet segments can be further segmented, duplicated, lost, or any combination of the above, reassembly is significant. Each packet segment will contain its length and its offset from the original (unsegmented) datagram. The last segment will be so indicated by its more flag being set to "false." Until this segment is received, how large the reassembly space needs to be is unknown. Also, the first datagram fragment may have a different header size than the other fragments, so this amount of space is not known until the first fragment is received.

Some other mechanisms of the IP protocol are the "time to live" and the "next protocol" fields. The time to live field provides a self-destruct mechanism in each packet. Each intermediate system that handles the packet decrements this field, until such time as it is either delivered or it counts down to zero and is discarded. The original concept was that the remaining value of the time to live field after a segment was delivered to a host would be the number of seconds that the host should wait before discarding any un-reassembled segments. It was subsequently decided that the two issues, i.e., the number of store-and-forward hops allowed in the network and the number of seconds of wait time on reassembly, were quite independent. Therefore, current implementation guidance includes utilizing the time to live for the maximum allowed number of hops and setting a fixed duration timer for reassembly to be complete before discarding un-reassembled segments.

SECURITY AT THE NETWORK LAYER

The Network Layer provides a convenient location for the addition of security mechanisms, particularly those that involve insertion of encryption devices. Just as the RS-232 interface allowed the introduction of encryption units between the terminal or host and the modem, the network provides a well-defined interface between the host and the communications component.

However, encryption at the network interface, as opposed to the RS-232 interface, is more complicated. The first major complication is that not everything that goes across the interface can be encrypted. The control portion (e.g., the part that indicates where the packet is to be sent) must be readable by the packet switch. Only the data portion must be encrypted. An encryption device that passes some information in the clear, and encrypts other portions, is much more complicated to build than one that encrypts everything that passes through it.

The second major complication is that, unlike the point-to-point data link encryption, network level encryption may need many keys; for example, one for each host on the network with which communications are desired. This makes the key management problem much more complex. An alternative would be to use the same key for all hosts on the network. However, this loses the inherent source authentication that pairwise keying provides, and also loses the access control capabilities that are implicit in the set of assigned pairwise keys.

The Network Layer security also may include integrity mechanisms, such as cryptographic error checks. Such checks ensure that if any of the data or control field are modified, there is a very high probability that the modification will be detected. The probability of not being detected is the random chance that the N-bit error-check will pass the test despite data/control modification. Because the probability of passing the test based on random chance is approximately one in 2^N, this can be made arbitrarily small by making N large. Making N equal to 32 bits is common.

Service assurance mechanisms also may be added at the Network Layer, although such technology is less common than for confidentiality and integrity protection. The first step in service assurance is to detect potential denial of service threats. This may be by noting an increased number of retransmission attempts, which also could result from acts of nature. Once the loss or partial loss of communications is noted, recovery measures can be initiated. These may include addition of reserve communication resources or the prioritization of traffic. The goal of service assurance is to eventually restore the service level to that before the disruption.

TEST TOOLS AT THE NETWORK LAYER

Test tools at the Network Layer fall into three broad categories:

1. Tools that allow one to determine if communications are possible.
2. Tools that provide broad insight into the nature of the communications process and problems.
3. Network protocol conformance tests.

Communication Feasibility Tests

Tests of the communications capability typically appear as "echo-back" tests. A packet is sent to a selected destination and is returned. This test demonstrates three things. Can you reach the other site? Can bits be sent and returned without error? How long does it take for the transmission and reply?

Communication tests at the network level may also be oriented toward measuring throughput. What level of Kbps or Mbps can be sent and received? Data integrity tests may be included here as well.

Tests Which Provide Detailed Insights

Network Layer testers are typically PC-like devices that operate either as one end of a communications channel or monitor the communications channel between two other correspondents.

A device that operates as one end of the communications channel is assumed to be a proper implementation of the protocol(s), and is utilized much the way a platinum meter bar is to check a distance measuring device. In addition, the tester will conduct a series of scenarios that are intended to determine if the device under test properly obeys the protocol(s). Such testers are often used to determine if a host should be allowed to connect to a network.

Network protocol analyzers can monitor the flow of commands, responses, and data between two devices. Typical devices of this sort are LAN protocol analyzers, which can capture packets and decode the various higher level protocols. These decoded results can then be displayed for analysis.

Network Protocol Conformance Tests

Any organization responsible for ensuring that implementations of protocols properly correspond to the specifications and implementation guidelines can elect to perform conformance tests. Such tests are expensive to develop and are still the exception rather than the rule. Organizations that have developed such tests include the MAP/TOP community, the Corporation for Open Systems, and the Defense Communications Agency.

SUMMARY

The Network Layer is one of several layers that can be divided into sublayers. Two such sublayers include the X.25 network interface protocol and the IP. Both or either one may be included in any given network implementation. The choice of the proper transport protocol may depend on which of these combinations is selected. The transport protocol is the subject of Chapter 6.

6

THE TRANSPORT LAYER

The basic purpose of the Transport Layer is to provide end-to-end integrity of higher level protocol packets. In official OSI terminology, the ends correspond to the OSI end systems. However, the usual interpretation of the ends of a Transport Layer connection are the processes in the two communicating computers.

ALTERNATIVE TRANSPORT LAYER APPROACHES

The association between the two end points at the Transport Layer can be a connection or it can be connectionless. The general distinction between connection and connectionless is essentially the same that we have seen at the lower layers.

The end points are identified by reference numbers or port numbers that distinguish one communication from another. In a typical example, the X.25 address is adequate to get a packet delivered to the correct end system (host), and the internet protocol gets it to the correct transport protocol module. Then, the Transport Layer address (reference identifier or port number) provides the internal software address of the process within that host. One aspect of this additional addressing granularity at the Transport Layer is that it allows one to multiplex several transport associations across one network association, e.g., across one X.25 connection.

The Transport Layer communications are most frequently by means of a connection-oriented protocol, which provides reliable, sequenced delivery. However, connectionless transport protocols are also utilized. Both will be described here. Connection-oriented transport protocols are described in the following section, and connectionless transport protocols are described later in the section "Connectionless Transport Protocols."

Connection-Oriented Transport Protocols

Like any other connection-oriented protocol, the distinguishing characteristic of a transport connection is that it maintains state information about the data transfers. This state information includes the sequence number for the next transmission and the next expected sequence number upon reception. It also includes the current flow control allocation.

Connection-oriented transport protocols almost always provide end-to-end integrity of the data transfers. In some cases, all or a part of this integrity is provided by the network layer and is simply passed on by the transport layer. Integrity is utilized here in the sense of reliable, sequenced delivery. No bad bits are delivered; no packets are lost, duplicated, or out of order. Acknowledgments are delivered to indicate that packets have been received successfully. However, this ACK means that the packet contents are in RAM and still may be lost if the system crashes. Higher level ACKs and/or recovery mechanisms are necessary when crash recovery is required. These higher level mechanisms may also include checkpoint recovery.

The services that the Transport Layer provides are built upon error, sequence, and flow control mechanisms. Although these mechanisms have the same names as similar mechanisms at lower layers, they are considerably more complex at the Transport Layer. For example, the timeouts utilized for error recovery need to be selected based on the delays of the actual end-to-end connection, which may vary from connection to connection, and from time to time on any given connection. Therefore, the timeouts are typically based on the round-trip time that has been experienced on the connection, i.e., the delay from the time of packet transmission until the ACK arrives.

Similarly, sequence controls tend to differ from those at lower layers. The sequence numbers tend to be larger, being as long as 32 bits (in TCP). Flow controls build on this same sequence number base but have dynamic window sizes, unlike the fixed window size of lower layers. (Data Link Layer window sizes are sysgen parameters and X.25 Network Layer window sizes are negotiated at connection openings.)

Like the Network Layer, the Transport Layer can negotiate connection characteristics at connection establishment. At the Transport Layer, negotiations may include the maximum packet size, the sequence number size, and whether error checks will be utilized. However, the number of possible negotiations is typically fewer than that of the X.25 connection establishment.

TRANSMISSION CONTROL PROTOCOL (TCP)

TCP provides reliable, sequenced delivery of a byte stream of higher layer data. It is a connection-oriented protocol, with most of the usual connection-oriented service characteristics.

TCP was the first transport protocol to address the concerns of internetworking (interconnected networks). In fact, TCP was originally defined with the IP functionality included within TCP. IP was "surgically" removed from that TCP to form the existing TCP and IP. Some of these early origins can still be seen in TCP. For example, it uses a sequence number for every byte, not every packet. The sequence number that is assigned to a packet (called a segment in TCP) is the sequence number of the first byte in the packet. The idea was that an internet packet could be cut into fragments at any byte boundary and still be able to assign each fragment a meaningful sequence number for acknowledgment and reassembly. (The ACK is the next expected sequence number, which is the number of the byte immediately after the last byte of a packet.)

TCP Protocol Mechanisms

TCP seems deceptively simple upon first inspection. As seen in Figure 6-1, the protocol mechanisms in a TCP header are straightforward and include the usual

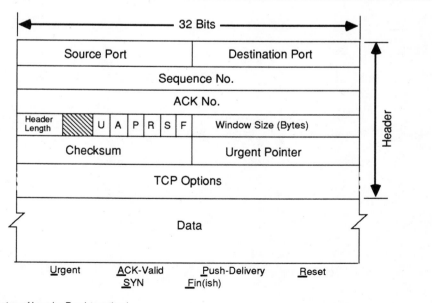

Graphic courtesy of Learning Tree International.

FIGURE 6-1   The header format of TCP.

sequence number, acknowledgment, flow control window size, error-check, and port number mechanisms. Unlike many protocols, there are no special formats for control packets versus data packets. There are no classes of TCP, as with the OSI variations (called "transport protocol," classes 0 through 4). TCP takes a "one size fits all" approach to protocols. It may be overkill in some applications, but it certainly simplifies matters.

TCP provides the functions of control packets by using special flags in the protocol header. When the connection is established, one sets the **S** SYN flag. The exchange of SYN flags by the two ends causes a connection to be considered to be open and ready for business. Actually, data could be sent with the SYN flag packets but should not be delivered to an application until the entire exchange is completed. This exchange is called a three-way handshake. The handshake synchronizes the initial sequence number values. An example of a three-way handshake is shown in Figure 6-2.

TCP also provides a symmetric open capability in which the two ends simultaneously attempt to create the connection. Each sets the SYN flag and selects its initial sequence number. Then each SYN flag segment is ACKed.

The more common approach is for the three-way handshake to be initiated at one end by an "active open," which is matched at the recipient's system by a "passive open." The match may be for a specific port number or for any, in which the passive open is available for any connection. The passive open is often called a "listen."

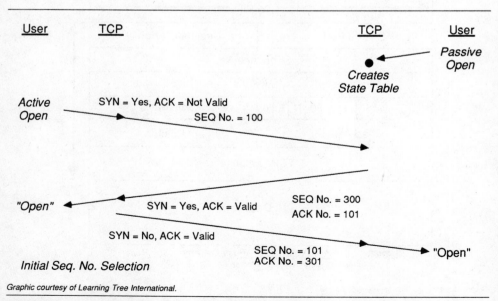

Graphic courtesy of Learning Tree International.

FIGURE 6-2 TCP initializes a typical connection with a three-way handshake.

The opening of a TCP connection is shown in state machine form in Figure 6-3, which illustrates the active and passive opens as well as the intermediate states involved in the three-way handshake. The state transitions are indicated by the arcs between the states. Each arc shows the event that causes it to happen and the output or other effect.

The TCP protocol provides the capability to negotiate options at the connection establishment. However, very little use is made of this capability. The principal usage is not really a negotiation at all, but rather is advisory in nature. Each end system can advise the other of the maximum packet size it is capable of receiving. The maximum size can be different in the two directions.

After a TCP connection is open, application data can be delivered. This delivery service should be viewed as a byte stream, not as a sequence of well-defined blocks of data. In particular, TCP has no equivalent of the OSI Service Data Unit. For example, an application may send 100 bytes, followed by 1,000 bytes. The TCP protocol may send these as two separate packets or combine them in a single 1,100-byte packet. Or it might decide to send the data as a 600-byte packet followed by a 500-byte packet. In addition, a retransmission might be a different block size than what was transmitted originally.

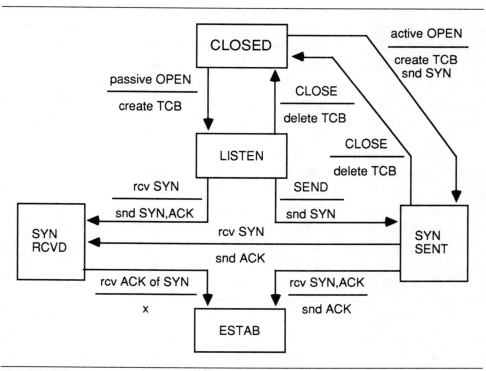

FIGURE 6-3   The state machine for a TCP connection establishment.

The same kind of flexible delivery rules apply at the receiving TCP implementation. In the above example, the receiving TCP could deliver 600 bytes to the application, followed later by 500 bytes. Alternatively, it could bundle both together into an 1,100 byte delivery, or into any other splitting or combining.

Because TCP has such flexibility in deciding when to transmit data, the application needs some way of telling TCP that it should send data **now**. Suppose, for example, you were transmitting several large blocks of data, followed by a very short block. TCP might hold onto the short block, expecting to receive more to send. Because no more is coming, however, that could be a problem. TCP includes a "push" flag to allow the application to tell TCP that it should send the bytes it has received up to this point.

Some implementers have erroneously attempted to utilize the push flag as an end-of-record delimiter. That might work if you controlled both ends of every connection you ever make, but it is not suitable for general interoperability and is not consistent with the protocol's intent. If you must define record boundaries, the application program must provide that capability. TCP does not have anything comparable to the more flag of X.25.

TCP packets contain 32-bit sequence numbers. As mentioned previously, TCP considers each byte to have an associated sequence number. The actual sequence number that is carried in a TCP packet is the sequence number of the first data byte. Therefore, if you were to look at the sequence numbers of TCP packets as they arrived, they would not be consecutive numbers such as 67, 68, 69, 70, etc., but would have gaps depending on the packet size. An example is shown in Figure 6-4. Note that the first packet contains bytes corresponding to sequence numbers 101 to 110, and that it is ACKed by indicating that the next expected sequence number is 111. The next packet is indeed sequence number 111, as shown in Figure 6-4.

The TCP sequence numbers are very large (32 bits) for two reasons. First, they are used up rapidly, with one number per byte. Second, there was considerable concern that packets from two different connections should not be misdelivered, even if the connections utilized the same port numbers.

Flow control in TCP is based on the number of bytes that one can accept. This byte count becomes the window size in a sliding window scheme in which the left edge is the last ACK number to be received. The window size can be updated dynamically by utilizing the window size field in the TCP header. An example is shown in Figure 6-5, which sets the left edge of the window at 111 and establishes the window size as being 30 bytes. In practice, the window normally would be at least a few thousand bytes. This example relates to the packet flow in Figure 6-4 and shows that the 20-byte (octet) packet with sequence number 111 could be sent, because it fits within the 30-byte window. Note that the next

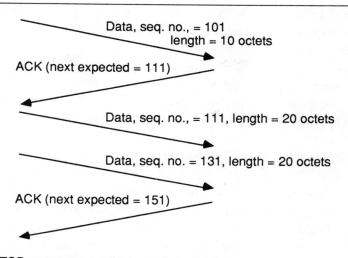

- TCP sequence numbers apply to octets
- TCP ACKs are the next expected octet number

Graphic courtesy of Learning Tree International.

FIGURE 6-4　TCP sequence numbers are not simply sequential numbers.

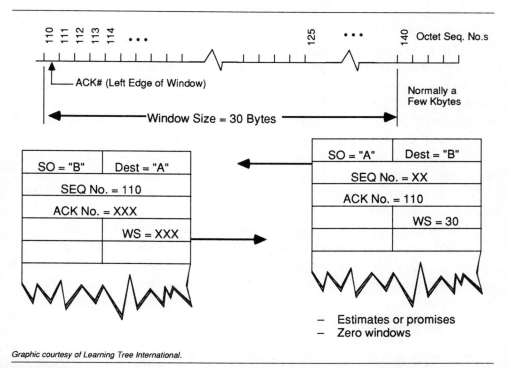

Graphic courtesy of Learning Tree International.

FIGURE 6-5　TCP flow control is by means of dynamic changing of the window size.

packet, with sequence number 131 and a length of 20 bytes, could not be sent until a further flow control allocation is received.

The byte stream orientation of TCP also shows up in a protocol flag called the "urgent pointer." If it is meaningful in a packet, the urgent pointer flag will be set. In that case, the urgent pointer provides an offset from the initial byte sequence to point to "special data." The semantics of "special" are application specific; TCP merely carries the news. A typical application of the urgent pointer is to resynchronize the processing of a data stream after the user has indicated a desire to abort processing or data output.

The error-check of TCP is a 16-bit 1s complement sum. An arithmetic error check is not as strong as a CRC, but is considerably better than a 16-bit Exclusive-OR. The latter will fail to detect any even number of bad bits in a column. This form of error is detected by TCP as a result of the loss or gain of arithmetic carries. The 1s complement form of error-check has a carry from even the most significant bit, and allows efficient generation (e.g., using 32-bit arithmetic). The 1s complement error-check may also be utilized when the check is optional, because there is an alternative representation of zero that is never generated in an arithmetic operation, and therefore can be used to indicate that there is no error-check. However, the error-check is always required in TCP implementations.

The error-check is very important for two reasons. First, it provides the end-to-end error checking that is required for data integrity. It is also important in the implementation, because the error-check computation can be a major portion of the TCP protocol processing and limit the achievable throughput.

The TCP error-check includes the TCP header, the TCP data, and the pseudo header, which includes the IP source address, the IP destination address, and the IP data length (i.e., the TCP segment length). These values are passed between TCP and IP as parameters, and their integrity is protected by the TCP error-check as well as the IP header error-check. Although this may seem a bit like wearing a belt **and** suspenders, it is part of the end-to-end integrity aspect of TCP; it does not rely on or necessarily trust the intermediate systems (routers) to perform these checks.

TCP was designed to recover from some exception conditions, such as damaged packets. However, it was not intended to handle certain other exception conditions, such as crash recovery. If one end of a TCP connection crashes and is subsequently rebooted, it typically will lose all information about its previous TCP connection(s). When a packet arrives on one such connection, the TCP implementation sends back a packet with the **reset** flag set. This will cause the other end to force its connection state back to **closed**.

There are periods of inactivity during which a TCP implementation may want to ensure that the connection is still available, that is, that the other end has not crashed and rebooted. A "keep alive" mechanism can be called upon for this purpose. The idea is to be able to send a packet without any data. The usual approach is to resend the most recent ACK. This is an example of an implementation detail that is not an explicit part of the protocol specification.

To release (close) a connection, one can either force an abrupt termination (abort) or cause an orderly closure, in which all data are transmitted and ACKed before the connection is officially declared to be closed. The orderly close, called "graceful close" in TCP, is started when one end sets the **F** FIN flag to indicate that it is finished sending data. However, with TCP's graceful close, the connection is not actually closed until both parties indicate that they are finished sending data by setting their FIN flags. Only then will TCP consider the connection to be closed, but each end will retain the connection state information to handle the situation in which the ACK to the last FIN flag is lost. Note that the FIN flag "consumes" a sequence number, just as a data byte does. This allows it to be ACKed. The graceful close sequence of message exchanges is shown in Figure 6-6, and the state machine for the close is shown in Figure 6-7.

Note that in the graceful close of the connection, the two ends will hold the state information for twice the worst case delay across the internet, and if it is not needed during that time, it will then be discarded. This should handle any

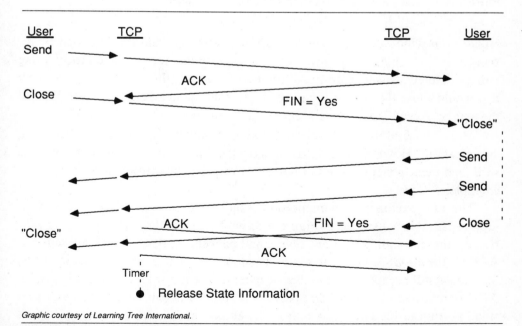

Graphic courtesy of Learning Tree International.

FIGURE 6-6 The "graceful close" of TCP ensures that all data are delivered before a connection is actually closed.

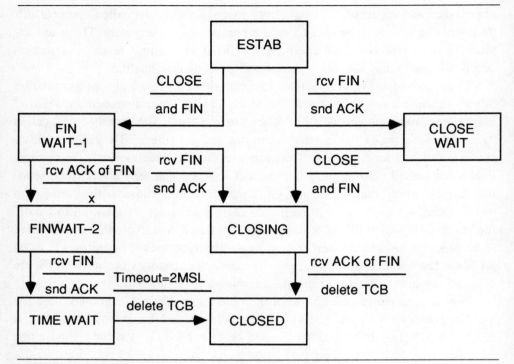

FIGURE 6-7   The state machine for closing a TCP connection.

situation in which the ACK for the FIN flag was lost, and the FIN will be retransmitted. The point, of course, is that if the side that received the last FIN flag simply deleted its state information without waiting, then a retransmitted FIN flag would cause the connection to be reset, resulting in a confused state. Was all the data received? Do we have to retransmit some part or all of the data?

Most of the above TCP services and mechanisms are defined in the TCP specifications. However, one needs to understand many implementation issues as well, and these generally are not described in protocol specifications. Two such examples follow.

The first example implementation issue is called the "silly window syndrome." It is demonstrated in Figure 6-8, which shows the transmission of TCP packets into the sliding window. Four small packets, A, B, C, and D, are sent and ACKed. Each ACK conveys the same window size; that is, the receiver indicates that it can still accept some number of bytes. After transmission of packet A, an ACK is returned indicating that packets B, C, and D can be sent, as well as a small portion of the large data unit E. When packet B is ACKed, another small portion of packet E can be sent, etc. for the entire data unit E. This is very undesirable! We would have preferred to send E in one or more large packets, not a sequence of very small packets. Our achieved throughput will have been reduced by the large number of packet processing steps that have been required, losing many CPU cycles that applications could have utilized.

The implementation solution to the silly window syndrome is for the sender to wait for a larger flow control allocation before sending and for the receiver to hold the right edge of the window fixed until it can offer a substantial increase in window size. Recall that this is an implementation issue, not a protocol design issue. Both sets of issues are important and must be addressed at each protocol layer.

A second example of a protocol implementation concern is the need for dynamic timeouts in an end-to-end protocol. Clearly, the retransmission timeout needs to be different for the distinct cases of two nodes on the same LAN versus two nodes that are separated by many low-speed, high-delay networks. The timeouts are determined based on the observed round-trip times of packets and their associated ACKs. Thus the two nodes on the same network will see ACKs

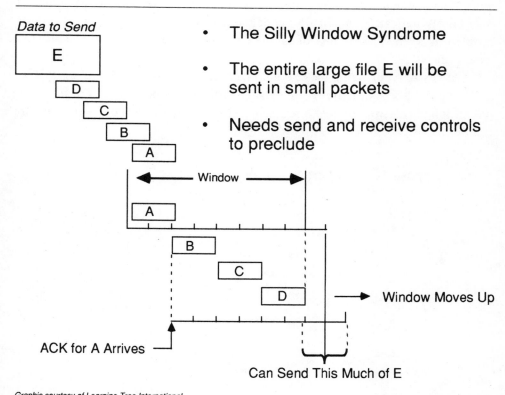

Graphic courtesy of Learning Tree International.

FIGURE 6-8 Many TCP systems suffered the "silly window syndrome" implementation problem.

returned very quickly and make their timeouts correspondingly short. In contrast, the two widely separated nodes will observe a long delay from transmission to the returned ACK and make their timeouts very long.

The dynamic timeout determination works fine except in cases such as shown in Figure 6-9, in which one node thinks that the timeout should be short and retransmits prematurely. (Perhaps a routing change caused a delay longer than previously encountered.) In any case, the ACK is returned from the first transmission shortly after the retransmission. The sender believes the first packet was lost, that the retransmission has now been ACKed, and that this ACK apparently came back very quickly. This further reinforces the setting that the timeouts should be short, leading to the same problem on all subsequent packets. Every packet is transmitted twice, which is a waste of communications resources and may be expensive based on a cost-per-packet billing algorithm.

The above example shows that robust delivery protocols can cover up a number of delivery problems, some of which you should know about. Network management should be doing something about these problems. But, if the network management operation is based on the observed retransmission count, it may falsely indicate problems in the delivery mechanism. That is not where the problem is in this case! How does one determine which problems result from which causes?

The key to recognizing the real culprit here is the number of duplicate ACKs that are received. As Figure 6-9 shows, each packet is being ACKed, including both original transmissions and retransmissions. This would not be the case for

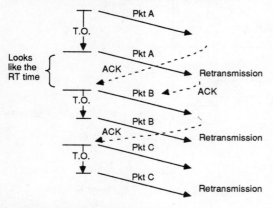

- As a result, TCP retransmits every packet!

- The "clue" is the number of multiple ACKs received

Graphic courtesy of Learning Tree International.

FIGURE 6-9   The dynamic timeout of TCP may cause every packet to be transmitted twice.

an error-prone delivery mechanism. This observation should point you in the direction of a timer problem, not a delivery problem. However, you should not have to rely on network management to solve this problem. Why couldn't the transport protocol implementation observe that it was receiving duplicate ACKs on each packet and automatically readjust the timeout? A likely mechanism to determine what the timeouts should be would be to revert to the same method used when connection was established.

This section has attempted to describe the TCP protocol, including its specified services and mechanisms and implementation concerns. The OSI transport protocol, or more correctly, the set of classes of OSI transport protocols is discussed next. You will find many similarities with TCP, but there also will be many differences.

THE OSI TRANSPORT PROTOCOL

The basic intent of the OSI Transport Protocol (TP) is the same as that of TCP: to provide connection-oriented, end-to-end, data delivery with a high degree of data integrity. However, unlike TCP, the OSI TP has several variations, called "classes" of the transport protocol.

The Classes of OSI Transport Protocol

The OSI TP is a set of protocol classes, most of which provide the same OSI Transport Layer service, but which differ based on how the Network Layer services are involved. For example, a very lightweight set of TP mechanisms may be all that is required when the network provides acceptable integrity of the delivered data. At the other extreme, the network or cascaded set of networks may introduce errors, lost packets, or other forms of data integrity problems. In the latter case, the TP mechanisms must be expanded to provide the required level of end-to-end data integrity.

The TP may also differ in terms of its mechanisms based on whether or not a network connection is shared by several simultaneous transport connections. This is a form of multiplexing. The combination of adapting to differing levels of network service and deciding to multiplex or not leads to the five different OSI classes of transport protocols. They are shown in Figure 6-10.

As shown in Figure 6-10, classes 0 and 1 do not multiplex transport connections over an X.25 connection. Instead, there is a one-to-one correspondence between transport and network connections. Class 0 is intended for X.400 electronic mail. Class 1 can be ignored, at least in North America, and probably elsewhere as well. Class 1 is a typical mutation of the standardization process.

Candidate Transport Protocols

- The type of network determines the required level of transport support

	Network Type		
	Type A (Acceptable, Low Number of Errors)	Type B (Errors Occur, But Host Is Notified)	Type C (Errors Occur Without Notification)
Single User Per Network Connection	TP Class 0	TP Class 1	—
Multiple Users Per Network Connection (Multiplexed)	TP Class 2	TP Class 3	TP Class 4

Note: ARPA/DoD Transmission Control Protocol (TCP) could be used in any of the above, but it has more features than would necessarily be needed

Graphic courtesy of Learning Tree International.

FIGURE 6-10   OSI provides five classes of transport protocol.

Classes 2, 3, and 4 all multiplex two or more transport connections across one X.25 connection. In class 4, there is no reason to limit the networks to X.25; they can be any form of network. TP class 4 is similar in this and many other regards to TCP.

To help ensure interoperability, the National Institute of Standards and Technology (NIST), formerly the National Bureau of Standards (NBS), has devised a strategy in which only transport protocol classes 2 and 4 would be utilized in the U.S., plus the use of class 0 for international uses of X.400 electronic mail. The latter is mandated by CCITT.

This discussion will focus on TP class 4, with a summary view of how classes 0 and 2 can be combined with class 4 from an implementation point of view. The protocol class to be utilized on any given connection is negotiated at the connection establishment.

TP Class 4 Protocol

TP class 4 (or TP4) is the heavy duty transport protocol of OSI. In that regard it has many similarities with TCP, and these will be noted in the following discussion. However, it also has several differences. Some of these differences are definite improvements; others may or may not be better than TCP, depending on your perspective. Other differences have no apparent advantage or disadvantage.

All of the five classes of OSI TP considered here are connection-oriented. As such, they require that a connection be established and that certain options be negotiated. A *connection request packet* begins the connection establishment process and contains the fields, which are summarized in Figure 6-11. A more detailed version of this packet is shown later.

The connection request packet can be compared to that of X.25, in which a connection identification number is defined. In X.25 it was a channel number; in TP it is a reference number. Unlike X.25, the reference number will have end-to-end significance. The connection request packet in Figure 6-11 indicates that the originating end system will call this connection "XXXXX". The other end can select its own number, and it is shown in the connection request as 0 (zero).

There also are some similarities in the negotiated values, such as the maximum packet size and the selection of the size of sequence numbers. However, many different aspects need to be negotiated at the TP, such as whether or not error checks are to be utilized. X.25 relied on the lower layer LAPB link protocol for this function, but it was only between a host and a packet-switch. In TP, the error check is end-to-end and at the Transport Layer, not relegated to a lower layer.

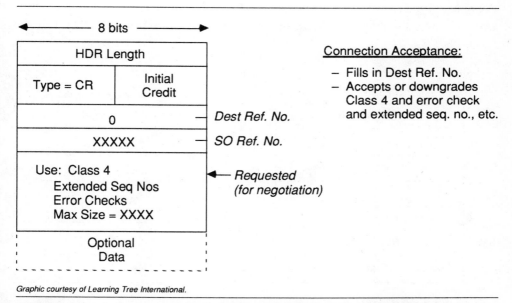

Graphic courtesy of Learning Tree International.

FIGURE 6-11 A simple example of an OSI transport connection request packet.

There also is a difference in flow control between X.25 and TP. In X.25, window size was negotiated when the connection was established and remained fixed for the duration of the connection. In TP, the window size varies continuously. The initial window size (the "initial credit" field) is included in the connection request packet and indicates how many packets can be sent before waiting for ACK(s) to come back to slide the window forward.

In both X.25 and the TP, there can be a small amount of optional user data in the connection request packet and in the returned connection confirmation packet.

Just as there are similarities with the connection establishment of X.25 connections, there are also some differences, a few of which have been mentioned above. These differences will be discussed later during a more detailed description of the connection request packet (Figure 6-16).

After the connection has been established, data packets can be exchanged. The formats of these data packets and their corresponding ACK packets are shown in Figure 6-12. These examples assume that the extended sequence numbers and error checks were negotiated when the connection was established. This means that the sequence number field and ACK number field each will be 31 bits long, and that the credit (window) field will be 16 bits long. The latter will be carried in the variable part of the packet. Otherwise, it would have been a four-bit field in the same location as in the connection request.

Note that only the destination reference number is listed in each data and ACK format. These values are what the receiving end selected for this connection. The word destination, therefore, must be interpreted in the context of the

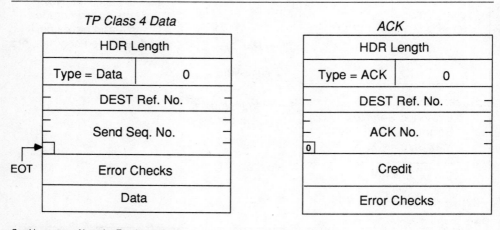

Graphic courtesy of Learning Tree International.

FIGURE 6-12   TP class 4 data and ACK packet formats.

sending end system. A separate ACK packet is sent, unlike TCP, which piggy-backs the ACK number in data packets. The ACK approach is similar to the supervisory packet of HDLC. The ACK provides the left edge of the window, and the credit field provides the window size, which is the flow control value. The equivalent of saying "receiver not ready" would be to state that the window size is zero. However, the implementer generally should not reduce the window below any previously advertised size, as discussed later.

The TP service is in terms of Service Data Units (SDUs), which are the data units (blocks) that are passed between the Session Layer and the Transport Layer. Figure 6-13 shows an SDU being received from the Session Layer, segmented into some PDUs for transmission, and being reassembled for delivery as the exact same SDU that was received. The End Of Text (EOT) boolean is used to indicate the last PDU of such a sequence, which is like the X.25 more flag in that regard. Recall that TCP has no such capability.

The error-check mechanism of TP class 4 is shown in Figures 6-14 and 6-15, which indicate its location in the header and its algorithm, respectively. The error-check consists of two one-byte checks. One is the module sum of the bytes in the packet and the second is the sum of the bytes, multiplied by their relative location in the packet. This algorithm would detect swapped fields; such as if the first two bytes were exchanged in location with the second two bytes. The TCP

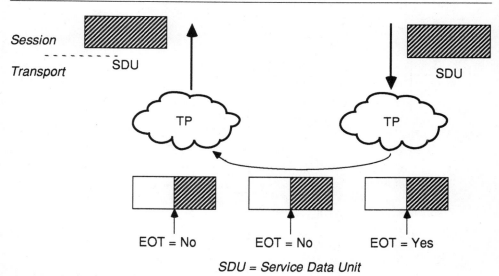

SDU = Service Data Unit

EOT = End of Text (block)

Graphic courtesy of Learning Tree International.

FIGURE 6-13 A Service Data Unit (SDU) may be segmented into multiple Protocol Data Units (PDUs).

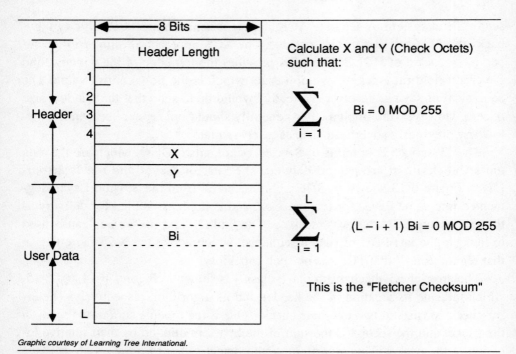

Graphic courtesy of Learning Tree International.

FIGURE 6-14   The TP class 4 error check consists of two one-byte fields.

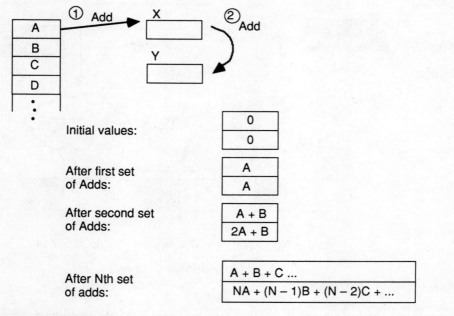

Graphic courtesy of Learning Tree International.

FIGURE 6-15   The TP4 error check requires two additions for each byte.

error-check algorithm would not detect this form of error. On the other hand, this does not sound like a very common error.

The negative side of this error-check is that it can be computationally demanding. Its direct implementation is shown in Figure 6-15, which indicates that at least two additions are required per byte of the packet. Even with clever algorithms to expedite the computation, it is still slow compared with a TCP error check. This can be a major limitation when attempting to implement high throughput systems, because the error-check is often the major component of Transport Layer protocol processing.

Figure 6-16 returns you to the connection request packet for additional detail. As before, there is a reference number, which will be utilized by the other end in future packets to identify this connection. This is a shorthand form for the connection identifier. The negotiated fields include the protocol class (e.g., a request to run class 4), sequence number size (e.g., request 31-bit sequence numbers), use of error checks, maximum transport PDU size, and the version number. The parameters field also includes a Service Access Point (SAP). The

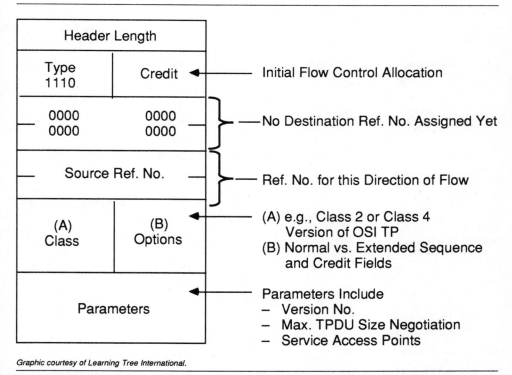

Graphic courtesy of Learning Tree International.

FIGURE 6-16   The TP4 connection request packet contains several fields which are to be negotiated.

latter seems to be an unusual parameter. Why wouldn't the SAP be a part of the fixed (always utilized) connection request header like the TCP port numbers are? It turns out that the OSI committees believed that there would be some use of TP connections in which the SAP would be implicit. You would only connect to one service. Thus they made it an optional parameter. One wonders how long the debate was that lead to the possible savings of a few bytes on each connection request.

Figures 6-17 and 6-18 show more detail on the data and ACK packets of TP class 4. The data packet utilizes the 31-bit sequence number, the boolean flag to indicate the end of a sequence of packets that belong in one SDU, and the *checksum*. The ACK packet of Figure 6-18 shows the next expected PDU sequence number and the credit (window) allocation carried as a 16-bit integer. Other parameters in the ACK packet include the check sum and two other interesting fields.

The first is the *sub-sequence number field*. It allows you to put sequence numbers on ACKs. Suppose that you sent an ACK with a credit field of 10 and then later sent another ACK with a credit field of 20, attempting to increase the size of the window. The receiver could get them in either order and would not

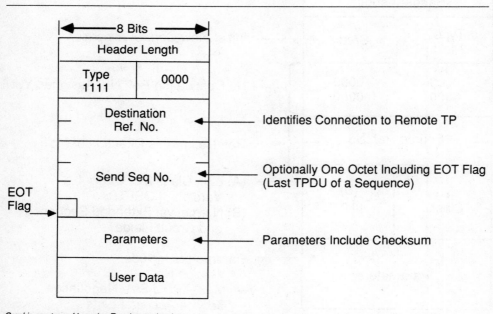

Graphic courtesy of Learning Tree International.

FIGURE 6-17 A TP4 data packet.

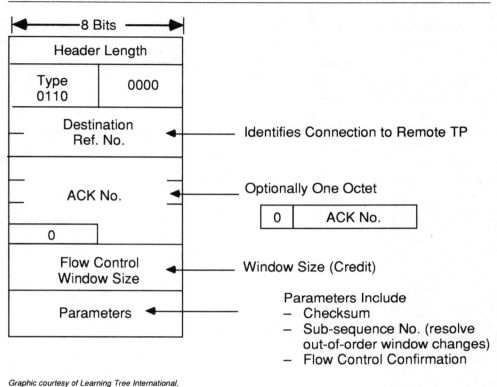

Graphic courtesy of Learning Tree International.

FIGURE 6-18 A TP4 ACK packet.

know which one to follow. The sub-sequence number resolves this problem (the credit of 20 packets will have a higher sub-sequence number).

The second of these fields is the *flow control confirmation field*. It allows the two ends to reconcile their respective values for flow control similar to the way the bank reconciles monthly statements of your deposits and checks written.

In TP class 4, we found that ACKs were not piggybacked on data packets. This is surprising, because ACKs were piggybacked at the Data Link and Network Layers. Why not at the Transport Layer? Did its developers foresee the probability of having returned traffic for piggybacking versus having to send a supervisory packet to deliver the ACK? They may have, but it seems more likely that they simply invented a more general way of piggybacking. As shown in Figure 6-19, an ACK may be piggybacked with a data packet if both are going to the same destination, without having to be on the same transport connection. This seems like a good idea, because processing time and communications overhead will be reduced as a result of the more general piggybacking.

- Transport protocol ACKs are not necessarily "piggybacked" on return traffic

- An ACK PDU may be concatenated with data PDU to form a network service data unit

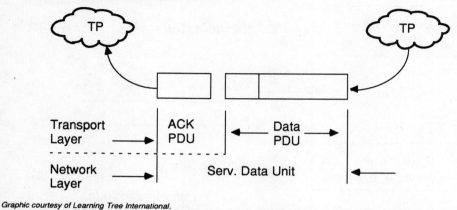

Graphic courtesy of Learning Tree International.

FIGURE 6-19   A TP4 ACK PDU can be concatenated with a data PDU.

TP class 4 has two forms of data transfer: normal data, which has been discussed; and expedited data, which is shown in Figure 6-20. Expedited data is in the form of a special control packet. Unlike normal data, expedited data is not limited by flow control, although only one expedited data packet can be outstanding at any given time. After sending an expedited TPDU, you must wait for its ACK before sending another expedited data TPDU or any normal data packets. This ensures that no subsequent normal TPDU can get ahead of the expedited TPDU. The purpose of expedited data is not of concern to the Transport Layer. This layer only knows to get data delivered as quickly as possible, and to indicate that the data is special. It is then up to the higher layer protocols to process it expeditiously and to accomplish whatever the sender had in mind, based on the particular application context and protocols involved.

Most of this discussion has focused on the TP class 4 protocol. Figure 6-21 compares the functions of this protocol with classes 0 through 3 and indicates that class 4 has all of the functions of the lesser classes. This may be misleading, because it implies that the other classes should be obtained as direct subsets of class 4. This is not the case and, unfortunately, it is not that simple.

Class 0 is one of the biggest exceptions in the subset concern because of its origins and intended purpose. It was included because CCITT wanted it for the support of X.400 electronic messaging (e.g., electronic mail), and for backwards

- For expedited data, the format and mechanisms are

- Only one expedited data unit can be outstanding

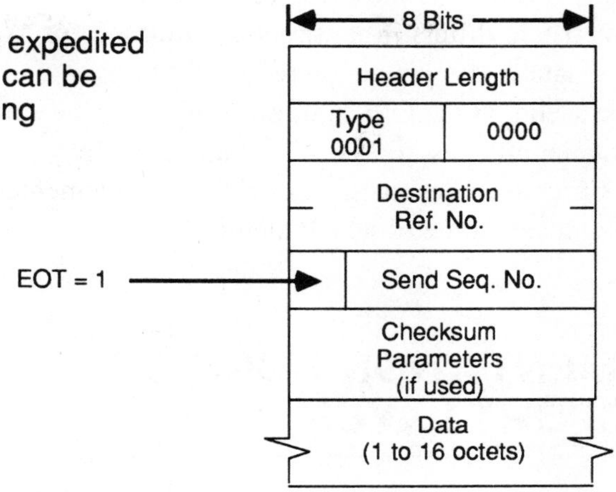

```
|◄──── 8 Bits ────►|
┌──────────────────────┐
│    Header Length     │
├───────────┬──────────┤
│  Type     │          │
│  0001     │   0000   │
├───────────┴──────────┤
│     Destination      │
│      Ref. No.        │
├───────────┬──────────┤
EOT = 1 ──► │     │ Send Seq. No.  │
├──────────────────────┤
│      Checksum        │
│     Parameters       │
│      (if used)       │
├──────────────────────┤
│        Data          │
│   (1 to 16 octets)   │
└──────────────────────┘
```

Graphic courtesy of Learning Tree International.

FIGURE 6-20   A TP4 expedited data packet is a form of the control PDU.

Transport Protocol Functions

Function	0	Transport Protocol Class 1	2	3	4
Connection Establishment	X	X	X	X	X
Option Negotiation	X	X	X	X	X
Connection Refusal	X	X	X	X	X
Transfer TPDUs	X	X	X	X	X
Handle Protocol Errors	X	X	X	X	X
Segmenting and Reassembly	X	X	X	X	X
Normal Release		X	X	X	X
Expedited Data		X	X	X	X
Sequence Numbering of TPDUs		X	X	X	X
Extended Sequence Numbering			X	X	X
Multiplexing (e.g., Over one X.25 Con.)			X	X	X
Explicit Flow Control			X	X	X
Reassignment After Failure		X		X	X
Retention Until ACK		X		X	X
Resynchronization		X		X	X
Frozen Reference Numbers		X		X	X
Error Checks (Checksum)					X
Retransmission on Timeout					X
Resequence TPDUs					X
Inactivity Control					X
Splitting and Recombining					X

Graphic courtesy of Learning Tree International.

FIGURE 6-21   Functions associated with TP classes 0–4.

compatibility with the Telex system. Class 0 differs from transport functions in that it does not send disconnect confirmation packets, it does not use any flow control, and it disconnects the transport connection when the X.25 connection is closed. Class 0 also differs in its service definition; for example, it does not support any user data in its connection request packets.

We have seen that the OSI Transport Layer can be similar to the current TCP transport functionality, as in class 4, or that it can be quite different, as in class 0. The network architect, designer, and software implementer must be keenly aware of these differences, some of which are very subtle.

IMPLEMENTATION CONSIDERATIONS AT THE TRANSPORT LAYER

As indicated before, the implementation of protocols at all layers goes beyond the issues of the protocol specifications, and must include how resources are utilized, how data are passed between layers, how timers are handled, and a number of other considerations. These are the subject of this section. They apply to TCP, TP, and other transport protocol implementations. The following paragraphs are organized by generic issues in the implementation.

The Robustness Principle

The robustness principle was first stated in the early versions of the TCP specifications, although it applies to the implementation of any protocol layer. It states that the implementer should:

Be liberal in what you accept, but be conservative in what you send.

This is the single most important rule for implementers. It is a major extension of the golden rule. Do unto others as you would have them do to you, but do not expect them to behave with the same concern for you!

As an example of the robustness principle of implementation, a robust TCP implementation should not send a packet unless all of the packet fits within the current window, but it should be able to cope if another TCP implementation sends when any part of the packet is within the window. This does not mean that the proper TCP implementation can actually accept data under the above circumstances. It only means that the proper TCP implementation will operate properly even when others go beyond the original intent of the rules.

Buffering Issues

The most important issue related to buffering within the transport mechanism is the form of buffering. Is it a large circular buffer, a set of linkable small buffers, or a set of fixed size (maximum packet size) buffers? The importance relates to the granularity of the flow control allocations. Suppose that a TCP implementation advised you that you could send 20,000 bytes. It may expect you to send as many as twenty 1,000-byte packets, but what if you send 1,000 packets of 20 bytes each, or even worse, 20,000 packets of one byte each? Would the receiver be able to handle any of these situations equally well? Probably not.

One common buffering approach is to set aside a maximum length packet size buffer for each new packet. This handles the worst case packet size. Any packet will fit within this buffer, but unfortunately, many packets are much shorter than this maximum size and will result in significant waste of buffer space. For example, consider a packet with one byte of data in a buffer that can accept up to 4,096 bytes of data.

In contrast, a circular buffering approach implies that each incoming packet takes its place in a sequence of storage locations. Pointers handle the differences in packet size without any wasted space that would occur in fixed (maximum length) buffers.

A hybrid scheme is to allocate storage in small multi-byte units that can be strung together by pointers to handle either short or long packets. This provides a middle ground position between the other two extremes.

The final choice of buffering schemes is frequently based on the need to minimize the copying of packets from one part of memory to another. Our circular buffer example would almost always require this copy operation, while the pre-defined maximum block size might require a simple memory map operation to get the block to the next protocol processing.

Packet Processing Issues

The software required to process a packet can be quite large because of the number of possible exception conditions that may occur. However, very little of this software is required for normal packets—those that arrive in the proper sequence and without errors. The transport processing should be organized to look for the most likely arrivals first and to only check for, and call in, special processing routines when actually needed.

Interoperability Testing Issues

The ultimate form of testing of protocol implementations is to demonstrate that they interoperate with other vendors' products. This is called *interoperability testing.* Ideally, this is conducted as a form of stress testing in which abnormal as well as normal networking requests are made. For example, our TCP connection request might have its SYN flag set (as would be expected), as well as its FIN flag set (which would not be expected), and could include an urgent pointer that pointed to a byte beyond the actual byte stream that was sent (which would appear to be an error). The receiving TCP implementation should handle all such occurrences without any negative effects on the system or other connections. This behavior was typical of the "TCP/IP Bakeoffs" in which different TCP/IP implementations challenged each other in the spirit of seeing which ones could survive anything that the others could send. This type of stress testing is more difficult to perform in a multi-vendor, commercial environment. It is essential, however, to provide the same level of confidence in the robustness of protocols as we have in the TCP/IP implementations.

Retransmission Strategies

The TP must be able to retransmit any particular data unit(s) based on the failure to receive an ACK within a prescribed time, called a *timeout.* A basic concern about the retransmission strategy is whether or not each packet is handled separately (with its own timer), or if sequences of packets are handled together. For example, if packet N is retransmitted, are packets $N+1$, $N+2$, and so on, automatically retransmitted as well? The protocols typically do not tell you what to do in these cases. The implementers are left on their own to develop a strategy.

An implementation detail is whether there is a timer per packer or a timer per connection that has one or more outstanding packets. These two implementation choices tend to lead to retransmission strategies of sending selected packets or all packets respectively.

The timeout values also are an issue in the retransmission strategies. At the transport level they should be dynamic, based on observed round-trip times for packets and ACKs. The most recent round-trip times should have more emphasis or weight than older round-trip times, but they should not be utilized exclusively. Exponential smoothing of new and old data is typically utilized.

A matter related to retransmission strategies is the receive strategy. What should the receiver do if an error-free packet arrives, but it is not the next expected sequence number? The first issue is: Is it before or after the next expected sequence number? If before, it is a duplicate and should be ACKed but discarded. However, if after, should it be kept or discarded? If you keep it, you can reduce the number of retransmissions, but will then need another timer to be able to eventually discard it if the other intermediate data packets do not arrive.

ACK Strategies

A matter that is closely related to the retransmission strategy is the ACK strategy at the Transport Layer. As expected, ACKs are utilized to confirm the receipt of PDUs, but they also are used for updating the credit (window) flow control allocation and provide a minimum level of activity on otherwise unused connection. The latter is called a "keep alive" function.

The major concern of ACK strategy is deciding when to send an ACK. The simplest conceptual approach is to send an ACK packet in response to each data packet received. Although simple, this approach requires more CPU processing than would otherwise be required. We need a more efficient scheme. In the telephone person-to-person analogy, you do not acknowledge every word, or even every sentence. You find points in the conversation when it is necessary to say "yes," "OK," or some other indication that you have understood everything up to that point. The Transport Layer does not have that same level of understanding of the semantics, so it must rely on more syntactic boundaries. You may ACK every packet, or perhaps every second or every Nth packet, each of which ACKs all previous packets. Sending an ACK for every second packet or on a timeout, whichever comes first, is a common approach.

We have seen examples of piggybacking ACKs with normal data traffic; in the case of TP4, a special form of piggybacking by concatenating an ACK packet with a data packet. Care must be taken in this latter approach, because combined ACK and data packets may exceed the maximum internet packet size, resulting in segmentation and reduced network performance.

Flow Control Strategies

Flow control at the Transport Layer is intended to allow the receiver of the data to control the rate at which it is sent. This is conceptually very simple, but in reality it is much more complex. For example, what is the metric that limits the receiver's ability to accept data? Is it the number of bytes that are sent, the number of packets that are sent, or some other unit such as N byte sub-blocks? Regardless of the metric, there are three basic strategies that can be implemented, which are described below.

The first strategy is the simple stop and wait approach to transmission: after sending a packet, wait for the ACK before sending the next packet. Of course, retransmissions may be sent based on a timeout. The rule applies to the next new packet. This is a very pessimistic flow control strategy, and it will not provide very high performance, but it is simple to implement.

The next level of improvement in the flow control strategy is the use of a window, which may be a number of bytes or packets. This much data may be sent before having to wait for an ACK. The stop and wait strategy is a special case of this strategy in which the window size is fixed and is equal to one. In the more general case, the window size can be varied at any time and is based on the currently available storage. This is often considered to be the best approach to flow control.

One can go beyond the simple window-based scheme by providing a so-called optimistic allocation, in which the totality of all outstanding flow control allocations could not **actually** be met. This is a form of statistical multiplexing in which you take advantage of the very low probability that all senders will transmit an entire allocation at the same time. If they do, the receiver must discard some data, relying on the fact that it will be retransmitted when not ACKed. This results in a tradeoff between storage (memory) and communications utilization and cost. In some earlier systems memory was very limited and this tradeoff was chosen in favor of conserving the use of memory space. In today's environment of decreased memory cost and of support for large memory address spaces, this tradeoff almost always is determined by the high cost of communications, especially when these communications are provided by public carriers. For LANs, with their very low communication costs, the tradeoffs may differ.

We have seen that the basic components of connection-oriented protocols, error control, sequencing, and flow control all have significant implementation considerations as well as protocol issues. The next section considers the corresponding concerns of connectionless transport protocols.

CONNECTIONLESS TRANSPORT PROTOCOLS

Connectionless TPs are not as common as connection-oriented protocols, but they are being used increasingly to support transparent user services. Many of these uses are in transaction-oriented services that cannot always tolerate the overhead of opening a connection. The reliability and sequenced delivery assurances of the connection-oriented TP are either not needed or are provided by higher level protocols, such as a remote procedure call mechanism.

The services provided by the connectionless transport protocol are usually minimal, often being limited to multiplexing and demultiplexing. Error detection may be provided as an option, but error recovery is typically not provided.

The Connectionless User Datagram Protocol (UDP)

Associated with TCP/IP is a connectionless transport protocol, the User Datagram Protocol (UDP). It is utilized to support a number of higher level protocols, including the Trivial File Transfer Protocol (TFTP); the Network File System (NFS), with its Remote Procedure Call (RPC) and External Data Representation (XDR) protocols; and the Network Directory Services (NDS).

UDP provides very minimal services beyond those of IP. As seen in its header, which is shown in Figure 6-22, the only additional services are an optional check sum over the UDP header and the data and port numbers for multiplexing/demultiplexing at the Transport Layer.

The error-check can be made optional, and properly interpreted by the receiver, because of the use of a 1s complement error-check. In this error-check form, there are two representations of the value 0, one of which can never occur in arithmetic computations of check sums. This illegal value is utilized to indicate that no check sum is included in a UDP packet.

The port numbers are essentially the same as used in TCP and are numerically equivalent whenever they might be utilized by either transport protocol. The unique aspect of UDP port numbers is that the source port number may be set to 0 in UDP, indicating no specific port. This is for use when no

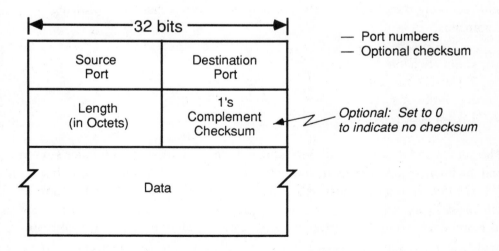

- A connectionless (Datagram) Transport Protocol
- User Datagram Protocol (UDP) has very few mechanisms

- The optional checksum includes the "pseudo-header" of TCP, including the source and destination addresses

Graphic courtesy of Learning Tree International.

FIGURE 6-22 The User Datagram Protocol (UDP) header has almost no mechanisms.

response is expected and hence no port number is required. However, this makes the port numbers of UDP seem deceptively simple, because the source port number may also be utilized as a transaction identifier and thus will differ on each transmission to a server port. It becomes difficult, if not impossible, to track any sequence of UDP-based transactions as being a part of a particular user-to-server dialogue, which you might want to make for security auditing purposes.

The OSI Connectionless Protocol

The OSI connectionless transport service and protocol are defined in ISO 8072 and 8602, respectively. The fact that connectionless operation is foreign to OSI even appears in the numbering scheme. In almost all other cases, the service definition and the protocol specification are consecutive integers. In the case of the connectionless transport, they have no such relationship. This is partly because of the variations that OSI considers between the Transport and Network Layers.

Because any connectionless operation, including that of OSI, has no connection setup phase, the only primitives for the connectionless transport are **UnitData.request** and **UnitData.indication**. These correspond to sending and receiving data, respectively. Each such primitive has the following four parameters:

1. Source address.
2. Destination address.
3. Quality of service.
4. UserData.

The source and destination addresses include the specific host computer system and the internal software address to get to the connectionless transport service.

The connectionless transport service is not expected to provide any form of reliable delivery, sequencing, or flow control. This is consistent with the concept of being connectionless. As was the case with the UDP protocol, the OSI connectionless transport protocol may (optionally) include an error-check. If an error-check fails upon receipt of a packet, the packet is discarded. There is no retransmission at the Transport Layer.

Because items such as the check sum are optional, the connectionless TP header is encoded as a series of type-length-value sequences following a length indicator and a TPDU code field. The resulting PDU structure is shown in Figure 6-23. Note that here it is similar to that of UDP, containing the TSAPs (similar to port numbers), the length field, and the optional error-check field.

FUTURE HIGH PERFORMANCE TRANSPORT PROTOCOLS

There is still considerable debate as to whether or not existing TPs will support gigabit/second networking. Some evidence indicates that it will, but other work indicates that new protocols may be needed, even to the point of putting them in high performance silicon chips.

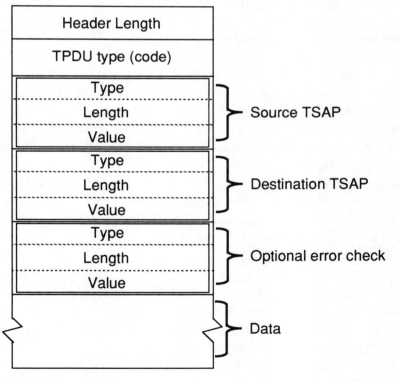

Graphic courtesy of Learning Tree International.

FIGURE 6-23   OSI Connectionless Transport PDU.

Any new TPs may implement both connection and connectionless capabilities within the one protocol. If these are developed, it will be the result of very high speed LANs and/or fiber-optic telephone company links. They will undoubtedly take advantage of the inherently low error rate of such media as well as its high data rate. The protocols may also be lightweight, carrying little protocol overhead and having an easily re-created set of state information in the case of a crash at either end.

SECURITY AT THE TRANSPORT LAYER

The Transport Layer is usually considered a prime location for security mechanisms. First of all, it is the location of end-to-end integrity mechanisms in the overall network architecture. Integrity is one of the three basic network security concerns, with confidentiality and service assurance. Perhaps the other two concerns can be applied here as well.

The usual end-to-end integrity controls act to counter problems introduced by nature, such as bad bits or lost packets. However, security concerns relate to problems introduced (perhaps maliciously) by humans. Can the Transport Layer also ensure that these threats are countered? The solution is in terms of control mechanisms that cannot be faked (i.e., the sequence numbers, error-checks, and other control mechanisms can be verified by secure, non-forgeable means). This involves cryptographic protection of these fields, not only for confidentiality but also for integrity. There may not be a need for confidentiality in terms of these control fields—maybe all that is needed is the ability to protect against their undetected modification.

Thus, confidentiality and/or integrity of the control and data fields can be ensured at the Transport Layer. These protection mechanisms could be negotiated; for example, in terms of cryptographic error checks and encryption for confidentiality when the connection is opened. These form(s) of protection could then be supplied on a per connection basis.

The protection of protocol control information at the Transport Layer could ensure that the sequence numbers are correct. This could help to avoid a number of forging threats, such as the replay of valid packets with their sequence numbers changed to be within the current window. Similar checks could be made against changes in other control fields.

The major negative aspect of security at the Transport Layer has two concerns. First, the Transport Layer is implemented in software; thus the security mechanisms, including the cryptographic components are computer programs—can their implementations really be trusted? Second, the Transport Layer protocol is rather complex, and the security mechanisms are scattered about this implementation. How do you identify a "trusted computing base" that includes the parts you have to ensure are correct, always invoked, and never bypassed? These concerns are typical of "future research required" developments.

TEST TOOLS AT THE TRANSPORT LAYER

There are two principle methods of capturing the traffic at the Transport Layer: software records of the control and data packets that were sent, and protocol analyzer records of traffic. The first may be limited to the control traffic, such as connection establishment and closure, or it may include the data transmissions as well. Both are useful, especially because control information, such as flow control, may be piggybacked on data packets.

Some of the packets of concern to the Transport Layer may be at a lower layer, such as ICMP messages. For example, a source quench ICMP message may cause the Transport Layer to cut back on its transmission rate. If one only observes the transport traffic, this control message is not seen, and the reason for the transport behavior is lost.

Observation of the Transport Layer should include sufficient detail to be able to determine the existence and cause of abnormalities. Suppose, for example, that every TCP packet is being transmitted twice. What information is required to determine that this is actually happening? What additional information is required to determine why it is happening in this specific case? Beyond that, what other information may be needed to fully understand what is causing the general problem that is being observed in the network behavior? All of these issues must be considered in developing the monitoring tools at the Transport Layer. The usual concerns of collecting the right amount of data still apply, otherwise you get too much of the wrong information.

The second general tool at the Transport Layer, as well as others, is the *protocol analyzer*, which is usually available in LAN environments. The protocol analyzer can be set up to watch for specific values in one or more protocol fields. For example, a LAN protocol analyzer can be set to watch for packets that are destined for site XYZ, and for the TCP/IP protocol at that site. Even more specifically, the protocol analyzer can be set up to record all Telnet (remote login) traffic sent to that site from site ABC. This allows a very selective investigation of the traffic across the network.

The Transport Layer is a particularly important layer of the network protocol stacks, because it provides end-to-end insight into what is happening. Is the data actually getting from system XYZ to system ABC? If so, the problem must be in the higher level protocols in the hosts. If not, it must be a problem in the delivery mechanism. These are quite different forms of problems, and different personnel are generally responsible for their resolution. Therefore, it is very important to be able to resolve the nature of such problems as quickly and as definitively as possible. The test tools described above should provide convincing evidence to all parties as to where the problems are being introduced into the network system.

SUMMARY

Unlike the lower layers, the Transport Layer is not divided into sublayers, but does have two alternate types of service, namely connection and connectionless. The connection-oriented OSI transport protocols consist of five classes, but these different classes of service are primarily due to the different degrees of service that may be provided by the Network Layer below it. The connectionless service provides very little beyond that of the Network Layer.

The Transport Layer's connection-oriented service is primarily responsible for the end-to-end integrity of communications. The aspects of integrity include error-free delivery and proper sequencing. Flow control is also included to ensure that the transmission rate matches the receiver's ability to accept data.

7

HIGHER LAYER PROTOCOLS IN END SYSTEMS

The top three layers of the OSI RM differ considerably from the bottom four layers, which were discussed by this point. The focus so far has been on the delivery of data, with varying degrees of concern about the reliability and integrity of data transfer. Now we will begin to look at other issues relating to the nature of the data being transferred and to the control of the interprocess communications involved.

THE SESSION LAYER

Most protocol layers of the OSI RM existed in one or more protocol suites before development of the model. The Session Layer is unique in its differences from one suite to another. Some suites, such as that of TCP/IP, had no Session Layer; others, such as DECnet and SNA, had very different Session Layer functionality. Although there was some agreement that many of the security mechanisms associated with networking should be at the Session Layer, in OSI there are no security services at the Session Layer. Therefore, you should not expect the Session Layer to be an intuitive carry-over from any previous networking protocol experience that you may have had.

The OSI Session Layer

The OSI Session Layer is documented in the usual service definition and protocol specification documents. The ISO and CCITT documents are as follows.

Service Definition	ISO 8326	CCITT X.215
Protocol Specification	ISO 8327	CCITT X.225

As with other OSI documentation, these are important reference works for the implementer but definitely are not tutorials. Thus they need to be augmented by textbooks, each providing a different perspective and some insight into the service and protocol. Implementer guidelines are also very useful. These additional sources of information are helpful and probably required for the upper layers, which differ so much from earlier protocol stacks. The upper layers are generally considered to be the Session, Presentation, and Application Layers.

The Session Layer did not exist in the TCP/IP protocols, and many early OSI architects argued that it should not be a separate layer in the OSI implementation as well. Although DECnet and SNA have functions one can associate as being at a session-like layer, no previous protocol stack had anything like the OSI Session Layer. Therefore, the approach to this layer will be from the perspective of an analogy with a tool kit, which it provides.

The OSI Session Layer provides a wide variety of tools that can be used by application programs. All of these tools are propagated up to the application programs with no further value added by the Presentation or Application Layers. One might wonder why they were not made Application Layer services initially, thus giving a six-layer model. Only a few OSI pioneers apparently know.

The Session Layer provides a set of tools that might be envisioned as being very broad in scope. One analogy would be a craftsperson's tools. An electrician's tools would differ from those of a plumber or carpenter. However, there is some total set of tools available that might be found in any hardware store. The proper set would be chosen for a given need. Similarly, the proper subset of Session Layer tools would be negotiated for each application. For example, there are different sets of Session Layer tools for check point recovery, electronic mail delivery, half-duplex transactions (e.g., enquiry/response), and for ensuring that all data are delivered before a connection is closed. The latter is called an "orderly release" of a connection.

Associated with the set of tools are a set of rules. For example, half-duplex tools ensure that only one end of a connection is allowed to talk at any given instance—you can only talk if it is your turn. The tool enforces this rule.

But for every rule there is an exception or a way around the rule. An example exception in the Session Layer relates to the half-duplex rule. The ability to utilize this exception can be negotiated when a session connection is established. It is called *typed data*. (OSI terminology is not always intuitive, but because most people only use such terms in OSI context, the words tend to be recognizable and have a specific meaning. This can be of considerable benefit, although it does make the learning process more difficult.)

Although details of the Session Layer are deferred until book three of this series, this book describes the basic components of the OSI Session Layer. These are formulated in what the higher layers call *functional units*. Each of these functional units is a tool within the Session Layer. These tools or functional units are organized into a kernel functional unit that must be supported, and a set of negotiable functional units that are optional in each implementation. We return to these functional units after discussing some of the basic session services that utilize them.

Session Layer Services

One of the Session Layer services is *dialog management* or *data flow control.* This is not flow control in the sense discussed earlier; this relates to the control of the direction of flow. Whose turn is it to talk? This service may appear to be for supporting old-style half-duplex data communications, but actually it provides applications with a way of doing one thing at a time. After an application sends a request, it can be made to wait for the response before issuing the next request. This is known as Two Way Alternate (TWA). The functional units that are able to provide this TWA service resemble the tokens of a token passing LAN. The other approach is to continue to send consecutive requests without waiting for each response, which is known as Two Way Simultaneous (TWS).

TWA implies a strict one-at-a-time rule for the communication, but there is a way around this rule. This exception is called typed data. If the typed data functional unit has been negotiated, then some data can be sent even when one does not have the token. This would be useful in an emergency in which one side needs to signal some important event but does not currently have the token.

A second category of session services relates to how sessions are released. There are three variations. A session may be aborted by either the user (the application) or the provider (the Session Layer). In this case data may be lost. Second, the session may be released in an orderly manner at the request of either side in which all data are transferred in both directions. This is comparable to the "graceful close" of TCP. Finally, the ability to release the session may be based on ownership of a token. This is called "negotiated release". Only the side that currently owns the token can release the session. The other side can request the token, but may not necessarily get it.

A third category of Session Layer services is synchronization, which has two forms:

1. The major sync point.
2. The minor sync point.

Both allow the sender to mark points in the message exchange with a serial number. They differ in terms of how these marked points affect the data exchange and how they are utilized. When a major synchronization point request is sent, no further PDUs may be sent until confirmation of the synchronization has been received. In contrast, a minor synchronization does not require a confirmation on every PDU. The Application Layer negotiates a window size during which a minor sync confirmation must be issued. Otherwise, lack of a confirmation does not impede the flow of data interspersed with minor syncs. The Session Layer is not aware of or involved with this window mechanism. It is not intended for usual flow control but rather to avoid inefficient use of the network if some component is unable to sustain the data flow. (A back-pressure form of flow control, in which any component along the path can signal its need to reduce the flow rate, would seem to do this even better.)

The major and minor synchronization points also differ in their use as rollback points. The sender can never be required to rollback beyond the most recent confirmed major synchronization point. The confirmation implies that data up to that point are safely stored to whatever degree of safety is appropriate in a given transfer. A minor synchronization point does not have this restriction. Both major and minor synchronization points use a common (sequential) number scheme for the sync points. The initial value of the sync number can be negotiated when the session is established. The default is to start at number 1 and to count up to 999,999. The sync number is sent with the data request, and a confirmation number is returned indicating the last received sync number. Confirmation number 98 indicates that request sync number 98 was received. Decimal digits again! You can see the influence of the PTTs (telephone companies).

Synchronization points are directly related to other Session Layer concepts, namely *dialog units* and *activities*. An example of a dialog unit is shown in Figure 7-1. It begins and ends with a major sync point and may have some internal minor sync points. As shown in the figure, the major sync points must be confirmed, and the flow of PDUs must stop until this confirmation is received. This delay may be required to get data stored safely on disk, to change the magnetic media that is receiving the data, or to obtain a new machine part in a factory example. Its use is general.

An activity is a further expansion of the dialog unit; that is, one or more consecutive dialog units prefaced with an "activity start" major sync point and terminated with an "activity end" major sync point. This is shown in Figure 7-2.

The rules associated with an activity state that no data are to be sent until the activity start major sync point has been issued, and no data are to be sent after the activity end major sync point. Ways to get around the rules are shown in Figure 7-3. So-called *capability data* can be sent either before the activity start and/or after the activity end.

As indicated in the Figure 7-3, capability data are intended for control purposes. This data can be utilized to determine if the two ends are both capable of performing the activity. As indicated in this figure, a common relationship

- Synchronization and dialog units

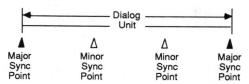

- Example usage (numbered boxes represent files being transferred)

- Resynchronization (recovery)
  - Can only go back to the last confirmed major sync
  - Can go back to any minor sync within the dialog unit

Graphic courtesy of Learning Tree International.

FIGURE 7-1   A Session Layer dialog unit.

- Activity and dialog concepts

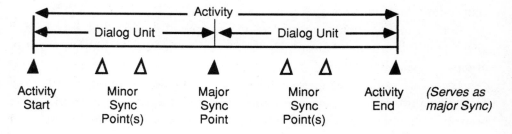

- Example usage
  - The transfer of one or more X.400 E-mail messages per activity

- The activity mechanisms can also provide the quarantine service

- An activity can also be interrupted, resumed or aborted

Graphic courtesy of Learning Tree International.

FIGURE 7-2   Example of an activity.

- The usual relationship between activities and session
  connections is one-to-one

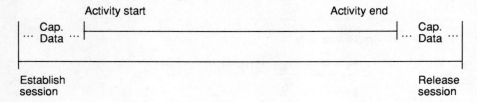

- Capability data can be sent before or after an activity
  — Intended for control purposes
  — Capability data transfers are ACKed

Graphic courtesy of Learning Tree International.

FIGURE 7-3   Capability data can occur either before or after an activity.

between the activity and the session is one-to-one. This is not required, however, as shown in Figure 7-4, which indicates that several activities can sequentially utilize one session; or conversely, several consecutive sessions may be involved in one activity, by interrupting and later resuming a single activity.

The examples of relationships between activities and sessions can be taken one step further by considering the relationship between sessions and transport connections. There also are many options, as shown in Figure 7-5. Although the likely case is one-to-one, one session could involve several consecutive transport connections, and vice versa.

Activity management is more than an example of dialog units, because it is also a significant functional unit itself. The subject of functional units will be discussed again momentarily.

The remaining form of Session Layer service is the exception reporting service. Exceptions are special events that need rapid attention. Exceptions can be from either the user (the application, Application Layer, or Presentation Layer), or the provider (the Session Layer itself). Exception reporting is also a functional unit.

Token Controls

Before discussing the functional units in more detail, the *tokens* that are involved at the Session Layer must be discussed further. The use of tokens includes the following operations:

- TWA communications
- Negotiated release of a session

- Several activities can sequentially utilize the same session connection

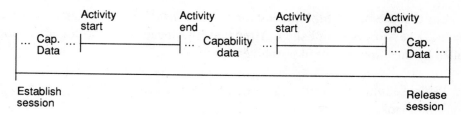

- A single activity can span across several sequential sessions

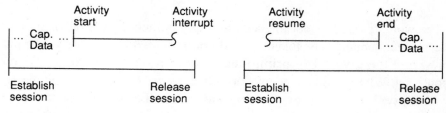

Graphic courtesy of Learning Tree International.

FIGURE 7-4 The relationship between activities and sessions.

- Typically, the session and transport connections are established and released at the same time

- However
  - One session connection may utilize several consecutive transport connections

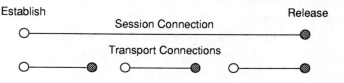

  - One transport connection may support several consecutive session connections

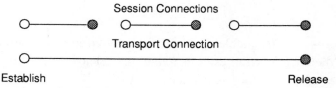

Graphic courtesy of Learning Tree International.

FIGURE 7-5 The relationship between sessions and transport connections.

• Minor synchronization
• Major/activity synchronization

Initial placement of the tokens for each of these operations is determined when the session is established. After that, the location of the tokens is controlled by three token control primitives:

1. **Please token request:** Asks for, but does not necessarily get, one or more tokens.
2. **Give token:** Passes one or more tokens.
3. **Give control:** Passes all tokens.

The word "please" is not intended to imply politeness, but rather that it is a request, not a demand. The token(s) need not be passed immediately. The please request and the give token primitives seem to provide a complete request/ response set. Why is the give control primitive needed? This is an example of the Session Layer's need to provide backward compatibility with earlier systems, such as Telex. In this case, all controls are passed in one unit, as expected in such prior implementations.

Functional Units

Many of the Session Layer functional units have been discussed briefly in the preceding descriptions. Functional units and services are closely coupled because the functional units are the protocol mechanisms that provide the services. In this section, we attempt to bring all of the functional units together and to describe the negotiation process that determines which functional units will be applied on a given session.

The fact that functional units are negotiated makes them appear as options. In one sense they are, but they are optional in terms of what is utilized on a per session basis and also on what is implemented. Not all networks or nodes on a network will implement all of the Session Layer functional Units. As in the hardware store analogy, not every craftsperson needed all of the possible tools. You implement what you need.

The total set of functional units is shown in Figure 7-6, with each item discussed below.

• The kernel is non-negotiable; that is, it is required in all implementations. It provides the basic session establishment and release (including abort), and the transfer of normal (non-expedited) data.
• Negotiated release provides token control over the release of the session.

Kernel (non-negotiable)	Session connection Normal data transfer Orderly release User-Abort Provider-Abort
Negotiated release	Please tokens *Token-controlled* Give tokens *connection release*
Half-duplex	Please tokens *Two-way alternate* Give tokens *transfers*
Duplex	Duplex operation
Expedited data	Expedited data transfer (up to 14 octets)
Typed data	Data transfer not subject to token
Capability data exchange	Data exchange outside of an activity
Minor synchronize	Minor synchronization point Please tokens Give tokens
Major synchronize	Major synchronization point Please tokens Give tokens
Resynchronize	Resynchronize to previous sync point
Exceptions	Provider exception reporting User exception reporting
Activity management	Activity start Activity interrupt Activity resume Activity discard Activity end Please tokens Give tokens Give control (all tokens)

Graphic courtesy of Learning Tree International.

FIGURE 7-6   Session Layer functional units.

- Half-duplex and duplex refer to the TWA and TWS dialogue control as described earlier. TWA involves token controls.
- Expedited data is data, usually relatively short in length, which is to be given special attention in delivery at the lower layers and in processing at the other

end system. It was originally limited to a maximum of 14 bytes to fit within the expedited data length limitations at the Transport and X.25 Network Layers. A subsequent amendment is removing this restriction without indicating how longer length data are to be handled at lower layers. This apparently means that the lower layers will treat such data as if it were normal, and the only difference will be in the expedited processing at the other end system.

- Typed data is data that can be sent in a half-duplex mode without having to "own" the token. It is only a meaningful option if the half-duplex functional unit is also negotiated.
- Capability data exchange refers to the ability to send some data before and/ or after the activity. It is only meaningful if the activity management functional unit is also negotiated.
- The minor and major synchronization functional units provide the corresponding sync point capabilities. Either or both may be negotiated. Both are token controlled and include the please and give token primitives.
- The resynchronize functional unit allows the application to resynchronize to a previous sync point (either major or minor). It is meaningful only if one or the other (or both) of the sync point functional units are negotiated.
- The exceptions functional unit allows the user and provider to signal the existence of special events that need immediate attention.
- Activity management is a large functional unit that supports the general concept of an "activity"; that is, a related set of PDU exchanges. Although the idea of activities was initially limited to electronic mail exchanges, it has become a widely utilized tool. Note that it is the only functional unit to include the give control (all tokens) primitive, which was used for backwards compatibility with Telex, further indicating its original intent to support electronic message communications.

In the past, the Session Layer functional units have been combined into subsets called the Basic Combined Subset, the Basic Synchronized Subset, and the Basic Activity Subset. These subsets are strictly advisory (i.e., for OSI applications implementers to consider for their uses). They are shown in Figure 7-7. These subsets are not negotiated as a group, and their separate functional unit components must be individually negotiated when desired.

In addition to negotiating the functional units, the session establishment also may negotiate the initial location of the token(s), the initial serial numbers for the synchronization points, the protocol version number to utilize (i.e., the highest common version), and the maximum TSDU size.

Defined Subsets of Functional Units

- **The Basic Combined Subset comprises**
  - Kernel functional unit
  - Half-duplex functional unit
  - Duplex functional unit

- **The Basic Activity Subset comprises**
  - Kernel functional unit
  - Half-duplex functional unit
  - Typed data functional unit
  - Capability data exchange functional unit
  - Minor synchronize functional unit
  - Exceptions functional unit
  - Activity management functional unit

- **The basic synchronized subset comprises**
  - Kernel functional unit
  - Negotiated release functional unit
  - Half-duplex functional unit
  - Duplex functional unit
  - Typed data functional unit
  - Minor synchronize functional unit
  - Major synchronize functional unit
  - Resynchronize functional unit

Graphic courtesy of Learning Tree International.

FIGURE 7-7   Subsets of functional units.

Session Layer PDUs

The basic form of a Session Layer PDU is simple, being a "type-length-value" encoding. However, the actual PDUs that are exchanged can be complex because of the ways the multiple type-length-value encoding forms are combined. One such example is shown in Figure 7-8, along with the simple (single) type-length-value encoding. The rules for concatenation of SPDUs can become very complicated. Many of the unusual aspects result from the desire for backward compatibility with Telex systems.

Implementation Considerations

The Session Layer of OSI can be complicated to implement, because not **all** of the Session Layer functional units must be implemented. The selected subset can be implemented according to the state machines that are defined in the ISO and CCITT specifications.

- Session PDUs have a common top-level format

- In the simplest form, the parameters are encoded as a set of type-length-value entries

- However, due to the variety of inputs (CCITT, ECMA, ISO, etc), the session layer PDU formats have many optional ways of expressing the parameter list

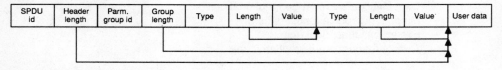

Graphic courtesy of Learning Tree International.

FIGURE 7-8   Typical encodings of Session Layer PDUs can become complicated.

The major area of complexity of the OSI Session Layer is the number of PDU variations, especially the ways in which they can, cannot, or must be combined. The specifications and the later volumes in this series should be referenced for this level of detail.

Trends at the Session Layer

The current trend at the Session Layer in its non-OSI equivalent protocol stacks is the Remote Procedure Call (RPC). This is an entirely different paradigm than that of a strict peer-to-peer connection. In fact, the RPC may concern either connection or connectionless lower layer services. In the latter case, the RPC must provide the required robustness and integrity mechanisms, although these are not necessarily the same mechanisms or services as typically expected of connection-oriented services. This is discussed later.

The RPC paradigm was originally developed as a part of the Xerox Network System (XNS), about the same time as the ARPAnet TCP/IP developments. However, it did not really catch on until recently. It is utilized heavily in systems such as the Sun Microsystems Network File System (NFS) and Yellow Pages (YP), as well as Apple's AppleTalk network remote transaction protocol.

The RPC approach is common in *client-server systems*, which are also called frontend-backend systems. In both cases, the client (frontend) work is performed in a workstation; the server (backend) work is often performed in a minicomputer or mainframe that is also attached to the network. The existence of the network is usually transparent to the user of the client (frontend). The important aspect is that the computational work can be divided in a way that optimizes the workstation and mini/mainframe capabilities, makes best use of the network, and ensures the integrity of the data being manipulated.

Client-server systems are not limited to the workstation and mini/mainframe configuration, but can apply to any arrangement of computer systems in which an application is divided into two pieces for operation across the network. In fact, the terminology is reversed in the case of X windows, in which the client refers to the remote application, and the server is the code that runs the display at the workstation based on commands from the client.

A typical RPC mechanism must ensure that the request/response data are transferred without error, and that the desired operation happens either **exactly** once or **at least** once. An example of an exactly once operation is a debit of a bank account; of an at least once operation is a deposit to an account. (The bank would probably insist that this deposit should also be exactly once and would argue that a better example would be a request through an automated teller for an account balance—if a second read operation occurs, there is no problem.)

Security at the Session Layer

No OSI security services have been identified at the Session Layer, although some non-OSI protocol stack designers have felt that this was a logical place for security because control of sessions is basic to controlling access across the network. For example, DECnet's equivalent of the Session Layer has had several security mechanisms, including authentication and access control. IBM's SNA also has included the option for encryption of sessions.

Test Considerations at the Session Layer

No special test considerations are identified here for the Session Layer other than to verify that all of the state machine operations are performed properly and that conformance, stress, and interoperability tests are conducted.

THE PRESENTATION LAYER

Like the Session Layer, the Presentation Layer is primarily an invention of OSI. Presentation-like functions appear in the TCP/IP file transfer and remote log-in (Telnet) protocols but without having a special layer. Although DECnet and SNA designers can point to a defined set of presentation-like functions, neither of them had anything comparable to the context negotiation and abstract syntax of the OSI Presentation Layer.

The OSI Presentation Layer

This section is a general introduction to the OSI Presentation Layer. A more detailed description is deferred until book three in this series. However, it is felt that this introduction will be sufficient for many persons whose responsibilities require an understanding of the purpose and operation of the Presentation Layer, without having to know the bit-by-bit details of its mechanisms.

Development of the Presentation Layer Standards

The Presentation Layer was late in coming into place; consequently, early OSI implementations (such as MAP/TOP) had a null implementation at this layer. The delay was partly the result of getting a false start in its development. Indeed, its name reflects this false start. The original concept was of **presentation** of information to the consumer (e.g., a user at a terminal or a computer program). What would be needed to make a screen of information presentable to the user at the terminal? First it had to be converted into the proper character set, then the line lengths had to be made compatible, then the end-of-line conventions had to be mapped, and so on, to be able to see the results. These same concepts applied to making data presentable to a computer program.

But then it was agreed that these terminal and program-specific mappings were the concerns of the Application Layer; for example, as a part of the virtual terminal and file transfer protocols. This left the concerns of the Presentation Layer to be those of data **representation**. Examples of data representation differences include the internal representations of data within computers, such as 1s versus 2s complement integers, floating point numbers, and byte ordering. These representation differences span across the range of application needs and provide a generic need for this layer.

Given that different end computer systems have different internal representations of data, how can information be transmitted meaningfully between them without losing the intent? Some syntax is required that can transfer the information while preserving its semantic content.

With the exception of the special case in which the two end systems have identical internal data representations, some transformations are clearly required. There are three possibilities for where and how these transformations could be done:

1. The initiating end system could perform the transformations to match the internal representations of the other end system.
2. Just the opposite could be done: the associated system could perform the transformations.

Neither of these approaches is satisfactory, because we would have a large number of translations required—about n^2, where n is the number of different types of end systems.

A more satisfactory approach is:

3. Perform translations at each end, to and from an intermediate form.

This is not new. Terminals from different vendors have connected to computers of different vendors using this method for more than two decades. The revelation brought about by OSI was the generality with which this intermediate representation could be managed. In particular, the generalization was from one of extending from terminal characteristics to general data structures, including those of complex PDUs, such as utilized by the Application Layer protocols.

Abstract Syntax Notation and Transfer Syntax Negotiation
The new approach to describing Application Layer PDUs is by using a technique that is very similar to that of defining primitive data types, and subsequently complex data structures, in programming languages like Pascal, C, or Ada. In OSI, the data representation is in Abstract Syntax Notation.One, or ASN.1, which is a notation for defining PDU structures. A PDU structure is an "abstract syntax." As its name implies, ASN.1 is the first one of several possible notations for defining an Abstract Syntax (AS). If abstract syntax sounds like foreign terminology, think of a particular abstract syntax as an Application Layer PDU.

Each Application Layer PDU is defined as an abstract syntax. Utilize a notation that PDU(n) is defined by AS(n), for $n = 1, 2, \ldots$. The originating Application Layer protocol will notify its Presentation Layer of the set of AS(j), AS(k), etc. which it expects to utilize on an Application Layer association. Its Presentation Layer entity already knows about these AS, as should the corresponding end system with which it intends to communicate. It is now up to the Presentation Layer to negotiate a Transfer Syntax (TS) that both end systems can utilize.

This negotiation will take the following form. When the originator of the Application Layer association requests a set of AS, the Presentation Layer determines the set of possible TS that could be used by it to provide a TS (encoding). For example, the originator's Presentation Layer connection request might include the following possible TS for each AS; that is, for each PDU type.

PDU_type(1) = AS(1) with TS(a), TS(b), or TS(c)
PDU_type(2) = AS(2) with TS(a), or TS(d)
PDU_type(3) = AS(3) with TS(b), TS(d), or TS(e)

The associated end system might respond with the following negotiated values.

PDU_type(1) = AS(1) using TS(*a*)
PDU_type(2) = AS(2) using TS(*d*)
PDU_type(3) = AS(3) using TS(*d*)

Each "AS(*n*) using TS(*x*)" pair is called a Presentation Layer "context." The combination of all such contexts is called a Defined Context Set—the set of pairs that can be utilized. Note that a single TS may be utilized for more than one AS. Also, it is possible that no common TS may be mutually acceptable. In this latter case, the association will not be able to interoperate. Let us assume that an acceptable defined context set was established. Unlike the negotiations at other layers, the Presentation Layer may continue to add to or delete contexts at any time. This is necessary at the Presentation Layer, because it must be able to support a changing set of needs by the Application Layer. Like negotiations at other layers, a default context exists if there is no negotiated defined context set.

Sending Data Across the Association
After establishment of the association, session, and connections of an end-to-end communication, the application programs can pass information units to each other. The Application Layer passes the identifier of the AS (APDU type) for each information unit that it sends to the Presentation Layer. The information unit becomes a PSDU, which is encoded in the local system's representation. It in turn may be sent as one or more PPDUs, each of which will convey the Presentation Layer context (AS:TS pair) of the PSDU of which it is a part.

Services and Protocols of the Presentation Layer
There are two general categories of services the Presentation Layer provides: pass-through services from the Session Layer and context management. These are defined in the following ISO and CCITT documents.

Service Definition	ISO 8822	CCITT X.216
Protocol Specification	ISO 8823	CCITT X.226

In addition, the Presentation Layer relies very heavily on AS and TS documentation, which are:

ISO	**CCITT**	
ASN.1	ISO 8824	CCITT X.208 or X.409
Encoding Rules	ISO 8825	CCITT X.209 or X.409

The ISO and CCITT versions of these documents evolved along slightly different lines. ISO developed separate specifications for the two, while CCITT defined both in a single document, X.409, which was a part of X.400 electronic messaging. Later, CCITT developed two separate documents as well, as indicated above.

Abstract Syntax Notation.One (ASN.1)

ASN.1 previously was related to the choice of a negotiated TS. This discussion now takes a detailed look at the particulars of ASN.1 and the TS.

ASN.1 is a notation for describing AS, where an AS, for these purposes, is an Application Layer PDU. The APDU is a syntax because it has a format and structure that describe it. It is an abstract description because it is independent of any particular implementation.

As discussed earlier, the description of an APDU in ASN.1 is like the definition of a data structure in a modern programming language. Primitives such as integers and booleans are defined. From these primitives, more complex structures such as arrays (sequences) can be developed. More complex structures can be developed with mixed types, such as integers and booleans.

The primitive types can be identified by a *tag*, where the tag consists of a class and an identifier. The class is one of the four types indicated below, with their respective encodings.

00 = Universal Class—Types defined within ASN.1
01 = Application Class—Types defined in OSI standards
10 = Context Specific Class—The context defines the type
11 = Private Class—Types for use by a vendor

The primary concern here is with the universal class. A brief listing of some of its defined types is shown below.

Identifier = 1: BOOLEAN
            2: INTEGER
            3: BITSTRING
            4: OCTETSTRING
            9: REAL
           18: NumericString
           19: PrintableString
           22: IA5String
           28: CharacterString

All of these types are primitives, as well as being universal in their definition. Note that ASN.1 is case sensitive. All of the above type names, like all other types, begins with a capital letter. Some types are expressed in all capital letters. These are reserved words.

In addition to the above listed primitives, there are others that are *constructors*. They can be of any of the four classes mentioned earlier. The universal class constructors include the following.

Identifier = 16: SEQUENCE and SEQUENCE OF
            17: SET and SET OF

The constructor type SEQUENCE allows you to define an ordered list of data elements of arbitrary types. SEQUENCE OF is similar, except that all of the elements must be of the same type.

Constructor type SET differs from SEQUENCE in that a set does not require ordering. SET OF is similar, but requires that all of the data elements in the set be of the same type.

Another form of constructor that is primitive, but does not have a tag assigned to it is CHOICE, which allows a selection from a list of different candidates of possibly differing types. The type of the resulting field depends on the choice that is made, which is why it does not have a specific type assigned to it.

The above primitives have been of two forms: the kinds of elements you would expect to be primitives, such as integers; and constructors, which allow you to build more complex structures. These more complex structures are called *constructed types*, and include a wide variety of data structures such as records and protocol headers.

Current usage dictates that all Application Layer PDUs be defined using ASN.1, but it also could be used for other protocol layers. For example, recall the PDUs associated with TCP/IP and you will see many examples in which protocol control information fields could have been described in ASN.1. The first two fields in the TCP header were 16-bit port numbers. These were of type INTEGER. Later, there were a number of flags, such as the SYNchronize flag to establish the connection. These were of type BOOLEAN, and they were an example of a SEQUENCE OF constructor, because their order was important. In IP, there were a number of possible options. Because their order is not important, this would be an example of the SET constructor type. They need not all be of the same type, so it is not SET OF.

The Transfer Syntax Encoding

During the negotiation exchange at the Presentation Layer, a specific (concrete) TS is selected for each AS that that will be utilized. The key that relates a TS to an AS is the tag field (i.e., the class and identifier field). For example, an AS may have a tag of "Universal 2," which means INTEGER. You will see this same "Universal 2" in the TS as well, where it will also mean INTEGER, but it will have a specific encoding, something it did not have in the abstract form. The TS is expressed in type-length-value form as shown in Figure 7-9. Note that the "type" is the tag. In the INTEGER example, the class was universal and primitive, and the identifier was 2. This fits within the one-byte format shown in the figure. If an identifier value in excess of 30 is required, the extended format of Figure 7-10 is utilized. The length field is also extensible, providing an open-ended, network-wide mechanism for describing the data that are being transmitted.

Non-OSI Equivalents of the Presentation Layer

The equivalent of the Presentation Layer in other suites (e.g., the logical units in SNA) can be found, but they are somewhat unusual. The Presentation Layer is primarily an invention of OSI, not something that came out of other protocol approaches.

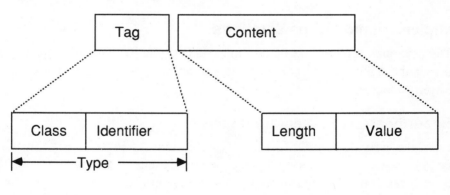

- Information may be represented as

- Example
  — Class = Universal and Primitive
  — Identifier = 2
  — The content is then the length and value of the integer
  } Represents an integer

- This is Type-Length-Value encoding

Graphic courtesy of Learning Tree International.

FIGURE 7-9   An example of encoded information for the transfer syntax.

- The tag format is either
  — For identifiers that can be represented by 5 bits

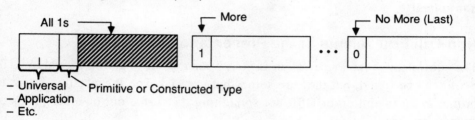

— Or, for larger identifiers (≥ 31)

- The length field can be extended in a similar manner

Graphic courtesy of Learning Tree International.

FIGURE 7-10   The extended form of the transfer syntax.

Implementation Considerations

The principal implementation considerations of the Presentation Layer relate to use of the AS notation. This has become an essential part of all Applications Layer protocols.

Security at the Presentation Layer

From the early days of OSI, it was expected that the Presentation Layer would be performing character-by-character manipulations of the data stream. Therefore, it seemed like a reasonable place to perform functions such as character translation, data compression, and encryption. The latter would be a substitution for each character, like character set conversion, but with a varying substitution to avoid frequency analysis on the cipher text stream. The OSI security committee decided, however, not to place security services at the Presentation Layer.

Test Considerations

Much of the job of the Presentation Layer is handled by the use of ASN.1 to define Application Layer PDUs. This ensures that the syntax differences between the two end systems will be managed by the encodings that are negotiated. Therefore, the testing aspects focus on verifying the proper operation of these negotiations.

Like all other negotiations we have discussed, the Presentation Layer can perform its negotiation when the connection is established. However, unlike the other layers, these negotiations also can be performed at other places in the dialogues, altering the defined context set. This presents a more challenging test situation because of its dynamic nature. Many more test conditions must be simulated.

Testing at the Presentation Layer also must take into account which subset of the available functional units are to be included in the implementation. This includes the pass-through services from the Session Layer and the selected portions of its functional units. The tests should verify the proper operation and adequacy of the offered services (i.e., that all of the prerequisite services are also available). An example is the inclusion of typed data only if the half-duplex functional unit is available.

THE APPLICATION LAYER

In many earlier protocol suites, such as TCP/IP, the application protocols sat directly on top of the TCP transport protocol. Therefore, these application protocols provided their own equivalents of the Session and Presentation Layer functionality, but only to the extent that they needed such services. Each application protocol would develop its own set of mechanisms.

The OSI approach is to develop a set of common Session and Presentation Layer services upon which the Application Layer can build. The concept is to avoid "reinventing the wheel" for each application. The TCP/IP community addressed this problem from a different perspective. A core group of persons developed the TCP/IP protocols and were involved in all such application protocols. They ensured that common services were utilized by guiding the developments, not by rigidly partitioning the services into layers, as with OSI.

For example, the FTP file transfer protocol needs a remote log-in capability. Rather than invent its own, it builds on the Telnet protocol, which provides this service. Similarly, FTP needs an out-of-band control channel, and Telnet is utilized for this purpose. The SMTP (Simple Mail Transfer Protocol) needs to move messages from place to place. Although this is not the same service that is needed for file transfers, it is close enough that considerable similarity is seen between the internals of FTP and SMTP.

The small core group approach probably would not work in OSI, in which the committee size, composition, and continuity cannot be controlled as it was with TCP/IP. Neither approach is optional in all cases.

The General Nature of the Application Layer

The Application Layer of OSI is intended to provide services to application programs. These application programs need to perform remote accesses to resources, move records or files from one place to another, and exchange electronic messages. Application Layer protocols have been developed for each of these purposes, and are described in the next section, *The OSI Application Layer Services and Protocols*.

The OSI Application Layer Services and Protocols

A detailed description of the Application Layer services and protocols is deferred until book three of this series. This discussion provides an introduction to the Application Layer and each of its major components.

There are certain capabilities that are commonly needed, such as the opening of a connection. At one time these functions were grouped together into a Common Application Service Element (CASE), which was considered to be a sublayer of the Application Layer. The idea of making this a sublayer has changed, and CASE has been replaced by a set of service elements, each of which may or may not be utilized in a given application. They provide a set of reusable modules, providing services needed by a number of applications. The existing service elements include the following:

Association Control Service Element (ACSE)
Reliable Transfer Service Element (RTSE)
Remote Operations Service Element (ROSE)

Each of these service elements is discussed in the following paragraphs.

- **Association Control Service Element (ACSE)** provides the capabilities that are required to establish and release an association, which is the name given to the concept of a connection at the Application Layer. The intent is that only the ACSE should be allowed to invoke the service primitives to perform these functions.
- **Reliable Transfer Service Element (RTSE)** is not what you probably expected from its name. The word reliable means that crash recovery protection is the service provided. An ACK meant simply that the reliable delivery

mechanisms of TCP and TP4 ensured that data were reliably delivered into RAM memory. But if the receiving system crashed after the ACK was returned, the data would be lost, and no recovery mechanism is built into the transport services.

This is where the reliable service of RTSE comes into play. The equivalent of an ACK in RTSE is a Session Layer sync point confirmation, which is propagated up to the sending Application Layer protocol. At that point, the sender knows that it will not have to resend that data, and its local copy can be discarded.

The RTSE uses the services of the ACSE to establish an association, and then provides its reliable delivery to another Application Layer protocol. This is an example of the modularity and reuse within the Application Layer.

• **Remote Operations Service Element (ROSE)** is intended for request/ response operations. The primitive operations of ROSE are very simple. One can issue a request using the invoke operation. The response is either a result, a rejection, or an error report. This forms the basis for a Remote Procedure Call (RPC) form of dialogue, which is becoming increasingly popular. However, ROSE is intended to be considerably more general than just an RPC mechanism. ROSE is currently used by network management, message handling systems, and directory services.

ROSE provides its services to the more visible Application Layer protocols mentioned above, and it in turn can build upon the RTSE services. This is another example of the reuse of the service elements.

Commitment, Concurrency, and Recovery (CCR)

The Commitment, Concurrency, and Recovery (CCR) services are another commonly utilized element within the Application Layer. CCR provides a set of controls over what are called "atomic actions." The concept of an atom is not that it necessarily is very small, but rather that it cannot be sub-divided, at least not in the thinking of physicists of years gone by. The atomic action may consist, for example, of the earlier analogy of debiting one account and crediting another. The desired end result is that either the **entire** operation happened or none at all. You specifically would not want one account debited but the other not credited.

This mechanism also applies to multi-party operations such as updating a distributed data base. You would want to ensure that either every copy of the data base is updated, or none at all. CCR does this using a classical mechanism known as a "two-phase commit." In the first phase, the master, who wants to make the update, gets an agreement from every slave copy of the data base that the change will be made. They have each stored this on safe (crash recoverable) storage. After they all have agreed to make this change, the master orders the change to be made. Otherwise, the master orders a rollback to the original condition without making the update.

Electronic Message Handling Systems

The most common electronic Message Handling System (MHS) in OSI is known as X.400 (CCITT's designation). ISO developed a similar system called MOTIS (Message Oriented Text Interchange System). The two have been merged in the 1988 version of X.400 and ISO 10021. They provide a capable means for the exchange of multimedia information, multimedia meaning text, graphics, images, and digitized speech. All can be combined in a single document if desired. More typical near term uses will be the exchange of desktop publishing quality documents.

X.400 is based on four basic components:

1. The User Agent (UA).
2. The Message Transfer Agent (MTA).
3. The Message Store (MS).
4. The Access Unit (AU).

The UA is the portion of the message system that supports the user in the generation of messages. It does not include a text editor and file system. They are assumed to exist but are not the subject of standardization. The UA provides a standardized way of stating the recipient(s) of the message, the sender, the subject, the "carbon copy" and "blind carbon copy" recipients, and other information that is typical in inter-office memoranda. The UA distinguishes between this control information and the actual text of the message.

The MTA serves in the role of post office. There may be many such MTAs, and a message may be sent through several along its path to the recipient(s). An MTA may simply forward the message or copy it for a local recipient as well as forwarding it. The MTA interprets the control portion of the message, paying no attention to the body part. This is consistent with its role as the electronic post office.

In the 1984 version of X.400, the MTAs would hold onto a message for some time, such as a few days, and return it to the sender if it could not be delivered within that time. If the user did not log-in to read his/her electronic mail, it would be sent back. This was a problem, because people often go on vacation or business trips and are out of contact with their electronic mail system for weeks. In the 1988 version of X.400, the concept of a Message Store (MS) was added. An MTA could now include an MS facility, which would provide the longer term storage for undelivered mail.

The 1988 version of X.400 also added a link between the worlds of electronic mail and the paper-oriented postal system. The latter is often called "snail mail" by the electronic community, because of its slower pace. However, it seems desirable to include someone as a recipient, even if that person does not have an electronic mail account. This link between the two worlds is called an Access Unit (AU). The AU provides the capability to either printout the message or to have it written to a floppy disk; in either case it is delivered by the regular postal system.

The specification of X.400 involves several CCITT recommendations, i.e., several separate specifications. A few, such as X.409, have become widely known outside of the X.400 environment, but most have little visibility from the non-X.400 world. X.409 was CCITT's version of ASN.1, which was discussed in the section on the Presentation Layer. CCITT's X.410, Reliable Transfer Service, eventually became the RTSE discussed earlier in this section.

CCITT has identified several protocols that are important within the X.400 message system. They are defined in the CCITT recommendations, but they are known by a shorthand form, such as P1, P2, and P3. The P1 protocol deals with the delivery of a message. This is the portion that involves the MTA postal systems. The P2 protocol defines the header and body portions along with their formats and fields. The P3 protocol is a variation of the P1 MTA-MTA protocol and is intended for workstation-to-MTA transfers of messages. These protocols control the internal operation within X.400 for the creation and exchange of messages.

File Transfer, Access, and Management (FTAM)

You might frequently want to move files from one location to another across the network. One approach would be to convey the file as the body part of an electronic mail message. This is done often, but has some limitations. Message systems usually have some upper limit on the message size. If the file exceeds this limit, you either cannot send it, or have to segment it into pieces. You might utilize this approach if you need to send a file to someone and you don't have a log-in account on their system, which is needed for a file transfer. (Some systems do provide a guest account with an anonymous log-in, but it usually restricts you to reading files in certain directories without allowing write access.)

Another example in which electronic mail does not really meet the needs for file transfers is when a certain control mechanism in the message system might be triggered by something in the file. For example, the dot commands of Word-Star have a period in the left-most column, which would erroneously signal the end of a message over Telenet's TeleMail facility. This means you would have to remove such commands or send an ASCII formatted version of the file. You might also object to the delay that may occur between the time you send a message containing a file and the time it arrives in the recipient's mail box. Also, you are limited to receiving files that are sent to you. You cannot request that a file be sent, except by sending an electronic message asking for the file to be sent at some later time.

For a number of such reasons, you need a more general way of moving files than simply sending them as electronic mail messages. You also might like to be able to perform other file system related functions, such as looking at the contents of a directory to select the file you want.

The OSI network protocol for handling files provides a large set of capabilities. It is called File Transfer, Access, and Management (FTAM). As its name implies, it is used to transfer files, access individual records, and manage files. Examples of file management include copying, deleting, renaming, and changing access attributes. Therefore, FTAM provides more services than typical pre-OSI file handling protocols.

The decision to make FTAM capable of performing such a wide variety of operations is consistent with the conscious decision on the part of the developers to make FTAM a top-of-the-line file handling system. They were willing to accept the ultimate complexity, large program size, and implementation difficulties to provide a system that would support a wide variety of vendor approaches. A simplistic approach was viewed as limiting interoperability and not meeting future needs.

The FTAM specifications reflect its complexity and consist of four separate documents which have more than 400 pages. These documents are:

General Approach
Virtual File Store
FTAM Service Definition
FTAM Protocol Specification

The general approach document provides an introductory overview of FTAM. It is unusual for OSI to provide a tutorial description as a part of its documentation. This would again seem to indicate the developers' awareness of the complexity of this protocol.

Like any use of the word "virtual," the virtual file store is something that you seem to see, although it does not necessarily exist in that actual form. Applications operate on the virtual file store using a set of commands and interprets the responses in the context of this apparent structure of the file server. It is up to the local implementation to map from the virtual file store to the real local file store (e.g., a file server).

You can consider the virtual file store to consist of a directory, a set of files, and the attributes of these files. The directory mechanism of FTAM was not defined in detail in the original specifications and is considered to be a flat listing of the files that are contained on the file store. The files themselves may have several structures, all of which are subsets of a general hierarchically (tree) structured file. This general structure in shown in Figure 7-11.

Each node in the structure may contain a Data Unit (DU), but only a leaf node is required to have a DU associated with it. An intermediate node may be accessed, including all of its lower level nodes and their DUs. This is an example of a general File Access Data Unit (FADU). Several possible FADUs are indicated in Figure 7-11. The tree structure of the file also determines the order in which DUs would be transferred if the entire file were to be copied. They are sent in the order of a leftmost traversal of the tree, in which you send whatever DU is leftmost in the tree, and has not yet been sent.

The common subsets of the general hierarchical structure are called *constraint sets*. The constraints relate to which nodes can have DUs, and which file system operations can be performed. For example, one cannot update information in the middle of a simple sequential file.

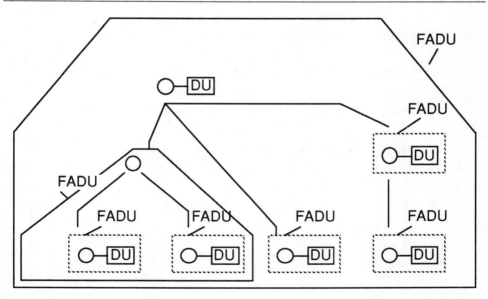

DU = Data Unit
FADU = File Accessing Data Unit

Graphic courtesy of Learning Tree International.

FIGURE 7-11   The general model of a file structure is hierarchical.

The files in the file store have attributes. Every file will have at least one attribute—its name. It will most likely also have attributes describing its size, the date and time of the last change, and its owner. Many other attributes are possible.

Operations on FTAM files are controlled based on a nested set of regimes. Certain operations are only valid in a particular regime. For example, you cannot read or write a file unless it has been opened, therefore you are in the open regime. An example set of nested regimes is shown in Figure 7-12.

The FTAM level of service can be selected to be either reliable service or user-correctable service. Reliable service implies that the system will keep enough context to be able to recover from major problems. This overhead may be eliminated by allowing the user to handle what are hopefully rare events.

Virtual Terminal System

The Virtual Terminal System (VTS) provides the ability for essentially any terminal to interoperate with any computer on the network. The terminal type is often a simple scroll mode CRT terminal, but the VTS supports page mode and forms mode terminals, complete with features such as protected fields, reverse video, and color.

• **FTAM defines a number of "regimes" or operational contexts**

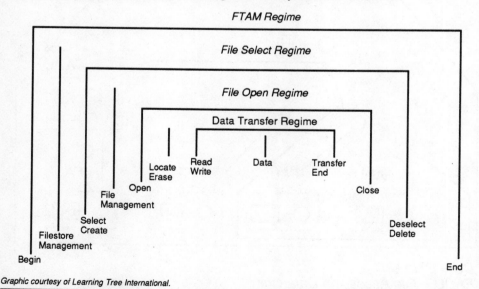

Graphic courtesy of Learning Tree International.

FIGURE 7-12   FTAM regimes are a nested set of states with the protocol.

The VTS provides a general purpose communications mechanism between terminals and processes. In addition to terminal-initiated connections to processes the converse could be true, or the VTS could be used for process-to-process or terminal-to-terminal communications. The intermediate representation for the communications in all cases is that of a virtual terminal. No company manufacturers such a terminal, but any terminal characteristic can be mapped into it for transmission and again upon reception.

The VTS also provides controls over which party can write at any given time, and on which part of the screen either party can write. This provides a split-screen option. These communications are called synchronous when there is a token mechanism to control the dialogue, or it can be called asynchronous when either side can transmit at any time. In the latter case, the split-screen would be utilized to avoid a situation in which both attempt to write on the same portion of the screen simultaneously.

Directory Services
The purpose of the directory or name server is to provide a network-wide capability to express a request in terms of a globally unique name, and to have this name mapped into a particular physical network address. The name is typically expressed much like the way you state the recipient's name of a letter sent via the post office. The address placed on the envelope of such a letter could be interpreted to be in the form:

```
John Doe @ 123 Cherry Tree Lane.Your City.Your State.ZIP.USA
```

The directory service, or name service as it is also called, provides the mapping from this form of address, called a name, into a physical network address, which in the postal analogy would be the official plot map location of the address. The network directory service maps a convenient user-provided name into a node address such as **[country].[network].[node]**.

Security Services
OSI security services have been identified in the security addendum to the OSI RM. These security services are particularly pervasive at the Application Layer. In fact, all five of the OSI security services—authentication, access control, data confidentiality, data integrity, and non-repudiation—are listed as being services that could be provided by the Application Layer. Only the Network and Transport Layers have nearly this wide range of possible security services, and neither of them provides non-repudiation.

One of the principal reasons the Application Layer receives such high marks as a location for security services is that it is in the best position to accurately determine what needs to be protected and against what threats. At lower layers, this ability to determine needs is lost.

Each of the five security services is discussed in the following paragraphs.

- **Authentication** is provided for a number of network access needs, including file transfer, virtual terminal access, and remote procedure calls. This is done at the initiation of an Application Layer connection. On-going authentication may also be required in some applications, such as is implicit in the ability to encrypt/decrypt messages.
- **Access control** is required to ensure that only authorized users or applications access sensitive data. Lower layers typically do not convey the user identification that is necessary to provide individual user access controls and accountability.
- **Data confidentiality** is frequently provided at lower layers by encrypting the entire data field of packets, and in some cases, encrypting the headers as well. The Application Layer has the option of encrypting either the entire application data field or performing selective field encryption. The latter might significantly reduce the overhead due to the encryption/decryption operations, particularly when they are performed in software. However, the trust requirement is substantial in this case. The software must be trusted to always encrypt the selected fields and to perform the encryption correctly.
- **Data integrity** usually means that any attempt to modify the data in transit will be detected with a very high probability. This can be achieved at lower layers (such as the Network or Transport Layers) by forming a cryptographic error check. Since the lower layers do not know which fields of information are in need of protection, they must protect the integrity of every field. The Application Layer can reduce this overhead by applying integrity mechanisms to only those fields that need such protection.
- **Non-repudiation**, the last security service, has two purposes. First, it can ensure that the recipient of a message cannot prove later that the message was never received. Alternatively, non-repudiation can ensure that the sender cannot prove later not to have sent the message. Proof of receipt or transmittal is usually done by means of an electronic signature, using public key cryptography. Each user of the network has both a public key and a private key. Messages which are encrypted in the public key can only be decrypted by the owner of the private key. Messages that are encrypted in the private key can be read by anyone, but could only be sent by the individual who possesses the private key. This provides the basis for the electronic signature. Several variations build on this basic concept.

The Application Layer provides a wealth of opportunities for introducing security into networks. The OSI recommendations for the placement of security services indicate that the Application Layer is a prime candidate for implementing security. However, implementer agreements and actual software products are not readily available yet. Much work is still necessary to ensure that differing implementations of security services and mechanisms do not create multi-vendor interoperability problems.

The TCP/IP Application Layer Protocols

People often refer to the TCP/IP protocols when they really mean the application level support that is provided by TCP, and to some lesser extent, UDP. These application protocols include Telnet (for remote log-in), File Transfer Protocol (FTP), Simple Mail Transfer Protocol (SMTP), Network File System (NFS), the Domain Name System (DNS), and network management. Each of these protocols is described in a separate section below.

Telnet

The Telnet protocol got its name from the concept of a **Teletypewriter Network** in which users at dumb terminals could access any host resource on the network. The basic characteristic as seen by the user is a remote log-in capability. However, the internal concepts of Telnet are considerably more profound, especially considering the early phase of networking when they were developed.

The first of these concepts is that of a virtual terminal, which provides a minimal intermediate representation of terminal characteristics. Its defaults tend to be those that can be supported by any terminal, such as local echo. The idea is to negotiate any desired features beyond this minimal terminal representation, which leads to the second basic concept of Telnet, negotiated options.

Negotiated options allow extension beyond the limits of the default Network Virtual Terminal, such as to perform remote echo. The terminal support processor at the user end can request that the server Telnet perform remote echo by sending the request "Do remote echo." The server Telnet can then respond with either "Will remote echo" or "Won't remote echo." Alternatively, the server Telnet could have offered to perform the remote echo by sending "Will remote echo." The user side would then respond with either "Do remote echo" or "Don't remote echo." Note that the protocol was intentionally designed to handle the situation in which the user side requests "Do remote echo" and the server side simultaneously and independently offers "Will remote echo." Each side interprets the other's message as a response to its request or offer.

The negotiations described above are one example of embedded commands within the Telnet data stream. How does the receiving Telnet implementation know which incoming bytes are user data and which bytes are embedded commands? The answer is exactly the same as that used in the Bisync protocol years before. (Bisync preceded each command character with a Data Link Escape (DLE) character. The DLE character indicated that the receiver should escape from its current interpretation of data and interpret the next character as a command.) Telnet precedes each command character with an Interpret As Command (IAC) character. Telnet also has a set of user interface commands including edit functions. The entire set of Telnet commands is discussed in detail later in this section.

The final basic concept of Telnet is its symmetric operation. Telnet is not limited to the case of a terminal initiating a connection to a host. Alternatively, the host could initiate the connection to the terminal, or it could initiate a connection to another host for the purpose of character-oriented data exchanges. One such example that you will see later is the use of a Telnet connection to serve as a control channel for the File Transfer Protocol. In addition to terminal-host and host-host connections, one can have terminal-terminal connections in which users communicate in real-time "chat" sessions over their terminals.

Regardless of the nature of the Telnet connection, it is established by the user in a simple manner. A typical user interface to Telnet involves making a connection by typing the command:

```
telnet <host.name>
```

where **host.name** can be either a logical name or an IP address. If a logical name is used, it is in the domain name form (such as **computer.company.com**). If an IP address is entered, it is in dotted decimal form (such as **192.1.2.3**).

The command **telnet** results in a TCP connection being established to the well-known port (Telnet is decimal 23). The connection is between a user Telnet and a server Telnet. Each character that is typed by the user is processed separately and is sent in a separate packet across the network. This causes an ACK packet to be returned, and an echo data packet is also sent if remote echo is utilized. Network utilization is rather inefficient, but fortunately these transmissions are limited based on users' typing speeds. There is also a large amount of processing overhead, because each character must be processed separately as well, with frequent process (context) switching overhead.

As mentioned previously, Telnet has a set of commands that can be embedded in the character stream. These Telnet commands include those required for option negotiation, which are **Do, Don't, Will** and **Won't**. A request for an option is made by issuing a **Do** command. The response is either **Will** or **Won't**. An offer to perform an option is made by the **Will** command, and the response is either **Do** or **Don't**. Subnegotiation is also possible, with multiple character commands using the **Begin** and **End** commands.

There is also a set of commands associated with the user interface. These include editing commands such as **Erase Character** and **Erase Line**. Other commands allow the user to **Interrupt Process, Abort Output, Break,** and to enquire **Are You There**. For half-duplex operation, there is a **Go Ahead** command that passes control to the other side.

The remaining commands include a **No Op** and a **Data Mark**, which is utilized when one wants to synchronize the two ends to a specific location in the data stream. This facility is utilized in conjunction with the TCP Urgent Pointer to approximate an out-of-band signal. When received, it is processed as soon as possible, scanning the data stream, discarding data, and interpreting Telnet commands up to the data mark, where normal processing of data is resumed.

File Transfer Protocol (FTP)

The FTP is exactly what its name implies, a capability to transfer files from one computer to another across the internet. It does not attempt to be as general a capability as the OSI FTAM, but FTP meets a large percentage of needs between different kinds of computer systems. Unlike the OSI FTAM, FTP does not provide access to individual records and provides only minimal file management capabilities, such as being able to list directories.

FTP was designed to support both human user and computer program controlled file transfers. Each response has both a human and a computer readable returned value, such as **230 user logged in <cr><lf>** in which the **230** is to be utilized in a computer when it is executing this operation itself, and the **user logged in** is for display and human interpretation when the operation is being dictated by a person at a terminal or workstation.

FTP utilizes a separate control connection and a data transfer connection, which is typically opened and closed for each file transfer. The control connection is a Telnet connection. It is maintained for the duration of the FTP connection, which was established to a well-known port (decimal 21).

To request an FTP connection enter **ftp <host.name>**, where **<host.name>** can be either the logical host name or the dotted decimal internet address. The most common requests after having performed the log-in at the other host will be to **get** (read) or **put** (write) a named source and destination file. The defaults are that the source and destination file names will be the same, and that the transfer will be in ASCII.

There are several non-default options that can be selected for a file transfer. They relate to three principal differences: data types, file structures, and transmission modes, each of which can be requested by the user.

The data type differences can be divided into two major groups, printable and non-printable. The differences within the printable group include ASCII and EBCDIC representations and conversions, and also include different print conventions that can be either an embedded carriage return and line feed or FORTRAN. Non-print file differences are image and logical byte size files. An image file is a bit-for-bit exchange of information between machines of the same type. A logical byte size transfer is one in which the DUs may differ between the machines; for example placing 32-bit words into a 36-bit machine's memory. The reverse is also possible but obviously more complicated.

FTP support for different file structures is limited to three types: unstructured files, record-oriented files, and page-oriented files. The latter were placed in FTP primarily for the DEC PDP-10, which was a popular host in early ARPAnet days.

FTP supports three different transmission modes: compressed (in which replicated bytes are compressed), blocks (providing check-point recovery), and stream (as a sequence of bytes).

The mechanisms of FTP are clearly pragmatic, near-term solutions to problems of file transfers. There is limited support for file management and no support for individual record-level access. Its developers had a much different perspective than that of FTAM. History will indicate if perhaps both had the correct vision based on the needs and capabilities at the time each was developed.

Simple Mail Transfer Protocol (SMTP)

The SMTP provides the ability to distribute electronic mail across the network. SMTP does not specify any particular method for the creation or reading of such mail, only for its delivery. It is almost entirely limited to the MTA aspects of X.400 but has a few UA capabilities as well. It operates with the Domain Name System, which is described next.

Domain Name System (DNS)

The basic service that DNS provides is a mapping between node names and their corresponding internet addresses across a very large, hierarchical, name space. The system consists of a component that resides in each host, called a resolver, and a set of components called name servers, which accept requests from the resolvers and respond with mapping information. The name servers are actually a hierarchy of devices, no one of which has the entire set of mappings for the entire internet.

The DNS evolved after the internet outgrew the previous practice of having the mappings controlled by a Network Information Center (NIC). The concept of a NIC is a good one for many functions, such as being the central point for the assignment of internet addresses and for distribution of internet documentation. However, management of the extremely large internet mapping tables became too burdensome and had to be automated and distributed.

The DNS operates over either TCP or UDP. TCP is used for the transfer of large amounts of information, while UDP is utilized for simple request/response transactions.

Network File System (NFS)

The NFS is a set of protocols developed by Sun Microsystems and licensed to a few hundred vendors to provide transparent access to remote files. The "transparent" means that the files appear to be local to your workstation (they may even be listed in your directory), but they are physically located at another system.

NFS is machine- and operating-system independent, but it is modeled closely after the Unix file system. NFS assumes that the file is a sequence of bytes, and a typical NFS Remote Procedure Call (RPC) request might be "read 2,000 bytes starting 84,000 bytes from the beginning of the file." This might result in these 2,000 bytes being displayed on the active window of your workstation. The RPC mechanism provides the required, but minimal, delivery assurance. If it does not receive the data, it asks for it again. If it gets the same thing twice (i.e., a duplicate), there is no problem. You still have the same 2,000 bytes on your screen. Any bad bits are the concern of the LAN and/or the UDP transport protocol. Any bad packets are discarded and result in a retransmission of the request. Duplicates may occur because of delayed responses, but as indicated, do not matter.

The real benefit of NFS is that the server, which actually has the files, can crash and recover without any impact on the client workstations other than an additional delay in obtaining the requested information. There is no state information involved in NFS that must be recovered with user-initiated reconnection. This stateless operation can be achieved because, in most cases, the file has read/write access permissions set such that you can read and write your own files, and you may allow others to have read access as well. It is unusual to allow others to have write access to your files.

It may seem that because a file is open it is state information. NFS addresses this issue by providing the client with a "file handle" that allows the server to access the file without having to keep the usual stateful file-open tables. If the client crashes, you reboot and start from scratch. No one ever claimed that clients are stateless. The main concern is to keep the **server** stateless to ensure simplified crash recovery of this shared resource.

There are several other forms of distributed file systems in addition to NFS, and they should be mentioned at least in passing. One, the Remote File Sharing (RFS) system, was developed by AT&T for usage with Unix systems. It is specific to a particular operating system, rather than attempting to be independent of the operating system, as was the case with NFS. RFS operates over a reliable transmission protocol, such as TCP, and therefore does not have the stateless aspects of NFS. However, RFS maintains the client file system semantics; NFS does not.

The Server Message Block (SMB) capability is another alternative approach to that of NFS. It has been widely used with NetBIOS (Network Basic I/O System) of PC networks. NetBIOS operates over a combination of connection and connectionless transport protocols, using connections for reliable transmission and connectionless for broadcast support. Like RFS, SMB preserves client file system semantics, but SMB also introduces a variety of new file locking techniques which evolved in the Microsoft DOS release for networking.

Apollo also has introduced a variation of distributed computing called the Network Computing Architecture (NCA). Apollo adds a forwarding agent similar to the port mapper of NFS, but it is a part of a Location Broker. Like NFS, NCA operates over a connectionless transport protocol, such as UDP, but also includes an Apollo proprietary version of a connectionless transport protocol.

Often associated with NFS is a system originally called Yellow Pages (YP)—not to be mistaken for the telephone companies' trademarked Yellow Pages. YP provides a distributed data base service for data such as name/address mapping and user id/encrypted password pairs. These data change infrequently and seldom need the integrity and consistency mechanisms of a CCR-like protocol. YP does not provide any of these controls and should not be utilized with any data base which requires them.

A YP data base is updated by making the change at a master copy of the data base. Any node in the network can be designated to be this master, and it need not be the same node for every YP data base. When a change is made at the master, it is propagated to a set of slave servers by a YP Push operation. Because there are no CCR-like controls, there is no guarantee that all servers will receive every update.

A YP client "binds" to a YP slave server by utilizing the broadcast capability on the network, typically of a LAN.

Network Management

There are two accepted approaches for network management in the TCP/IP internet: Simple Network Management Protocol (SNMP) and Common Management Over TCP (CMOT). They differ in terms of the extent to which OSI protocols are applied for the collection of monitoring data and the transmission of control commands. SNMP utilizes a very simple set of get, set, and trap primitives operating directly over UDP. This simplicity is implied in SNMP's name. In contrast, CMOT operates with a much broader set of commands, utilizing the OSI Common Management Information Service and Protocol (CMIS/CMIP), and a "thin" Presentation Layer. This is shown in Figure 7-13.

SUMMARY

The higher layer protocols (sometimes called upper layer protocols) are different from those up through the Transport Layer. In layers 5, 6 and 7, the emphasis is on specific services that applications need beyond that of reliable, sequenced, flow-controlled delivery. These new services include dialog control (whose turn is it to talk?), synchronization (where do we resume processing in case of a crash?), data representation (what is the type of data being transferred and how is it encoded?), file transfers, remote log-in, and electronic mail exchange.

Unlike the lower layers, which tend to provide several different ways of getting the same service, the upper layers provide a wide range of different services. These different services can be selected as part of the negotiation process when connections are established. The services are grouped into functional units for

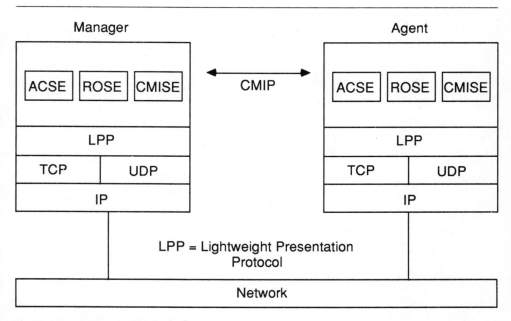

Graphic courtesy of Learning Tree International.

FIGURE 7-13   The CMOT Network management protocols combine OSI and TCP/IP protocols.

this negotiation. A given system might implement only the kernel and a small set of functional units that it needs for performing its specific set of processing requirements.

Protocol suites such as TCP/IP do not have the same upper layer modularization as OSI, and often have applications support protocols setting directly on TCP and/or UDP. As a result, the applications such as FTP and Telnet provide their own required subsets of Session, Presentation, and Application Layer services, all rolled into a single application such as file transfer.

Neither approach to modularization is inherently better than the other. The OSI approach builds upon the seven distinct layers of the OSI Reference Model, and the committee structure which produced the service definitions and protocol specifications at each layer. TCP/IP and other related protocol suites have less of this upper layer modularization and reuse, with a potential gain in performance by utilization of services which are tailored to specific application needs.

8

INTERCONNECTION, INTEROPERABILITY, AND MIGRATION STRATEGIES

Although this is a short chapter, it is not less important than the others. Instead it represents an area that is still in development. Its focus is how to interconnect computer systems, although they may have implemented different and incompatible protocols at one or more layers.

There are various ways to interconnect computer systems across networks and internetworks. *Interconnection* typically means to deliver bits from one place to another. For example, X.25 networks provide interconnectivity. One can deliver a packet of bits from an IBM computer to a DEC computer via X.25. This does not mean that the packet of bits is meaningful once it has been delivered in either direction. That requires *interoperability*.

Interoperability means that the bits can be interpreted upon arrival. There is either some common understanding of these bits, such as having implemented a common set of higher level protocols, or the bits have been specially created to emulate some device that the receiving host already knows about. An example of the former is that both end systems have implemented TCP/IP, or perhaps TP4/ISO IP. An example of the latter is 3270 terminal emulation, in which the originator of the packet appears to be an IBM 3278 terminal and a 3274 cluster controller. There is no IBM product with a "3270" label. It refers to a family of products, those listed being one such subset.

One of the issues considered here is how a common protocol stack can provide interoperability. You will see that a common protocol stack does not require common protocols at all layers. There will be several such examples, and they will attempt to extract some general principles about what it means to have implemented a common protocol stack. Sometimes these protocol stacks are called protocol suites. In any case, what is meant is a compatible set of protocols that can communicate between applications across the underlying protocol layers.

ALTERNATIVE INTEROPERABILITY APPROACHES

There are several different approaches to achieving interoperability. Some of the major approaches are described in this chapter.

Interoperability by Identical Protocols

One way to achieve interoperability is to implement the same exact protocols at all layers and in all nodes of the network. This is the approach taken in many small networks and in organizations in which there is strong, centralized control over networking. However, you will see that you need not be so strict in enforcing this policy of having only one form of communications at every layer, at least not for interoperability. It might still be a good idea for bulk purchasing, simpler maintenance, and a lesser need for spares. We will focus our attention on interoperability issues.

Suppose that our single form of networking is TCP/IP over Ethernet LANs, utilizing a certain type of coaxial cable for the interconnection media. Every department in the organization has one such network. What are the interoperability issues, and where could we relax the single approach constraint without affecting interoperability?

Going Beyond Our Identical Networks

The interoperability issues include one major concern. How do the separate departments interoperate? Each one can communicate well within its department, but how do they communicate across departmental boundaries? One solution is to add IP routers between the departmental networks. A common way of doing this is by means of a backbone network, which could be another Ethernet. If some departments are in other cities or even other countries, the routers can be utilized to form an interconnection across X.25 public, packet-switched networks. This goes beyond the initial constraint of using only one style of networking but breaks a distance barrier without any loss of the original goal of interoperability.

Other changes also could be introduced without any loss of interoperability. A mixture of forms of coaxial cable and twisted pair cabling could be utilized. Bridges could be used to connect some LAN segments. Some LANs could be Ethernet, with others being the somewhat different IEEE 802.3 form. All of these differences are manageable without a loss of interoperability.

You can conclude from this simple example that variations in the communications method do not affect interoperability. All are ways of delivering bits from one system to another without changing those bits or their meaning. Some adapters are needed, such as to convert from one form of cabling to another, but they are readily available.

The key to being able to handle this wide variety of bit delivery mechanisms is the usage of the Internet Protocol (IP). IP isolates TCP from any differences in the underlying protocols. All that IP provides, and all that it expects from the lower layers, is a best effort form of packet delivery. The lower layers could include LANs of any or all types, X.25 wide area nets, packet radio networks, and telephone company links.

Government OSI Profile (GOSIP)

Various differences can be tolerated in a network as long as the architecture plans for them. Many or all of these differences may be standards, but sometimes too many standards complicate interoperability. The solution is often one of having *profiles*. Profiles refine standards and limit the number of options that must be considered at each layer in the OSI model to those that are relevant to the real world. The most relevant profile is that established by the Government, which is a large procurer of networking devices and software. The *Government OSI Profile (GOSIP)* is the principal example of a profile that has become a major force in procurement.

GOSIP is being introduced in a phased manner, starting with GOSIP version 1, which specifies OSI protocols, but is limited to X.400 electronic messaging and FTAM file transfers as applications. Subsequent versions will expand this list of applications considerably. GOSIP version 1 is described in detail in the National Institute of Standards and Technology document FIPS Pub 146. It is further clarified in user guides and updates.

Relays at the Transport Layer

Could we have a mix-and-match at the Transport Layer that is similar to the flexibility that we saw at lower layers? Could some networks utilize TCP/IP while others utilize TP4/ISO IP? Can applications operate over either or both of these transport protocols in essentially the same way that interoperability became independent of the lower layer protocols?

The key to obtaining this desired form of mix and match is to do at the Transport Layer what was done at IP; namely, provide a common service. The approach that has been most widely applied to date is to add software on top of TCP to provide TP4 services, and then to support OSI upper layers over both TCP and TP4. This is shown in Figure 8-1, in which the left-most system operates with both the TCP/IP higher protocols, such as FTP, and with the OSI upper layer protocols, such as FTAM. In this figure, the right-most system operates with only the OSI protocols. Also shown is an intermediate system that implements both TCP and TP4 protocols and which relays upper layer PDUs.

This Transport Layer relay is technically against the OSI RM, which states that the Transport Layer is strictly end-to-end. This is another situation that may cause you to be visited by the protocol police, but you can argue your case based on this being only an interim measure. You do not intend to defy the OSI RM for very long.

Variations of the Transport Layer Relay

A variation of the Transport Layer relay is shown in Figure 8-2, in which the Telnet protocol is shown operating in both the usual TCP/IP environment and also in the AppleTalk protocol stack. The AppleTalk protocols are implemented in the Macintosh and in a VAX, which serves as the relay in this example. The VAX implements both the AppleTalk and TCP/IP stacks, just as our previous intermediate system had two stacks. In this figure, the VAX takes the Telnet packet from its AppleTalk protocol wrappings and places it in the TCP/IP protocol wrappings. These wrappings are often called *envelopes*. The envelopes are nested, because each protocol layer adds its control information on its particular envelope. The Telnet packet reaches the Cray, where it is processed as part of the Macintosh-to-Cray remote log-in. All that the VAX did in this example was to remove each Telnet packet from its incoming PDU and send it out in the other form of PDU. It would have been encapsulated initially in an AppleTalk PDU and then sent in a TCP/IP PDU, and vice versa.

A similar relay can be performed in the interconnection of non-SNA to SNA networks. In this case, instead of executing the Telnet protocol, the workstation

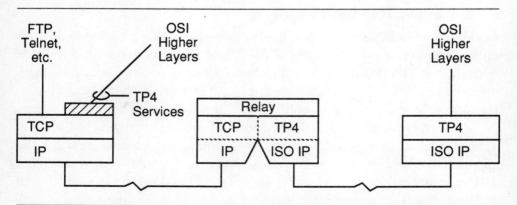

FIGURE 8-1   Special software can provide TP4 service over TCP, allowing interoperation between TCP and TP4 systems.

operates using the IBM 3270 protocols. They are called Logical Unit 2.0, which defines a Session/Presentation Layer-like set of capabilities in SNA. One part of the end-to-end journey is across TCP/IP, and the other portion is across SNA protocols. This is shown in Figure 8-3.

The key point is that the 3270 requests and responses are encapsulated in either TCP/IP or SNA packets, and the relay system simply changes the encapsulation from one form of delivery mechanism to another. No translation is required.

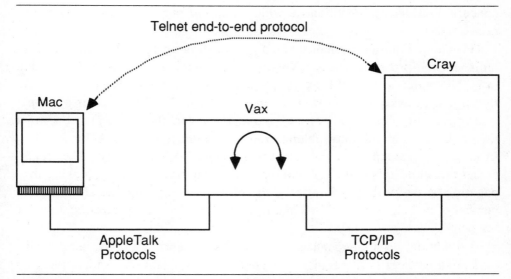

FIGURE 8-2 A relay function can forward application packets from one protocol environment to another.

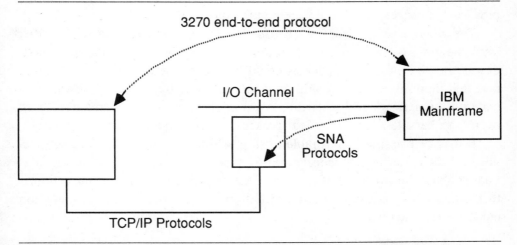

FIGURE 8-3 A relay function can forward packets between TCP/IP and SNA systems.

PROBLEM ISOLATION ISSUES

All of the above discussions were oriented toward how we could get packets across different protocol environments, with the concern being interoperability. An equally important concern that is often overlooked is *problem isolation*. Given that we can connect network A to network B, and therefore have interoperation between the two networks, how do we keep the problems of network A from coming over and becoming problems in network B? This becomes a major concern considering the extent to which many of our networks are interconnected today.

Problem isolation mechanisms vary depending on the nature of the problems and the protocol layers involved. Many good examples can be found in LANs, which are at OSI layers 1 and 2. LAN repeater devices regenerate the signal in passing it between segments of a LAN. This is their principal interoperability (interconnectivity) goal. However, they also guard against the propagation of certain problems from one segment of the LAN to another. In an Ethernet, a damaged cable can bring down an entire segment. The repeater can recognize this condition and disconnect the bad segment, blocking propagation of the problem. Similarly, the repeater can recognize an abnormal number of collisions on the LAN and keep that problem from spreading to other segments.

LAN bridges can interconnect two or more segments of a LAN, but they differ from a repeater in that bridges selectively forward packets, sending them on only if the destination is on another LAN segment. This selectivity reduces the load on the overall network. The bridge can provide the same problem isolation as the repeater, and the bridge can also be configured to avoid propagating broadcast messages, which can lead to major problems on LANs.

The worst case situation with broadcast messages occurred in some earlier implementations. In these cases, systems were vulnerable to Ethernet "meltdown," in which broadcast packets could lead to erroneous responses that perpetuated themselves. They could only be overcome by powering down every node on the network and restarting. Most of these major problems have been overcome, but a lesser form, called "broadcast storms," still occur.

It may or may not be desirable to stop broadcast messages from going beyond a bridge, because broadcast messages serve necessary functions, such as finding about the existence of a server. Each system administrator must address this issue based on the particular situation. An alternative interconnection mechanism is the router.

INTEROPERABILITY BY MEANS OF APPLICATION LAYER RELAY DEVICES

Until now, all of the examples have had an application protocol in common, such as Telnet in the Macintosh-to-Cray example, with a relay function being provided by the VAX. We now consider interoperability without having common application protocol. We now must translate between protocols.

With the exception of the lowest layers with examples such as Async to Bisync translations, you do not generally find protocol translations at intermediate layers. There is usually very little point in translating from one Network or Transport Layer protocol to another. Instead, we use the encapsulation technique. For example, we do not translate from one error or flow control scheme to another; we just obey the rules on each portion of the journey. In contrast, translation at the application protocol is often done when it is necessary to move data between two different environments.

An example of an Application Layer translating gateway is an SMTP-X.400 conversion device. It allows either form of message system to be converted to the other within the constraints that only common characteristics can be handled. The multi-media aspects of X.400 are not going to be translatable into SMTP text messages but can be conveyed in the body part of an SMTP message.

Another example of an Application Layer gateway is an FTP-FTAM conversion gateway. As with SMTP-X.400, only the intersection of their capabilities can be handled. In both examples, the Application Layer gateways provide the least service at the highest possible cost in terms of processing overhead, delay, and development of the relay device. They are clearly limited to the role of an interim device.

INTEROPERABILITY BY MEANS OF DUAL STACKS

The alternative to having to perform Application Layer protocol translations is to provide dual protocol stacks. For example, your host computer might implement the TCP/IP protocols, including FTP, Telnet, and SMTP, and might also implement the TP4 protocols including FTAM, VTS, and X.400. You could then interoperate with either form of host.

Your only problem now is knowing which protocol stack to utilize. You might learn this from trial and error. Try the OSI protocols; if that fails, try the

TCP/IP protocols. You might even keep a table in cache memory to remember what you have discovered using trial-and-error methods. Alternatively, the choice of which protocol stack to utilize at a given destination host could be integrated into the directory (name) server. In addition to the name-to-address mapping, you could discover which protocol stack to utilize.

INTEROPERABILITY BY MEANS OF APPLICATION PROGRAM INTERFACES

Interoperability in many systems is at least partly determined by the usage of a common Application Program Interface (API). There are many example APIs. NetBIOS is a commonly utilized API with PC-based LANs. A more recent API for PCs is the Named Pipes facility of OS/2 (not to be confused with the earlier named pipes of FIFO of Unix). IBM's Advanced Program to Program Communications (APPC) is the SNA-specific API. It is associated with LU 6.2 sessions in SNA. There are also vendor proprietary APIs, such as the NetEx (Network Executive) API associated with Network System Corporation's HYPERchannel.

APIs provide a set of application primitives to support network communications. Often there are both connection and connectionless communication primitives. The connectionless primitives are there to support needs such as broadcast transmission. There may also be other special capabilities, such as support of atomic operations in a transaction environment.

SUMMARY

Interoperability takes on many different forms, most of which are slight variations of the strategies described above. The two most important variations are the application protocol translation approach and the encapsulated delivery approach. Try to avoid the translation approach whenever possible, because it suffers from every possible problem, including performance, cost, and limited services. Variations of the dual stack appear to provide the most capable migration strategies from vendor proprietary approaches, as well as TCP/IP, to OSI.

9

DEVELOPING
NETWORK SYSTEMS

Network systems can be developed by any of a range of approaches. At one extreme, you get all of the networking hardware and software from one vendor with the idea of "plug and play" networking. It is not necessarily that easy, but that is the purpose of this alternative. At the other extreme, you could build the entire network yourself, including the hardware platforms for the routers, LAN bridges, terminal concentrators, and so on, and also develop your own software. The most extreme case would be to invent your own protocols as well, but few people have the time and budget to take this approach. What is typically found is a hybrid approach, often referred to as "buy and tie." You purchase those components that fit your needs and develop the rest, usually as software to run on an existing microprocessor-based platform. PCs are utilized in some cases, but the particular platform is not of major concern here.

This chapter goes through the development process and emphasizes those areas that tend to be at least partially unique to networking. You will examine each step in development, starting with the requirements definition and going through final test. The most extensive of these discussions is about the requirements definition phase, because that is the highest leverage point in development. It sets the stage for the functionality, performance, and human operability of the entire system.

REQUIREMENTS DEFINITION

The requirements associated with data communications and networking systems are similar in concept to four very common requirements of any information system:

1. What is the response time?
2. What is the number of work units that the system can process per second?

3. What percentage of the time is the system performing properly and available for use?
4. How well does the system protect our information from loss or corruption?

In computer networks, these become the delay, throughput, availability, and security, respectively.

There are two major concerns in this chapter: describing the network-specific requirements of systems and providing the tools needed to ensure that these requirements are reasonable and attainable. The first relates to the "shall statements" of a contractual document (e.g., for a procurement). How do you express these requirements? The second aspect is how one knows if a requirement can be met or if it is being stated too conservatively. You will analyze these requirements quantitatively using so-called back of the envelope calculations. They get their name from the limited computation required to get an order of magnitude result. It could literally be worked out on the back of an envelope.

Network Delay Requirements

The first of our performance metrics is *delay*. Like any other performance metric, delay is a measure, and a measurement, of a key performance attribute. It is the time required for a message to get across the network; or perhaps, the total time for a request to get across the network and for the response to come back. If our concern is the one-way delay across the network, you must consider how to actually demonstrate this attribute. Could you time stamp when a packet was sent and when it was received, subtracting the two to get the delay? What does this say about the need to accurately synchronize the clocks between the two systems? For high-speed networks, the delay could be the same order of magnitude as the expected clock skew. Instead, a round-trip time measurement may be needed, with both the time of transmission of the request and the time of receipt of the response being measured by a single clock. But then the problem is with how long it took at the remote system, after the arrival of the request, before the response was sent back. You should not attribute this part of the delay to the network. Perhaps you could arrange for the responder host to time stamp arrival of the request and sending of the response. You could then subtract this "delta" from the round-trip time. The clocks do not have to be synchronized in this case.

In addition to being able to measure delay, you could make some approximate calculations of it. Delay seems easy to determine for a point-to-point data communications link. If you knew the number of bits in a packet and the data rate of the line, is not the delay simply the packet length in bits divided by the data rate of the line in bits per second? Not necessarily—that is only one component of the delay. What if the line is busy when you want to transmit? There will be a queueing delay. What if the line is actually a satellite circuit with a quarter-second propagation delay up to the satellite and back down again? Finally, what about any processing delay that is associated at the computers involved at the sending and receiving ends? All of these factors also must be included. Each of these components of delay may or may not be a significant portion of the overall delay. You have to compute them to know.

You can extend the simple point-to-point circuit to include the processor(s) involved, in which case the processor(s) and circuit can be modelled as shown in Figure 9-1. This model can represent the sending end of a single point-to-point link, or it can represent one hop in a packet-switch network. In either case, the timing of interest starts when there is a need to handle a packet. In the packet-switch example, this is when an interrupt occurs, signalling the arrival of a new packet.

The first component of delay is the interrupt service routine, which will perform a minimal set of functions, such as queueing the packet for processing when the scheduler gets to it. Of course, you could have included a queueing delay to get to the interrupt service routine, because other interrupts could be pending at that same time. For these purposes, you have assumed that this delay will be small relative to the other components of delay on the link.

After queueing the packet for processing, the packet will wait for the scheduler to invoke it. When this is done, the packet will be processed, determining (among other things) which output line is appropriate for this store-and-forward operation. The packet is then queued on the selected output port. The total processing time is the concern in this component of delay. It could be estimated by examining the code, determining the approximate number of instructions that would be executed, and knowing the instruction cycle rate of the machine. Alternatively, it could be measured utilizing a test packet and seeing the delay from packet-in to packet-out in an unloaded processor. (This assumes that there is a single processor; i.e., no pipelining.)

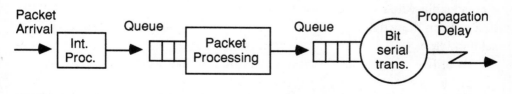

FIGURE 9-1 The transmitting computer and the transmission channel can be modeled by queries.

After processing is completed, there is some queueing delay (which we discuss later), and then the packet is transmitted, bit-by-bit, on the output line. The delay for this transmission is the first delay component considered; namely, the packet length divided by the data rate of the line. Finally, the bits of the packet are propagated down the line at a speed approximating that of light, which has a delay of about 1 nanosecond (nsec) per foot. This delay component is insignificant in many cases, but it is the reason for the quarter-second delay in a satellite link, which may be the dominant delay component in that case. Each component must be examined to determine whether or not it is a significant factor.

The delay calculated is for a single store-and-forward hop. For a point-to-point circuit, this is all you need, but in a packet-switched network, it is only one hop along the path. You need to multiply this per hop delay by the average number of hops. This assumes that all hops have the same delay; that is, that they have the same data rate for all links. If this is not the case, the average data rates need to be considered in the analysis, or the specific paths and their data rates need to be implemented for the calculations.

The queueing delays for processing and bit serial transmission will be the major source of variation in the delay time. They can be calculated based on classical queueing theory using the following equation.

$$\text{Delay} = \frac{p}{(1-p)}\text{Ts} + \text{Ts} \quad \text{where } p = \text{arrival-rate} \times \text{Ts}$$

arrival-rate = average rate of arrivals, e.g., in packets/sec

Ts = average service time in sec/packet

p = fraction of time the server is busy

You can see that the first term, which is the queueing delay, will grow without bound when the value p becomes close to unity; that is, when the server is busy most of the time. At very low values of p, the delay will be essentially that of the service itself. At p equal to 1/2, the queueing delay will equal the service time. You would generally like to keep the value of p less than 1/2 to keep the delay to a reasonable value relative to the service time. (Accountants would generally like to keep the value of p as close to unity as possible, so that the servers are seldom idle.)

To utilize the simple queueing equation, you had to make some gross assumptions about the queueing systems. A more complete description of such queueing systems and ways to overcome some of these assumptions are in book 1 of this series, *Mathematical Preliminaries for Computer Networking*.

For now, assume that arrivals to the system are random, and any knowledge about when the last arrival occurred provides no information about when the next arrival may occur. Similarly, assume that any knowledge about how long the server has been working on its current task tells nothing about how long it will be before the task is completed. Are these realistic assumptions?

You would expect that in an environment in which there was a maximum packet size, knowing the extent of processing up to this point would give some insight into about how long is required before its completion. This is the nature of the leap of faith you must make with this assumption. On the other hand, there are times when this model fits quite well. Suppose, for example, that you assigned a programmer the task of developing a new network protocol. You ask him or her how long it should take for completion and the answer is "about four months." Three months later, you ask how long it will be until the task is done. The answer you get is "about 4 months." A few months later you ask the same question, and you get back the same answer. Aside from demonstrating the eternal optimism of those in computer program development, it also demonstrates what is called the memoryless property of this form of system. You have no memory of how long you have spent on the task. The expected time to completion is always the same. A friend and previous customer once stated, "The only reason that you people stay in the software development business is that you have such poor memories. If you could recall all of the suffering and pain, you would get into some other line of business!"

Network Throughput Requirements

Throughput is the rate at which a network can sustain data flow over time, such as the time to transfer a large file. Because throughput relates to the time required to move information, it sounds like delay. The two are related in many ways. You usually gain on both counts by increasing the data rate of the lines. This reduces delay and increases throughput. However, delay and throughput are not completely interdependent. For example, you might obtain a satellite channel with a high data rate and high throughput but find that it increased the delay compared to a lesser data rate of a terrestrial circuit.

To begin the analysis of throughput, return to the model of a point-to-point circuit between two processors. The processors may be the end systems or they may be packet-switches, in which case the model is of one hop in the network. Which components of the model affect throughput?

Start with the processing time required per packet. This was a portion of the delay, but here you think of it in a different way. Suppose, for example, that the processing of each packet consumes two msec of CPU time. It not only adds two msec of delay, it establishes an upper bound on the number of packets that can be handled per second. A total of 500 packets per second would consume 100% of the machine cycles. (This assumes a single processor implementation. Otherwise, the computation needs to be performed for each separate processor in a pipe-lined system. It also ignores any lost cycles caused by I/O cycle stealing. These could be included in a more precise model.)

After you know the maximum packet handling rate, you can find the maximum throughput in bits per second by multiplying the number of packets per second by the packet size in bits. If you take the default X.25 packet size of 128 bytes, which is approximately 1,000 bits, you get a maximum throughput of 500,000 bps. This upper bound is caused by processor saturation. Note that the larger the packets the higher the throughput, because processing time per packet is independent of packet length. For the 128-byte packet size selected, there is no reason to connect these packet-switches together with megabit per second communication channels, but some number of 64-Kbps channels should be sufficient.

The data rate of each channel was also a part of the earlier model. It establishes an upper bound on each port of the packet-switch. About eight fully loaded 64-Kbps channels would saturate a 500,000 bps processor, so you could use this bit of arithmetic to get an order of magnitude on the number of channels that could be supported. However, the concern here is with throughput.

The example includes a processor that limits you to 500 Kbps aggregate traffic and links that are limited to 64-Kbps each. Does this mean that you should expect to get a 64 Kbps throughput across the links? Certainly the processor is not going to be what keeps you from doing so, but there are other factors to consider. The packets that are sent across the link include both user data and protocol overhead. Each of the 1,000-bit packets of user data also may contain about two hundred bits of protocol header information. This would reduce the achieved throughput in terms of user data by about 20%.

You have considered the effect of the processing and bit serial transmission limitations. What is the effect of the other components of the model, such as queueing delay and propagation delay? Initially, queueing seems to be a great help in achieving high throughput. It keeps resources busy most of the time. This is the same reason that a supermarket manager likes to see a queue at each checkout lane; it means that the checkout clerks are busy—they are achieving their version of high throughput.

Things are not necessarily this simple in networking. The apparently efficient use of the point-to-point circuit because of large queues may reflect poorly on end-to-end performance, causing premature timeouts and retransmissions.

The data may be getting through, but the extra long delays cause retransmissions. This adds to the problem of the point-to-point links, making them even busier. Thus there can be an interaction between the performance-related parameters of the different layers.

Another delay-related component of the model is propagation delay. What is its effect on throughput when there is a long delay, such as with a satellite channel? The first area of concern is, whether or not you can keep the channel full of packets. This concern can be met by making the window size large enough so the sender can continue to transmit until ACKs start returning. But that concern also must consider the error recovery strategy. In some links, if there is a bad packet, it and all subsequent packets are retransmitted. This would not work well with tens or hundreds of packets "in flight" at any given time. This leads to mechanisms such as the *selective reject* of data link protocols. Transport protocols do not have as explicit a mechanism. Instead, they rely on implementation strategies.

Up to this point, you have been considering the throughput of the aggregate traffic across a link. What is the effect for the end-to-end traffic? These users share the internal point-to-point links in a packet-switched network or other statistically multiplexed circuits. There are two concerns: do the users interfere with each others' access to the channel, and can any one user take advantage of the multiple channels to increase throughput?

Clearly, there will be interference between any users who would like to transmit at near the total data rate of the channel. This is fundamental to the idea of statistical multiplexing, and the result is added delay while the resulting queueing gets sorted out.

The second issue is much less obvious; can one user's data be spread across two or more of the multiple paths that mesh network structures provide? The answer is yes **and** no. Yes, the data can be spread across multiple paths in what is called bifurcating the traffic. But, no, the throughput does not necessarily improve. This is especially relevant in modern Transport Layer implementations in which the design is optimized on the assumption that the next arrivals are fairly predictable in terms of the order in which they arrive. Splitting the traffic into two or more paths increases the likelihood that packets will not arrive in order, possibly disrupting the throughput rather than improving it.

As stated earlier, throughput can be maximized by making the packet size larger. This is true when the per packet processing is independent of the packet length, which except for check summing is always true; and when the resulting larger size does not actually work against you, such as the increased likelihood of an error in a longer packet when transmitted on a telephone channel.

Yet another matter affecting throughput is the on-going dispute related to which bits count. Does the delivery mechanism get credit for getting the protocol overhead across the network, as well as the user's data? There is no clear-cut decision on this other than that the point to resolve the issue is sometime **before** making a commitment to provide a system with a given throughput. The same applies to determining the packet size(s) that will be implemented for the throughput tests. A typical throughput approach is to specify two requirements, one for very small (e.g., one-byte) packets, and one for maximum size packets.

Caution is still needed. You may feel that your network can provide a certain level of throughput for the maximum Transport Layer packet size, only to find that the large packet size causes Internet protocol fragmentation, significantly lowering achieved throughput. If you ran a test, measuring the achieved throughput as you made the Transport Layer packets increasingly larger, you would see throughput increase until the point at which IP fragmentation occurred. At that time, there would be a decrease in actual throughput.

Other protocol effects must also be considered. These include protocol implementation issues such as the retransmission strategies, ACK strategies, window size, and selective retransmission capabilities. These tend to be implementation issues rather than showing up as explicit requirements.

Network Availability Requirements

Availability is simple to define in terms of its concept, but difficult to apply to a given network environment. The concept is that availability is the fraction of time that a service can be utilized. If it is down, it is unavailable; if it is up, it is available. This simplicity is further noted in its calculation. The fraction of up time is the average time between failures divided by the sum of the average time between failures and the average time to repair when it is down. Simply stated:

$$\text{availability} = \frac{\text{MTBF}}{\text{MTBF} + \text{MTTR}}$$

where MTBF = Mean (average) Time Between Failures
and   MTTR = Mean (average) Time To Repair

In effect, a cycle is repeated over and over. The system runs until it breaks, after which it is down for some time. When it is repaired, it again runs until it breaks, requiring another repair, etc., for the life of the equipment. If you kept records of accumulated up and down time, you would have the actual availability of the system. The only problem with this is that you want to know what the availability is **going to be** on some new device, not what it was on some device that you are ready to discard. Discussion returns to this concern later.

High availability is achieved by making the MTBF very large (e.g., tens of thousands of hours), making the MTTR very short (e.g., less than an hour), and by introducing redundancy, which in effect makes the repair almost instantaneous. The only time that the system is down is when **both** the normal and backup units are down.

The availability of a network component can be estimated (calculated) from the above equation, given that data for the MTBF and MTTR. Where do these numbers come from? You might get them from experience, in which case you are probably using very old components, certainly not on the leading edge of technology. You might get them from marketing representatives, who believe that you will be awarding a large procurement if the numbers look good. You might get them from counting parts and computing the MTBF based on the individual part-level failure rates, degraded further by environmental factors. In this latter case, the MTBF will usually seem very low! A fairly frequent source of MTBF data is from product specifications.

There are similar problems with finding out what the MTTR should be for each component. You probably do not have previous experience with new components, and there may not even be an agreement on when MTTR timing starts and stops. Fixing the hardware is not always enough. The software must be loaded, self-tests may have to be run, and configuration data may need to be loaded before the networking device is really back up and functioning.

Analysis has to make the best of this imprecise world. Make estimates based on your best inputs and as improved by peer review. You have to remember that you are not looking for precision; rather you are trying to find the weak link in the chain. What is most likely to cause a network to be down, and how can you replicate that component or service to survive the failure? You make your best estimates, approximations, and sometimes, best guestimates.

Redundancy is the key to having any system survive in spite of failures. Consider a numerical example. Suppose a leased communications line has an availability of 0.97, and you need to improve this part of the system. Suppose further that you can purchase a modem that will automatically dial a backup line if the leased line fails, and that the availability of the direct dial line is 0.95. If either of these two lines is functioning, you can still operate. What is the probability that they are both down?

The probability that the leased line is down is one minus the probability that it is not down, or 0.03, and similarly the probability that the dialup line is not down is 0.05. If their failures are independent (and this is a big if), the probability that they are both down is the product of their individually being down, or

0.03×0.05, which is 0.0015. This says that the probability that at least one of them is up is one minus 0.0015, or 0.9985, which is a substantial improvement over either line by itself.

When some number of components must **all** work for the network system to be available, the system availability will be the product of the individual component availabilities. This assumes that the "Christmas tree light" effect applies —if any light is out, the entire string is out. (At least that is the way they used to work.)

Fortunately for your networks and unfortunately for your analysis, the network service is not entirely lost by a single failure. At least that is the way you should design them to operate. Alternate routing within the network is one such example.

Therefore, most network component failures will bring down only some portion of the network. How do you account for partial failures in calculating the availability? Consider the example network shown in Figure 9-2, which includes two terminal concentrators and two host computers. One terminal concentrator supports ten terminals and the other supports 20. Each computer is attached to the network by means of a front-end processor. You are to determine the availability of the network and its attachment devices including the concentrators and front-ends. What does it mean for the network to be down? This is an example of a system that can have partial failures.

One approach to deriving an availability value is to consider the service provided by this network. It is to provide terminal access to hosts. Therefore, you

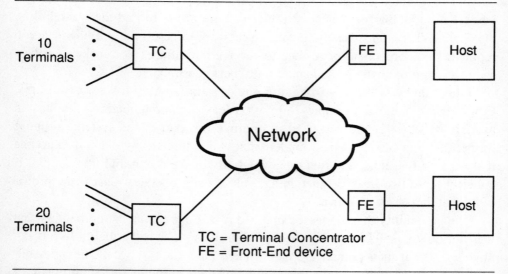

FIGURE 9-2   A simple example of network availability.

might model its availability in terms of the fraction of terminal support hours that are available to the users. For example, if everything performs well for an entire eight-hour shift, the system has supplied a total of 30×8, or 240, terminal hours of support, an availability of 100%. However, if the terminal concentrator that supports 20 users is down for two hours, we must subtract 20×2, or 40, terminal hours. Availability over this period can then be modeled as:

$$\text{availability} = \frac{\text{Total Term-Hrs} - \text{Lost Term-Hrs}}{\text{Total Term-Hrs}}$$

which would provide an availability calculation of 200/240, or 0.833, which is rather poor.

Even this simple approach to availability gets complicated when you consider other factors. For example, how many terminal hours of service are lost if one of the host front-end devices is down for an hour? That would depend on how many of the terminal users needed to access that particular host. This brings usage patterns into the calculation. You probably do not have such data, and if you did it might change with time. Instead, you might simply assume that the usage is evenly split between the hosts. Therefore, if a front-end device is down for an hour, 30/2, or 15, terminal hours are lost.

The same approach could be utilized with a PC- and server-based network, complete with multiple LAN segments, interconnecting bridges, and so on. In that case, the metric would be PC-hours of access. Each system will have one or more such metrics. The calculation can get complicated.

Network Security Requirements

The last of our four major requirements is *security*. As described in Chapter 2, security has three different aspects: confidentiality, integrity, and service assurance. You might attempt to quantify each of these aspects, providing some acceptably low fraction of messages that are mis-delivered, another acceptable fraction of messages that are corrupted without detection, and some acceptable fraction of time during which you have no service. You could perform calculations to determine if these numbers were met as a result of random chance, or perhaps even accidents. However, you cannot perform such calculations when the adversary is an intelligent and skilled intruder. After such a person finds a security hole, he or she will be able to penetrate the system at will with 100% success, in spite of all of your calculations related to probabilities.

Therefore, you must approach the specification of security in quite a different manner from that which you took for delay, throughput, and availability. Instead of attempting to specify acceptable numbers, you specify required security mechanisms and assurances. Security mechanisms are things like encryption and passwords. Assurances are quality control issues such as development in a clean room environment. Each of these are discussed below.

Confidentiality means that sensitive data are not disclosed to anyone who is not authorized to receive it. Typical confidentiality mechanisms include *encryption* and *access controls*. Encryption can be utilized to protect messages when being transmitted on the communications circuits, data while stored on media, and password files that are distributed and stored across the network. Access controls can include limiting access to network resources, such as by requiring a log-in, and by controls on access to host resources such as files.

Integrity of information can have several meanings, the most common of which is the ability to detect any errors caused by nature or any malicious modification that may have been made by an intruder. You cannot prevent the attempted modification, but you can detect the attempt with a high degree of confidence. For example, if a cryptographic form of error-check is utilized, and if the error check is N bits in length, then the probability that the intruder can make a change without detection is approximately 1 in 2^N. The same form of equation applies to the intruder's ability to guess the encryption key that is utilized for the cryptographic error-check.

Service assurance is the term utilized to express a system's ability to resist denial of service attacks, including having both nature and a malicious person as an adversary. Many of the service assurance mechanisms are those of fault-tolerant systems, which usually involve various forms of redundancy. Hardware sub-systems may be replicated, critical files may be mirrored, and spare resources may be available for restoration of system capabilities.

The security mechanisms to be stated as requirements should be based on the designer's attempts to meet a defined security policy. You should not simply string together a number of security mechanisms that have been selected arbitrarily. They should be selected because they meet some need expressed in the security policy. For example, the security policy may state that any communications over public networks must be protected by encryption.

In addition to the security policy and the security mechanisms, there are also security assurances. These three elements of security were discussed in Chapter 2. Security assurances are the quality control measures that you have taken to feel confident that your network system is secure; that is, that it meets your security policy. Some of the most important aspects of security assurance relate to the software development environment in which secure software is generated. Are the persons involved trustworthy, are the development tools known to be free from virus or other maliciously implanted programs, and is the configuration control process adequate? Measures can be specified as requirements to ensure that each of these concerns is addressed.

Requirements Allocation

System-level requirements may be met by either Commercial Off The Shelf (COTS) components, such as routers and bridges, and/or by developed software. Therefore, each system-level requirement must be specifically allocated to either COTS or developed software. This information is usually a part of the System Specification, a top-level representation that tells: of what does the system consist, what is it to accomplish, and what are the system-level requirements.

PRELIMINARY DESIGN

After the overall system requirements have been identified, quantified where possible, and determined to be demonstrable, you can take the design to the next step—preliminary design. The basic idea of the preliminary design is to further partition the system into identified software modules, to allocate requirements to these modules, and to unambiguously identify the data flows between the modules. The software modules that must be developed come about because you often need some capability that is not available in commercially available products. Your interest may be in producing such new products or in satisfying your internal needs. For whatever reason you have decided to develop networking software, what needs to be done at the preliminary design phase?

As a part of the normal preliminary design process, data flow diagrams are derived. These diagrams show the data stores and the processing elements that read and write them. They are a part of a general trend in design to put more emphasis on data—its structure, storage, and manipulation. The processing steps are derived from these needs to operate on data. For each data structure that is passed between modules, you need to define which module(s) set each field and which module(s) utilize each field. This is particularly important for networking software in which nested protocol headers are passed between modules.

Because the preliminary design establishes the top level modularity of the implementation, it is necessary to include all of the structurally related design concerns. For example, many security mechanisms must be isolated, such that they can be demonstrated to be always invoked, tamperproof, and correct. This separation needs to be defined in the early steps of the design.

Another aspect of the design that needs to be defined very early in the process is the approach to handling data packets from the network. For high performance, you need to avoid copying packets from one memory location to another and to avoid process (context) switching. To avoid copying packets, shared memory access is often required. An interface card may put the data directly in main memory where the protocol processing has access to it. This also raises the modularity issues of which network protocols should be off-loaded to an interface card. This point and the desire to avoid copying may work against each other.

Any user interfaces should be defined in the preliminary design. Some people feel that this should be taken to the point that the user manuals should be written before the Preliminary Design Review (PDR). This happens, but it seems like a good idea to at least have a first draft at that time.

DETAILED DESIGN

The operation of network systems is typically based on one or more state machine representations. The individual protocols often have their own state machines as well. This leads to a form of the design that can unfold naturally.

A state machine has an identified set of states and a set of events that are valid in each of those states. Any other event is an error and should be dealt with as such. The valid events are often the arrivals of control messages from a peer protocol implementation. For each event there is a defined action, sometimes including a state transition. The definitions of the states, the allowed events in each state, and the actions to be taken for each such event lead directly to a case statement form of pseudocode, which in turn leads directly to the actual coding in the next phase of development. It also makes the pseudocode easy to review.

It is particularly important that the detailed design indicate which software modules are particularly important to achieve high performance. The checksum routine is a classic example. Many transport protocol implementations spend well over half of their processing cycles performing the software error-check. This will be particularly true of the OSI TP4, which has a processing intensive error-check algorithm. It is common practice to tailor the code for these routines. This needs to be pointed out in the detailed design. Otherwise, someone will code from the design, follow good software engineering practices, and eventually have to recode it to get decent performance. You might as well get it right from the start.

Buffering issues are a matter for the detailed design to prescribe. Two common models to choose between are the circular buffer and the set of block-oriented buffers. Suppose that you have 100,000 bytes of available buffer storage. How do you advise a sender how much can be transmitted? If you state that 100,000 bytes can be sent, could you actually accept 100,000 one-byte packets? Or if you stated that up to 100 packets could be sent (knowing that a maximum packet size is 1,000 bytes), would that be efficient, especially for the one-byte transmissions? There is no safe, easy solution. Design what is best for your system, but do not defer the choice beyond the detailed design phase.

There are other areas in which the implementation can have a significant impact on the performance. These areas, such as the manner in which timers, retransmissions, and ACKs are to be handled, could be described at either the detailed design or the coding phase. This author's preference would be to include this information in the detailed design in terms of implementation guidance. This approach is preferred, because it provides early visibility and review of these important issues related to performance, and helps to ensure that these concerns are addressed between the detailed designer and the coder.

The detailed design is the place to bring out the *robustness principle* initially derived for TCP: "Be liberal in what you can accept, but conservative in what you send." This means that your design should not utilize obscure, rarely implemented portions of protocols. It also means that your design must handle all possible events, including all possible error conditions. It should also include damage limitation provisions wherever possible. You will see examples of damage limitation in routing algorithms that purposely do not propagate potentially erroneous routing data.

The detailed design is also the place to specify how the networking components will receive their initial configuration information. Higher level documentation may have called out the basic concepts for configuration, but the detailed design provides the detail as to how this is to be done. The default configuration parameters need to be defined, and the method for setting optional values needs to be specified.

There are also detailed design decisions about obtaining and keeping data that are needed, such as logical name to physical address mappings. Once determined, these mappings are often cached; that is, as each system learns this information, it is kept for future reference, writing new information over the least recently utilized data. This is another aspect of a self-configuring network system.

Somewhat the opposite of initial configuration is the need to specify methods of "garbage collection," when network resources get allocated, and then abandoned because of circumstances such as a system crash. Half-open connections are a typical example. The detailed design should specify how these conditions are detected and the resources are to be released.

A number of design tradeoffs in the network system need to be considered in the detailed design, and a particular approach must be selected for the subsequent coding step. In this author's opinion, implementation details usually should be determined in the detailed design, not the code generation phase. Detailed designs are easier to keep in an overall consistent state, and they are much more likely to receive detailed review. Examples of such implementation detail include the tradeoffs between node storage and network communications usage and are found in flow control and error control strategies.

CODING AND DEBUGGING OF MODULES

The pseudocode is used as a "code to" specification for the software in this phase of the development. Choice of programming language, however, should be made **before** writing the pseudocode, because the language constructs of the development language should form the basis for the constructs of the pseudocode. The language C is the most widely utilized language for networking software for several reasons, including its system programming characteristics and its portability.

Where the detailed design dictates a particular concern for efficiency in the implementation, the coding may need to drop into assembly language. These occasions should be minimized but definitely utilized in special cases. The error-check routine is the most common example, as mentioned earlier.

If the detailed design is done properly, the coding phase should be straightforward. The key decisions have been made and reviewed at the detailed design phase. The coder replaces the English language prose of the pseudocode with actual C (or other) program statements. Only local data structures should need to be defined during the coding phase; all others should have been developed in earlier phases and should be safely contained in configuration control before the start of the coding phase.

The end product of the code and module debugging phase is a software module that compiles correctly and meets the first level testing that can be performed. Such tests may be difficult in networking software, because each module (e.g., a layer) builds on the lower layer services, and it in turn provides services to a higher layer. This presents a lot of context that must be provided in the test environment software. In addition, much of the networking software handles exception conditions, which are difficult to simulate in the module test environment. This concern is discussed in the next section, which recommends a thread test approach that minimizes the need for special software test fixtures.

INTEGRATION AND SYSTEMS TESTING

Some developers take the approach of developing all of the modules separately and then bringing them together in a single integration test. This is sometimes called the "big bang" approach to integration. The problem usually is that the modules fail to work as one ensemble, and the troubleshooting problems are enormous.

A method that can be utilized, particularly in network software development, is to merge the back-end of module testing with the front-end of integration testing to form what is sometimes called *thread testing*. Like most terms, this one means different things to different people; therefore, it warrants explanation.

The initial thread testing operates with a small subset of the functionality of each software module. For example, a module like a TCP protocol might initially only be able to send and receive data across an existing connection. The connection establishment and clearing software portions might not even be implemented yet. The related modules would have also been developed to a certain stage of completeness, but that extent of completeness is of the same form in each module such that they can work together to simply move data from point A to point B. These partial modules are compiled, linked together, and form a test environment in which little simulation of inputs is required. The inputs come from the actual devices or modules that will be sending data in the final system.

Several benefits can be gained from this approach. First, it saves a considerable amount of throw away code that would otherwise be required to create the test environment. Second, and perhaps more important, it provides an early indication as to how well programmers are meeting the inter-module interface specifications, how well they are meeting their module functional specifications, and how well the set of programmers work as a team at debugging. Test input often can be generated by the actual terminal, workstation, or host devices that are to be supported by the network. Output monitoring is by means of breakpoints in the code and perhaps by the actual output devices as well. The latter are not sufficient by themselves, because until things work reasonably well, nothing meaningful will come out of the system to its normal output devices.

When a few threads have been completed, they can form the basis of a *build test*. At this point, you have clearly gone beyond the merged module and integration testing. In fact, that may be where you want to put the software modules into formal configuration control, at least for the portions involved in the build test.

The build tests continue to add more and more functionality until the entire system has been integrated and tested to see that it meets its official requirements. Then you are ready to perform the final set of tests, as described in the following section.

FINAL TESTING

At this point, the network system has been integrated and tested for functionality. You might expect that to be done, but several forms of testing remain. These tests may include one or more of the following.

There may be an official acceptance test. This test may simply repeat the tests that were previously passed at the last build test. Why repeat them? It gives Murphy's Law(s) a chance to indicate what things can go wrong. Many systems with and without networking have managed to find some new failure mode during such tests.

Perhaps what you should have done before this formal acceptance test was to have performed some stress testing—drive the network to its limits with traffic of all sizes and forms; mix normal and expedited data in unusual ways, try to clear connections before they are fully open, and send more data than the window size allows. Do not measure the throughput only. Force the system to try to make it get congested and fail.

Networking systems must interoperate with other systems. How do you know this will happen? Although you have met your specifications and your system has survived the rigors of formal acceptance and/or stress testing, it does not mean that you got all of the protocols right. You **may** need to pass conformance tests, but not all protocols have conformance tests. Where they are available, you can operate your networking software with a test protocol suite that has been deemed correct. If you pass, you get a certificate. This does not mean that you can necessarily interoperate with another system that also has obtained a certificate. Conformance testing has not yet reached that level of sophistication.

Therefore, you also have interoperability testing in which different implementations (e.g., from different vendors) attempt to interoperate under normal and stressful conditions. A grand example of interoperability testing was the TCP/IP "Bakeoffs," named after the nationwide event to find who could bake the best cakes. With TCP/IP, the competition attempted to see which systems were the most robust. Point counts were assigned for various operations. A few points were given for establishing a connection and transferring data. Many more points were assigned if you could cause another system to misbehave. And a lot more points were awarded if your TCP/IP packets could cause another system to crash. These became known as "Kamikaze packets." The end result was a robust set of protocol implementations, at least for those that survived.

The security-related equivalent of the TCP/IP bakeoffs is a series of penetration attempts. Skilled security penetrators who have access to the software listings and a wealth of prior knowledge on how to break system security attempt to subvert the network system. They usually win unless the system was designed from the beginning with security in mind.

MAINTENANCE OF THE NETWORK PROGRAMS

Life cycle maintenance of the network programs suffers from the usual concerns and costs of keeping a system running despite residual bugs and user-required extensions. Two important aspects are as-built documentation and an awareness of the networking concerns; another is application intent. Therefore, maintenance of network-related programs has the same problems as any other program, plus the added network-specific aspects. The addition of networking awareness, along with application awareness and programming awareness, makes maintenance activity a growing problem. The more disciplines a person must master to do the job, the fewer candidates there are to choose from and the harder it is to get the job done.

SUMMARY

Networking adds a new dimension to program and system design, development, and maintenance. On the one hand, it provides full-time employment for those who have mastered all of these disciplines. On the other hand, it makes life increasingly difficult for managers who must staff such positions. Networking has added dramatically to what we can accomplish but not without a significant price in the level of complexity of the resulting software systems.

You have seen that networking has a significant effect on system development, particularly on the software portion, because that is where most network protocols are implemented. The new capabilities come with an additional cost in terms of the development and maintenance complexity.

10

NETWORK MANAGEMENT

As networks become more and more important, or essential, to the operations of an enterprise, management of these networks becomes a critical matter. If the network is down, the enterprise is down, and hundreds of thousands of dollars may be lost per hour of down time. This was seen in the infrequent, but massive, outages of the telephone system. Enterprises are dependent upon communications. As such, communications must be managed as any other critical resource is managed.

Network management is like any other form of management in terms of its basics. You manage any entity by knowing what you expect to achieve, by monitoring to see if it is actually happening, and by taking control action when it is not. Unfortunately, this is not as easy as it sounds.

The first aspect of network management is to set expectations. This can be from history, analysis, or any other source of information. Network monitoring can be from data that are collected from the network, and/or from calls received from users on the hot-line. The former is definitely preferred. Network control requires knowing what the actual problem is and therefore involves diagnostics and problem isolation. All of these issues are addressed in the following sections of this chapter.

BASIC CONCEPTS OF NETWORK MANAGEMENT

Networks must be managed the same as any other complex system must be managed. Fault conditions, performance problems, and configuration changes must all be detected and controlled. Even automobiles have management subsystems in this regard. Some have complex computer systems to monitor and report on the current status of oil, gasoline, and other fluids, the gasoline mileage, the number of miles before service is required, and so on. Other cars have indicators for oil pressure, engine temperature, and gasoline supply. At least "idiot lights" are provided in all cases. You need similar, or often better, capabilities for monitoring networks.

The fact that parts of a network will fail from time to time is as sure as death and taxes. The threat of component failures raises the issues of reliability and availability. Reliability of a component part is measured in terms of the average or Mean Time Between Failures (MTBF). The larger the MTBF, the more reliable the component. Network components such as bridges, routers, and interface cards often have MTBFs of 5,000 to 50,000 hours, which with an approximate use of 9,000 hours per year, results in an MTBF of a few years. That's the good news. The bad news is that typical networks have **many** such components, so the likelihood that at least one component is down at any given time will be fairly high. Networks must continue to operate, in at least some degraded mode, in spite of these failures.

Failures of network components may be due to either hardware or software reasons. Hardware devices may fail in the sense that some part has burned out, and then a given set of inputs no longer produces the desired set of outputs. Software tends to fail in a different way. The code doesn't break or burnout; instead, a particular combination of processing state information with input results in a condition that was not correctly considered in the design. The software fails to handle the condition properly and may produce erroneous results. If the system administrator is lucky, the error will be noted immediately. Perhaps the system will even stop its operations at this point, leaving good clues as to what went wrong. More often than not, though, the error may be masked, and it may propagate before some second order indication is detected. Designing for the proper handling of all possible event conditions, and the collection of error reports are essential in this environment.

The situation is essentially that of a closed loop control system, as shown in Figure 10-1. Messages enter the system for delivery, but may be perturbed by disturbances including noise, component failures, and resource limitations. The system behavior is monitored and control action is taken as necessary to correct the effects of the disturbances. As shown in the figure, these corrective actions may be of three different categories:

1. The automated form of correction, such as dynamic alternate routing.
2. Human interaction, such as debugging a defective communications circuit, which is within the scope of network management personnel discretion.
3. Management decisions, including capital expenditures and long lead time items, such as adding lines or nodes to the network configuration

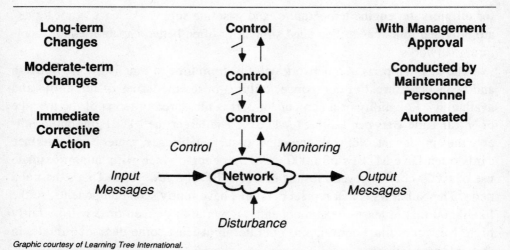

FIGURE 10-1   The Closed Loop Control System Model of network management.

(these go beyond the scope of normal network management personnel prerogatives).

The principal concerns about the differing time delays for automated changes, human debugging operations, and management decisions are about the responsiveness and stability of the closed loop control system. If responsiveness is too slow, the problem may escalate in the view of the network users. This lag time may actually result in instability and oscillation for sporadic loads. For example, occasional peak loads during a busy month may lead to network upgrades which are not made until after the peak load is completed. Later, the upgrade may be considered to be an over-kill, and management may decide to revert back to the previous configuration, only to encounter the peak load problem again later. Any closed loop control system may be subject to such instability.

So far, the closed loop control systems considered here have been about detecting problems and getting operations restored to proper levels of performance. Network management may include other factors beyond those of this simple model. In fact, OSI network management includes all of the following factors:

- fault management
- performance management
- security management
- configuration and name management
- accounting management

These factors may be subject to the same closed loop instability considerations that were discussed above. For example, accounting management could have a situation in which users are billed for network usage. To recover fixed costs, users may be charged a very high rate during a period of low network usage. As a consequence, users may cut back further on network use, leading to even higher costs, until the network becomes too expensive to utilize.

OSI network management introduces several aspects that are beyond the scope of this book, including security management, configuration and name management, and accounting management. These will all be considered in detail in later books of this series, but will only be described in passing in this book. This very broad range of network management concerns has been one of the factors delaying OSI network management specifications and implementations, which are not expected to be complete until the mid-1990s. The overall OSI network management protocol stack is shown in Figure 10-2. In addition to the ROSE and ACSE service elements which were discussed in Chapter 7, the Common Management Information Service and Protocol (CMIS/CMIP) are shown at the Application Layer. Also shown is the Management Information Base (MIB), which defines the management system variables using ASN.1.

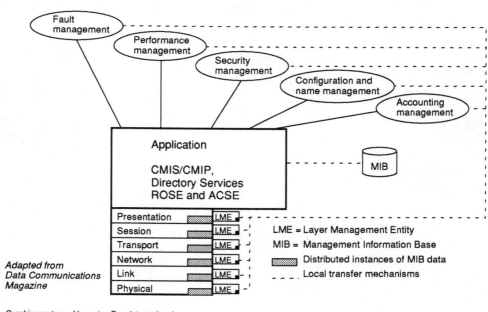

Adapted from Data Communications Magazine

Graphic courtesy of Learning Tree International.

FIGURE 10-2 OSI network management protocols.

ALTERNATIVE APPROACHES TO MANAGING A MULTIVENDOR NETWORK

The delay in the establishment of OSI network management standards has caused the development of a number of interim approaches. These developments and some of the alternative approaches are shown in Figure 10-3.

As OSI protocol implementations have become available, network implementers have found that the availability of OSI protocols from different vendors has not necessarily solved the problem of multi-vendor networking. Unless there is a way to manage the multi-vendor network, the consumer is often faced with the same single-vendor dilemma in networking. As a consequence, some groups have developed vendor independent network management approaches, such as the Simple Network Management Protocol (SNMP) and the CMIS/CMIP Over TCP (CMOT) strategies, while others have adopted vendor-specific approaches such as those of IBM, DEC, AT&T, and HP. A part of the motivation for the latter developments is the marketing proverb that "the company that controls the network, controls the account."

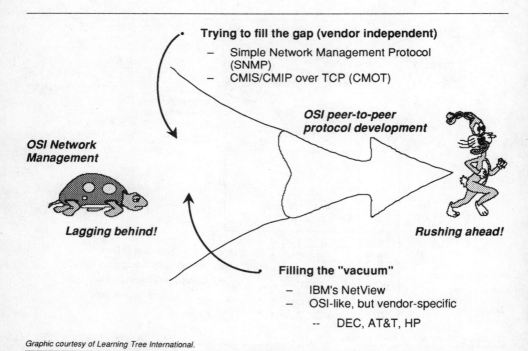

Graphic courtesy of Learning Tree International.

FIGURE 10-3   The slow development of OSI network management standards led to interim network management approaches.

A key element of the OSI network management approach is the MIB, which provides the data base for network management. Most of the alternative approaches for network management retain this information base, differing primarily in the way that information is transfered between the MIB, at the manager, and the agent devices, such as routers. The OSI approach is to utilize the CMIS/CMIP service and protocol, operating over the traditional OSI protocol stack. CMOT utilizes this same CMIS/CMIP, but over TCP/IP with a minimal (lightweight) presentation protocol, as shown in Figure 10-4.

The Simple Network Management Protocol (SNMP) operates with the OSI-like MIB, but utilizes a very simple (minimal) set of commands to communicate between the manager and the agents. The manager can read parameter values by a **Get-Request**, with a corresponding **Get-Response** being returned. These exchanges utilize the UDP connectionless protocol, and hence reliability must be ensured by SNMP itself. Since the amount of data that can be conveyed across UDP/IP exchanges is limited in many implementations, large read operations are performed by a **Get-Next-Request** variation of the **Get-Request**. This allows sequential portions of a large data item, such as a routing table, to be read.

The manager can write agent parameters by a **Set-Request**, which has a **Get-Response** returned to provide a read-after-write form of integrity. Again, SNMP is responsible for the reliability of the transfer, repeating the command as necessary. Note that both **Get** and **Set** operations require only at-least-once integrity, since duplicate operations do not cause any problems.

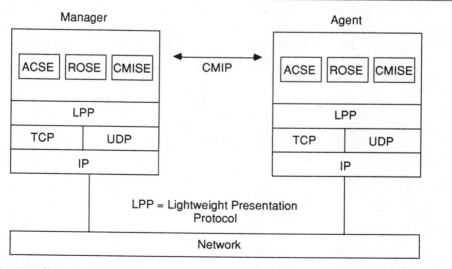

Graphic courtesy of Learning Tree International.

FIGURE 10-4 CMOT uses OSI network management standards over the TCP/IP Protocols.

The final primitive of SNMP is the **Trap** message. It is sent from the agent to the manager on an unsolicited basis. A typical use of the **Trap** function is to announce that an agent has encountered an exception condition such as a reboot.

The CMIS/CMIP capabilities include those of SNMP, and also add commands to initialize and terminate an agent, to cause a predefined action to be executed, and to create or delete an MIB parameter at the agent. CMIS/CMIP also provides several choices regarding the required integrity of the management operations.

Several vendors, including AT&T, DEC, and HP, have developed network management systems that utilize the CMIS/CMIP OSI network management tools and provide element management systems to interface to non-OSI portions of the system. The non-OSI portions may be single agent devices, but are more typically network management subsystems such as for a PABX network, a T1/T3 multiplexer network, or a modem-based network. Each of these subsystem network managers becomes an agent to the top-level manager, while being the manager of the subsystem network. This hierarchy can be extended to any arbitrary depth in some vendor approaches. An example showing the two-level hierarchy is presented in Figure 10-5.

IBM has a network management system called NetView that is specifically oriented toward the management of their proprietary System Network Architecture (SNA) network. Our concern here is not with NetView per se, but with how it can be integrated into a multi-vendor, multi-technology environment using NetView/PC. An example is shown in Figure 10-6.

The structure of the NetView and NetView/PC network management approach is very similar to that of the other vendor approaches shown in Figure 10-5, except that IBM utilizes SNA protocols between the top-level manager and

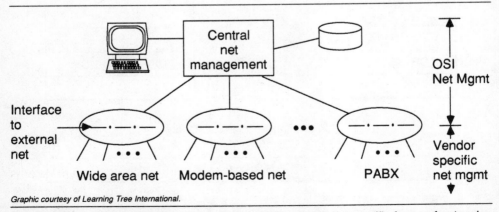

Graphic courtesy of Learning Tree International.

FIGURE 10-5   A typical approach to integrate OSI and vendor-specific forms of network management.

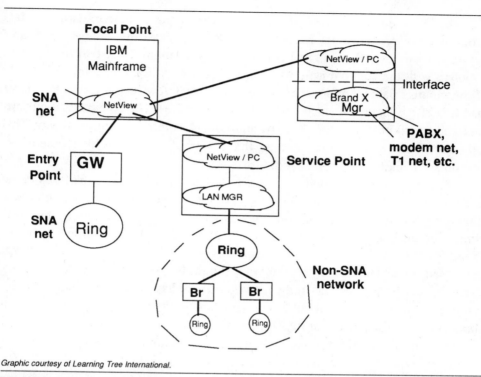

Graphic courtesy of Learning Tree International.

FIGURE 10-6   An IBM network management example with NetView/PC.

the second-level agent/manager, while the others utilize OSI protocols. Similarly, the other vendors provide interfaces to the non-OSI networks, while the IBM approach provides PC-based interfaces to non-SNA networks.

MONITORING NETWORK PERFORMANCE AND BEHAVIOR

The ability to monitor selected parameters within the network was one of the capabilities found in all of the network management systems discussed in the above section. This might be done, for example, by using the Get-Request of SNMP. Such monitoring will result in a very large amount of data as the network management system periodically reads values from the many agents in a large network. The fundamental point of this monitoring is to analyze the collected data to gain insight about the network's internal activity. Support programs should be available for this analysis: for example, to examine each set of data to determine if pre-set thresholds have been exceeded. One such threshold would be the ratio of packets with CRC errors to the total number of received packets.

The interpretation of the collected data often requires the correlation of data from two or more sites. For example, if node A indicates that a large fraction of its packets to node B require retransmission, you might think that there was a problem with the communications circuit. However, you might think differently if the monitor data from node B indicates that very few incoming packets have bad CRCs, but that many such packets were duplicates. The communications circuit appears to be operating properly, and node A is retransmitting anyway. This set of combined information indicates that the problem is more likely one of retransmission and/or ACK timer settings.

The above scenario shows the value of having data from multiple sites in the network, from which correlation can be made. However, such correlation is possible only when the data from the various sites cover approximately the same time interval. This poses another requirement on network management systems. If the SNMP Get-Request, or other such commands, is sent to each agent at approximately the same time, the intervals should be essentially the same. However, if a Get-Request is lost in the network, it will have to be retransmitted after a timeout. The intervals will not be the same unless the agent collects data over a fixed interval, independent of the polling time.

The type of **meaningful** data will depend on the kind of network, but the following are typical data of concern in packet-switched networks.

- The up/down status of each link attached to the node
- For each link, the total number of
  — bytes received
  — packets received
  — priority packets received
  — packets received with CRC errors
  — flow control "stop" indications received
  — bytes transmitted
  — packets transmitted
  — priority packets transmitted
  — packets retransmitted
  — flow control "stop" indications sent
- Any observable delay or response time data
- Number (by type) of exception messages sent and received
- Queue size and delay (periodic sampling)
- Number of active connections (such as in an X.25 net)

The above examples of monitored data are representative of that which would be collected, and are almost always either counts (such as the total packet count) or running totals (such as the total number of bytes sent or received). These data are relatively easy to collect in the agent device, and cause little network overhead to deliver to the centralized manager.

NETWORK CONTROL FUNCTIONS

The data that are collected by network monitoring and processed at the central collection site may indicate a problem within the network. Network control is then invoked to identify the nature and location of the problem down to a replaceable unit. This form of network control typically involves a semi-automated set of tools which an operator can utilize to diagnose the problem. Some other forms of network control may be completely automated and will be discussed later in this section.

When the monitoring software identifies a network problem the operator of the network management station is notified. This notification might be in the form of a color change on a network map, such as a displayed element going from green to red. If a network map is not always displayed, an icon can be utilized by changing its color or blinking it or by using an audible signal. Alternatively, a console message might be displayed, again using color or blinking or by using audible signals to get the attention of the operator.

The operator queries the system to obtain summary information about the problem. This query may be made simply by clicking on the icon or map item. More detailed information and recommended approaches for isolating the problem can then be brought up on another window of the network management workstation. The recommended approaches may include the isolation of one or more nodes of the network for test purposes and then generating artificial traffic to attempt to recreate the problem. Loopback tests are frequently utilized to determine which component is introducing the erroneous operation. When the problem has been isolated to a replaceable component, repair personnel can be dispatched to restore service.

The above scenario involved a human operator working with support tools at the network management workstation. In some other cases of network control, rather than being centralized, the control action should be entirely automated and distributed across the network. Dynamic alternate routing is one such example. Automation is needed for rapid restoration of service. Distributed control is needed for fault tolerance.

Many of the automated and distributed control mechanisms are based on watchdog timers. If an expected periodic event does not occur within the timeout value, control action is automatically initiated. Examples include packet-switch recovery from a program loop and LAN recovery from a lost token. While these automated control functions do not require the presence of the network management center for their operation, they do report their recovery activities to the centralized network control. The automated control may have restored operation, but the central controller may need to take other actions to ensure that the basic problem is handled and unlikely to repeat itself.

SUPPORT TOOLS AT THE NETWORK MANAGEMENT CENTER

The network management center usually consists of a collection of support tools. The number and capabilities of these tools depend on the size of the network, but there are several generally needed capabilities as discussed below.

The collected data from network monitoring often goes into a data base system, and hence a *DataBase Management System* (*DBMS*) is often required to extract information about the network. Relational DBMSs are most frequently utilized for this purpose.

Another frequently needed capability is a display of the current status of the entire network. This may consist of a wall-size electronic display, a CRT display on a workstation or PC, or a manually updated magnetic board with symbols for each network component. The purpose of this display is to provide network status at a glance.

The next level of detail that may be available with the workstation or PC approach is the ability to zoom in on the indicated problem area and obtain statistics about the faulty component(s). This is often accomplished by clicking on the portion of the display that indicates the problem.

As the problem becomes isolated to a box-level component, such as a bridge, router, or packet-switch, you need to perform tests on the component. One form of testing is to, in effect, operate as if you were at a directly attached console at the component device. Memory locations can be inspected using debug capabilities. Other such tests can be run from across the network, operating within a window at the network management center workstation. These diagnostic tests include artificial traffic generation and loopback.

Some problem analysis will require the availability of a protocol analyzer. These devices are available for either data link protocols or for LAN protocols, often displaying the entire set of higher layer protocols as well. The use of protocol analyzers has been described in other chapters of this book.

When network management concerns get to the level of the network cabling, a *Time Domain Reflectometer* (*TDR*) may be required. The TDR can display any imperfections in cabling such as opens, shorts, kinks, and improper taps. Other specialized cable testers are also available, with varying degrees of user sophistication required.

THE PEOPLE ASPECT OF NETWORK MANAGEMENT

Successful network management involves the technical and interpersonal skills of the network management team. The size of the team depends on the size and needs of the network, but must always include certain skills such as network planning and design, network installation, network operations, network troubleshooting, and help-desk support. In a small network, a few persons may share these responsibilities, while in a large network, there may be a separate group providing each aspect of network management. A key aspect of staffing the network management operations is to ensure that each person is aware of his or her role in the overall picture and that all aspects are explicitly assigned to some person or group.

The training of network management personnel presents a considerable challenge, particularly in multi-vendor, multi-technology networks. Any specific problem, although it may occur infrequently, must be identified and resolved quickly to bring the network back into full operation. The large number of **infrequent** problems makes training difficult, especially if there is significant turnover within the group, and cross-training becomes especially important with small groups of people who must service a variety of devices of different types.

The Help Desk provides an important link with the network users. The help-desk view of the network support system becomes that of a user, while it actually is far more complex. Those serving in the help-desk capacity must have a driving desire to help people, but also must have adequate understanding of the network operations. Support in terms of check lists and other problem resolution vehicles is important, since you want to be able to resolve 50 to 75 percent of the calls at the help desk.

In summary, the network management system includes people as well as technology—both must be provided for success. Although the principal focus of this chapter has been on technology, do not overlook the people aspects of this critical part of your network.

11

TRENDS IN
DATA COMMUNICATIONS
AND NETWORKING

A number of trends have become well established in data communications and networking and are discussed in the following sections. These are not intended to be predictions. Instead, they are already in place but are still growing in terms of their impact on technology and the marketplace. You can think of these areas as being at the edge of the usage curve. Five years ago they were just beginning. Today they are in place, but five years from now they will be dominant forces as their use grows exponentially.

HIGH DATA RATE NETWORKS

We have evolved from 300 bps communications to 9,600 bps, and then the giant step to LANs with 10 Mbps or more data rate. Each step has resulted in a major change in what can be done with networking capabilities. Today, 100 Mbps LANs are available, and 2 gigabit/sec LANs are coming.

There is a clear need for higher data rates and for uses such as graphics, image analysis, distributed computing, distributed data, and client-server methods of computing. The higher data rates are pressuring the capabilities of existing transport protocols.

The source of these higher data rates has been LANs, particularly fiber-optic LANs. This has produced a close tie to two other trend technologies, fiber optics and Integrated Services Digital Network (ISDN). These are discussed briefly in the next two sections.

FIBER OPTICS DATA COMMUNICATIONS

Fiber optics has become the data communications medium of choice for very high data rates—100 Mbps and above. Its use is based on its extremely high bandwidth and data carrying capacity, the long distances that can be run between repeaters, its small size (allowing many fibers to be placed in a conduit), and its inherently low bit error rate. The telephone companies have been replacing copper conductors with fiber for several years. Newer arrivals in the telephone business stress that their networks are entirely based on fiber-optic communications. It is a technology that has reached the masses, whether they understand it or not.

Fiber optics also may reach the masses through the "fiber to the home" expansion of the telephone plant. High definition television is apt to be the most visible aspect to users, but widespread availability of high data rate communications may be more important in the long run. It is not clear how this capability will be used, but if the past is any indication, it will be revolutionary. Like the famous quote associated with Rutherford B. Hayes and the telephone, "It seems like a good invention, but I'm not sure what useful purpose it will have." Only the future knows for sure.

INTEGRATED SERVICES DIGITAL NETWORK (ISDN)

Associated with other telephone company developments, ISDN will provide the capability to send very high data rate information from any location to any other location. Only the tariffs will limit how these facilities will be implemented.

ISDN will provide communications for digitized voice, data, video, and any other information that can be sent in digital form. Few, if any, sources of information are not digital today, making this a general purpose vehicle.

Sometimes ISDN is equated with 64-Kbps channels, which is the data rate for a digitized speech channel. This seems to be an obsolete communications data rate for most purposes. However, the ISDN channels include the capability for much higher data rates, with corresponding orders of magnitude more data rate capacity. Again, it becomes a matter of tariffs and economics as to what can be accomplished. In the past, some have stated that ISDN stands for **I Still Don**'t know, while today it means **I See Dollars Now**. ISDN is here, and more is coming.

Associated with ISDN are the Synchronous Optical Network (SONET, pronounced like sonnet) and the Asynchronous Transfer Mode (ATM). SONET provides a standard way of transmitting digital information at very high data rates across fiber-optic circuits. SONET provides standardized optical signals, a synchronous frame structure, and standardized procedures. SONET is expected to provide a 155-Mbps communications mechanism for FDDI 125 Mbps data streams across telephone company-provided circuits.

ATM, which is sometimes referred to as fast packets, is being developed to transfer bursty traffic over SONET circuits. ATM utilizes cells within the

SONET payload, with a 5-byte header and a 48-byte data field. The header fields include flow control, a virtual path identifier, a data type field, and a header error check. The ATM is a part of the proposed broadband (i.e., high data rate) ISDN services.

INCREASED USE OF CLIENT-SERVER NETWORK COMPUTING

Client-server (or frontend-backend) use of networking and computing is not new and has gradually made inroads into network and computing usage. It has become a significant part of protocol stacks, including those of XNS, TCP/IP, AppleTalk, and others.

Client-server computing is the basis for Sun Microsystems Network File System and several other forms of distributed computing systems as discussed in Chapter 7.

REMOTE PROCEDURE CALL (RPC) MECHANISMS

The Remote Procedure Call (RPC) form of networking and computing is one of many innovations in the early days of Xerox networking and interactive computing. The RPC has become a part of many protocol stacks, including those of TCP/IP and AppleTalk. With RPC capabilities, an application program can call upon the services of procedures on other networked machines using a simple procedure call. All of the network-specific aspects are provided in client and server stubs.

One attraction of the RPC is that it fits the needs of transaction processing protocols. The required robustness may be tailored to the task in the form of **at least once**, **at most once**, or **exactly once**. The client and server stubs are developed to provide the required level of transaction integrity.

Applications that use RPC capabilities will operate in the same manner as with local procedure calls except for timing considerations. Network operations will lessen this aspect of performance by one or two orders of magnitude.

LIGHT-WEIGHT DELIVERY PROTOCOLS

We can expect to see increased use of *light-weight delivery protocols*. Light-weight implies low overhead, which may be true, but it also means that the state information, if any, can be recreated quickly. The idea of not having any state information is associated with some connectionless protocols. You can expect to see an increased use of connectionless protocols as they become part of the approved set of OSI protocols and as system designers recognize the advantages of using them in selected applications. New protocols may have both connection and connectionless capabilities.

USE OF OSI PROTOCOLS

There will be increased use of OSI protocols, but they will not displace the TCP/IP, DECnet, and SNA protocols for many years. Just as Bisync continued to be utilized long after IBM's replacement SDLC was available, users will not replace their current protocols just for the sake of something new. You can expect that the 1990s will see a mixture of OSI, TCP/IP, and vendor-specific protocols. The migration strategy must account for this long period of coexistence. Migration strategies were discussed in Chapter 8.

MUTUALLY SUSPICIOUS NETWORKING

A principle that has existed for more than a decade in distributed processing is mutually suspicious networking, but you have yet to see its full implementation in any general way. The concept is that one node in the network should not blindly accept the claims of another node, either in response to a request or on receipt of unsolicited information. Routing problems have often resulted when this principle was ignored. Obviously incorrect routing data was often accepted and utilized, leading to network routing disasters.

Mutual suspicion implies that some "sanity check" should be made on all data that will be utilized in a distributed computation, network management, or other distributed operations. Advances in expert systems technology may be useful in this regard.

INTEGRATED NETWORK MANAGEMENT

As networks become more important or essential to the operations of an enterprise, management of these networks becomes critical. See Chapter 10 for a thorough discussion of network management.

This is another area in which expert systems technology can be expected to provide major improvements.

FAULT TOLERANT NETWORKING

As people become more dependent upon networks, they must become more fault tolerant. They should expect that portions of the network may be down, that servers will have disk head crashes, and other significant problems will occur. These problems should be considered in the network design, and counter-measures should be built-in for failures that are considered to be both reasonably likely and devastating in terms of their consequences. This is a judgment call, of course.

Current practice is most well defined in terms of LAN servers. Critical information such as File Allocation Tables and directories are stored in redundant form. Disk contents may be duplicated in so-called mirrored disks. Disk contents may be backed up periodically, and entire servers may be replicated. Almost any desired level of redundancy is available.

SECURE NETWORKING

Another view of the future is one of network security. Historically, worries about network security have been left for government agencies with highly classified information. Commercial practice has been limited to physical, procedural, and personnel security measures. Two major things have caused this to change. First, it is becoming well recognized that the major security threat is from the insider. The hacker has gotten much attention and has destroyed the previous good connotation of being a skillful programmer. However, the largest losses are from people who simply went beyond their assigned responsibilities and ripped off the organization. They represent the insider threat.

The second major change has been the availability of security mechanisms to counter the threats, both internal and external. Security-oriented systems have been developed and subjected to scrutiny by the National Computer Security Center, which assigns A, B, and C levels of security mechanisms and assurances. (There are also gradings within these levels such as B1, B2, and B3.)

Encryption has also emerged from the dark ages and become available for more widespread use to ensure a variety of security properties from confidentiality to source authentication. The more pervasive use of encryption will occur because of the use of algorithms and keying material that do not require the integrity and confidentiality of people, which have traditionally been the weak link in such systems. People-related matters have also caused expensive operational costs with respect to encryption, which now can be eliminated.

As people put more of their enterprise's "crown jewels" on the network, it is comforting to know that there are new and improved versions of the guards to protect these valuable assets. It is up to you to make intelligent choices as to which of these mechanisms should be utilized in each specific circumstance.

DISTRIBUTED COMPUTING

Distributed computing refers to the ability to utilize multiple, remote resources in a transparent manner. This is a very rich area for development, and it will be the subject of future books in this series. The basic idea is that one can access resources across the network without being aware of their remoteness and without having to perform any network-specific operations, such as requesting a file transfer.

To implement distributed systems, you must be able to provide general purpose interprocess communications, synchronization, robustness and distributed control, network-wide security protection, global naming, atomic transactions, remote procedure calls, and very high data rate communications. Many of these issues are discussed in other sections of this book. None are relegated to R&D, but all must be engineered together to make a truly transparent distributed system.

GOSIP AND ITS STAGES

The Government OSI Profile (GOSIP) has been developed as a series of steps or stages to account for the gradual release and availability of OSI protocols. In the first stage, only X.400 electronic messaging and FTAM are included. In the second stage, virtual terminal support will be added. Other stages will also add transaction processing, Electronic Data Interchange, Office Document Architecture, X.500 Directory Services, and network management.

CONFORMANCE TESTING

Conformance testing provides the equivalent of the Underwriter's Seal of Approval for networking protocol implementations. If a vendor's implementations pass the defined set of tests, that vendor has passed the conformance test and gets the seal of approval. With the Corporation for Open Systems (COS) in the U.S., this seal of approval is the COS Mark.

Conformance tests are typically run on an application-by-application basis. The first such tests to become available were the X.400 and the FTAM conformance tests. Others will become available as the protocols become firm and as the test suites are developed and approved.

Conformance tests do not guarantee interoperability, but they do provide a good step along that path. Actual interoperability testing is also required, like that performed using the OSInet facilities of the National Institute of Standards and Technology (NIST).

EXPERT SYSTEMS USE

Expert systems technology is essentially the computerization of knowledge of expert persons in a given field of interest. The systems are rule-based, with each rule representing input from a human expert or a rule that has been developed by the system based on its observations.

Expert systems have been utilized in network design, which involves the assignment of links and link capacities between switching nodes. A given network configuration is considered to be better than another if it meets all of the performance requirements and costs less. The analysis involves determination of the overall end-to-end traffic, allocation of that traffic to links based on the routing algorithm, sizing of the links, link costs based on differing fixed end costs, distance-related and capacity-related costs, and other factors. Expert systems technology is expected to continue to provide new tools for network design and optimization.

Network management is a second area that will benefit from expert systems. The idea here is to provide assistance in determining the most likely reasons for any given outage or degradation condition. The rule-based expert system can identify the problems to check for first and can recommend particular diagnostics to run, as well as assist in interpreting test results.

Expert systems also may be able to provide insight into the analysis of security audit data. Such data are often fragmented, distributed across the network components, and are represented in differing formats. Analysts of such data are usually confronted with having too much of the wrong information and too little of the specifics about a given suspected behavior. The expert system base may provide the needed clues as to what other audit data, like that accumulated at hosts on the network, should be requested.

NEURAL NETWORKS

In some ways, neural networks provide an alternative to expert systems. Although you expect that expert systems will be based primarily on human expert provided rules and have less ability to learn from experience, the opposite is true for neural networks. They will have learning capabilities based on observations (learning by example) and previous errors in decisions.

Neural networks are useful primarily in handling problems with complexities such as pattern recognition, artificial intelligence, and the approximate optimization of large-scale systems. Several of these areas relate to networking problems, and research in these areas is expected to provide breakthroughs in the 1990s.

T1 AND T3 NETWORKING

The direct use of T1 (1.5 Mbps) or T3 (43 Mbps) telephone company circuits for computer networking is becoming common. These circuits provide a high data rate, wide area backbone that can be utilized to interconnect networks and/or high performance computer systems. This approach overcomes the data rate limitations of other wide area alternatives, such as X.25 networks.

T1 or T3 circuits could be utilized to interconnect packet-switches, but a more likely network configuration would be to utilize them to interconnect routers on a point-to-point basis. This is consistent with the structure of several modern networks. Packet-switches, and X.25 networks in general, may be on their way to the computer network museum.

METROPOLITAN AREA NETWORKS (MANs)

Metropolitan Area Networks (MANs) are city-wide, and considered to be a large-scale, high-speed form of a Local Area Network. MANs are the subject of the IEEE 802.6 LAN standardization work and were delayed considerably because no clearly dominant approach was available for some time. The group started with the idea of utilizing satellite communications, and then moved on to cable television distribution systems. The CATV companies were not interested. The next approach was to utilize fiber-optics technology with a slotted access scheme that had been developed by Burroughs. This fell by the wayside because of cost-cutting when Burroughs and Sperry merged to form Unisys. Stability has finally arrived as a Telecom Australia development called *Dual Bus Distributed Queue* (*DBDQ*). This approach has been accepted by AT&T and the Bell operating companies.

DBDQ utilizes a dual fiber-optic cable bus, with transmission in opposite directions on each fiber. At each end of the bus a frame generator creates time-slot frames. Each unit on the MAN maintains a counter that represents the size of the current queue of requests for slots. Requests are sent to the frame generator on the bus going to the frame generator. The count kept at each unit is incremented whenever a request is observed and decremented whenever an empty slot is observed. The counter is the length of the queue as observed by a particular unit. If the counter at a given unit indicates zero, that unit can transmit in the next empty slot. This will happen when that unit's previous request is at the head of the queue, or it may occur when there is no other traffic contending for the network. The effect is to have an orderly passing of control under periods of heavy loading, but to have instantaneous access under very lightly loaded conditions.

MANs will be developed by the telephone companies and provide a new form of high data rate communication within the bounds of a city or telephone company administration. Data rates of 155 Mbps are expected. Devices that would attach to a MAN would typically be routers to allow the interconnection of networks, such as LANs, with other networks.

ELECTRONIC DATA INTERCHANGE (EDI)

Electronic Data Interchange (EDI) is an evolving set of standards for the electronic exchange of business-related documents, such as purchase orders and invoices. In the United States, EDI standards development is coordinated by ANSI, and the specifications are in the X12 series.

EDI is modeled after the paper forms approach to business information. A single form is considered to be an X12 Transaction Set. Each line of a given form is expressed as an X12 data segment, which has fields for quantities, unit of measure, unit price, product identification number, and so on. One or more Transaction Set(s), or electronic forms, can be placed in an X12 Interchange Envelope (header and trailer) and sent via electronic mail. X.400 electronic mail is commonly used.

Variations of EDI have been used for some time in large companies that need repetitive purchases and need to tightly control expenses related to purchasing operations. These include the automobile industry, large grocery companies, and discount merchandise companies. Development of the ANSI X12 standards and coordination of international equivalent standards will make EDI a rapidly growing use of networking capabilities.

ELECTRONIC SIGNATURES

Electronic signatures are a class of techniques for performing the equivalent of signing a document. Such electronic signatures will be increasingly important as the "paperless society" becomes more widespread. EDI will be one such example, because there will be a need for some signature mechanism in a contractual sense. Public key cryptography is a leading candidate for these signatures.

Many security mechanisms also will be based on electronic signatures to authenticate the source of information. Distribution of the public keys in a public key cryptography system is an example. Users of the system must be able to authenticate the source of such public keys to ensure that they are not being spoofed by a bogus source of keys.

PREPARING FOR FUTURE TECHNOLOGICAL CHANGE

This chapter has attempted to summarize some of the major technology areas that are beginning to come into use and are expected to become widely utilized within five years. The principal reason for identifying these areas is to alert designers to some new fields that need to be considered in any system that is being developed today. Migration strategies must be designed into these new systems, and better development tools and techniques are required to shorten the development cycle. Otherwise, you will almost always find that your new system is technologically outdated. This can be avoided by combining rapid development and identifying evolutionary upgrade paths for an on-going technology enhancement. One thing is certain. Development of networking systems will continue for the foreseeable future. It should be a challenging and rewarding experience.

BIBLIOGRAPHY

Bal, H., J. Steiner, and A. Tannenbaum, "Programming Languages for Distributed Computing Systems," *ACM Computing Surveys*, September 1989.

Black, U., "The X.25 Facilities," *Data & Computer Communications*, Fall 1989.

Bochmann, G. and P. Mondain-Monval, "Design Principles for Communications Gateways," *IEEE Journal on Selected Areas in Communications*, January 1990.

Braden, R., "Requirements for Internet Hosts—Communication Layers," *RFC* 1122, October 1989 (Network Information Center).

Braden, R., "Requirements for Internet Hosts—Application and Support," *RFC* 1123, October 1989 (Network Information Center).

Braden, R. and J. Postel, "Requirements for Internet Gateways," *RFC* 1009, June 1987 (Network Information Center).

Burger, Wilhelm, "Networking of Secure Systems," *IEEE Journal on Selected Areas in Communications*, February 1989.

Cargill, C., "Standards and Standards Organizations," *Data & Computer Communications*, Winter 1989.

Caruso, R., "Network Management: A Tutorial Overview," *IEEE Communications*, March 1990.

Case, J., et al., "Simple Network Management Protocol," *RFC* 1157, May 1990 (Network Information Center).

Cerf, Vinton, "Multivendor Connectivity and the Role of Standards," *Telecommunications*, January 1989.

Chappell, D., "Abstract Syntax Notation One, ASN.1," *Data & Computer Communications*, Spring 1989.

Claiborne, J. David, *Mathematical Preliminaries for Computer Networking*, Wiley, 1990.

Clark, David, "The Design Philosophy of the DARPA Internet Protocols," *ACM SIGCOM 1988 Symposium*, ACM Press, 1988.

Clark, D., et al., "An Analysis of TCP Processing Overhead," *Communications Magazine, IEEE,* June 1989.

Cole, R., "Experience and Analysis of Network Interconnection," *IEEE Journal on Selected Areas in Communications*, January 1990.

Comer, Douglas, *Internetworking With TCP/IP: Principles, Protocols, and Architecture*, Prentice-Hall, 1988.

Conard, J., "Bit-Oriented Data Link Protocols and Their Applications," *Data & Computer Communications*, Winter 1989.

Derfler, F., et al., "The X.25 Alternative," *PC Magazine*, May 1990.

Downing, A. and G. Popek, "Protocols for a Transparent, Internet, Distributed Operating System," *IEEE Computer Networking Symposium*, 1988.

Fernandez, J., "SNA and OSI: Which Manages Multivendor Networks Best?" *Data Communications*, April 1989.

Gilbert, W., "Managing Networks in a Multi-Vendor Environment," *IEEE Communications*, March 1990.

Halsall, F., *Data Communications, Computer Networks and OSI*, Addison-Wesley, 1988.

Haugdahl, J. Scott, *Inside NetBIOS*, Architecture Technology Corporation, 1986.

Heatley, Sharon and Dan Stokesberry, "Measurements of a Transport Implementation Running over an IEEE 802.3 Local Area Network," *Computer Networking Symposium*, IEEE Computer Society Press, 1988.

Held, G., "The RS-232 Interface," *Data & Computer Communications*, Winter 1989.

Henshall, J. and S. Shaw, *OSI Explained*, Halstad Press, 1988.

Hirsh, D., "Terminal Servers: Here to Stay," *Data Communications Magazine*, April 1990.

Huntington, J., "OSI Network Management: Is It Too Early or Too Late?" *Data Communications*, March 1989.

Hurwicz, Michael, "NetView Now," *LAN Magazine*, April 1988.

Jacob, A., "A Survey of Fast Packet Switches," *Computer Communications Review*, January 1990.

Jones, V., *MAP/TOP Networking*, McGraw-Hill, 1988.

Kent, C. and J. Mogul, "Fragmentation Considered Harmful," *SIGCOM 1987 Symposium*, ACM Press 1987.

Kessler, Alan, "Named Pipes," *LAN Magazine*, June 1988.

Kochan, S. and P. Wood, *Unix Networking*, Haden Books, 1990.

Krall, G., "SMNP Opens New Lines of Sight," *Data Communications Magazine*, March 1990.

Lewart, C., *Modem Handbook for the Communications Professional*, Elsevier, 1987.

Lide, David and David Walters, "A Functional and Performance Comparison of NetBIOS and APPC/PC," *Computer Networking Symposium*, IEEE Computer Society Press, 1988.

Lynch, D., "TCP/IP and OSI," *Data & Computer Communications*, Summer 1989.

Madron, T., *LANS: Applications of IEEE/ANSI 802 Standards*, Wiley, 1989.

Malamud, C., *DEC Networks and Architectures*, McGraw-Hill, 1989.

Malamud, C., "Streams Help Comm-based Services Go With the Flow," *Data Communications*, May 1990.

Martin, James and Kathleen Chapman, *SNA: IBM's Networking Solution*, Prentice-Hall, 1987.

Mayne, Alan, *Linked Local Area Networks*, Wiley, 1986.

Meijer, A., *System Network Architecture: A Tutorial*, Pitman, 1988.

Mier, E., "LAN Gateways: Paths to Corporate Connectivity," *Data Communications Magazine*, August 1989.

Minzer, S., "Broadband ISDN and Asynchronous Transfer Mode," *IEEE Communications Magazine*, September 1989.

Moy, J., "OSPF Specification, Open Shortest Path First," *RFC* 1131, October 1989 (Network Information Center).

Muftic, S., *Security Mechanisms for Computer Networks*, Wiley, 1989.

Nemzow, Martin, *Keeping the Link, Ethernet Installation and Management*, McGraw-Hill, 1988.

Neufeld, G., "Descriptive Names in X.500," *ACM SIGCOM 1989 Symposium*, 1989.

Notkin, David, et al., "Interconnecting Heterogeneous Computer Systems," *Communications of the ACM*, March 1988.

Partridge, C., "How Slow Is One Gigabit Per Second," *Computer Communications Review*, January 1990.

Parulkar, G., "The Next Generation of Internetworking," *Computer Communications Review*, January 1990.

Parulkar, G. and J. Turner, "Towards a Framework for High-Speed Communication in a Heterogeneous Networking Environment," *IEEE Network Magazine*, March 1990.

Perlman, Radia and George Varghese, "Pitfalls in the Design of Distributed Routing Algorithms," *SIGCOM 1988 Symposium*, ACM Press 1988.

Peterson, L. et al., "The X-kernel: A Platform for Accessing Internet Resources," *COMPUTER (IEEE)*, May 1990.

Preshun, R., "Considering CMIP," *Data Communications Magazine*, March 1990.

Purser, M., *Data Communications for Programmers*, Addison-Wesley, 1986.

Rose, M., "Transition and Coexistence Strategies for TCP/IP to OSI," *IEEE Journal on Selected Areas in Communications*, January 1990.

Satyanarayanan, M., "Scalable, Secure, and Highly Available Distributed File Access," *COMPUTER (IEEE)*, May 1990.

Schlar, S., "Shopping Smart to Save on Packet Networks," *Data Communications*, March 1990.

Schnaidt, Patricia, "The DECnet Direction," *LAN Magazine*, November 1988.

Scott, K., "Taking Care of Business With SNMP," *Data Communications Magazine*, March 1990.

Shirey, R., "Defense Data Network Security Architecture," *Computer Communications Review*, April 1990.

Sidhu, Gursharan and Richard Andrews, "Bridging the Design of Diverse File Systems" (AppleTalk Filing Protocol) *LAN TIMES*, February 1989.

Soha, Michael, "A Distributed Approach to LAN Monitoring Using Intelligent High Performance Monitors," *IEEE Network*, July 1987.

Soha, Michael and Radia Perlman, "Comparison of Two LAN Bridge Approaches" (Source routing and spanning tree) *IEEE Network*, January 1988.

Spanier, Steve, "Comparing Distributed File Systems" (NFS, RFS and SMB) *Data Communications*, December 1987.

Stallings, William, *Handbook of Computer-Communications Standards*, Vol. 1–3, Macmillan, 1987.

Stevens, W. R., *Unix Network Programming*, Prentice-Hall, 1990.

Sunshine, C., "Network Interconnection and Gateways," *IEEE Journal on Selected Areas in Communications*, January 1990.

Tannenbaum, Andrew, *Computer Networks*, Second Edition, Prentice-Hall, 1988.

Terplan, Kornel, *Communications Network Management*, Prentice-Hall, 1987.

Terplan, K. and J. Huntington-Lee, "Can Third Parties Change SNA Management Stripes?" *Data Communications Magazine*, April 1990.

Tillman, M. and D. Yen, "SNA and OSI: Three Strategies for Interconnection," *Communications of ACM*, February 1990.

Tittel, Ed., "The LANalyzer," *LAN Magazine*, December 1988.

Tolly, K., "Opening the Gateways to SNA Connectivity," *Data Communications*, March 1990.

Warrier, U. and C. Sunshine, "A Platform for Heterogeneous Interconnection Network Management," *IEEE Journal on Selected Areas in Communications*, January 1990.

Wells, G., "X.400 Migration Strategies," *Proceedings of the Third International Conference Information Network and Data Communication*, INDC-90, Norway, 1990.

Willett, Michael and Ronald Martin, "LAN Management in an IBM Framework," *IEEE Network*, March 1988.

INDEX